MANILA GAMBIT

MANILA GAMBIT

A Novel

JOHN F. ZEUGNER

RESOURCE *Publications* • Eugene, Oregon

MANILA GAMBIT
A Novel

Copyright © 2015 John F. Zeugner. All rights reserved. Except for brief quotations in critical publications or reviews, no part of this book may be reproduced in any manner without prior written permission from the publisher. Write: Permissions, Wipf and Stock Publishers, 199 W. 8th Ave., Suite 3, Eugene, OR 97401.

Resource Publications
An Imprint of Wipf and Stock Publishers
199 W. 8th Ave., Suite 3
Eugene, OR 97401

www.wipfandstock.com

ISBN 13: 978-1-4982-3862-5

Manufactured in the U.S.A.

For Emerson, Magnolia, Aster, and Thomas

"I cannot conceive why there is such an ardent desire to discover in a game of chess anything more subtle than it has to offer, for I am of opinion that the real beauty which it possesses should be more than sufficient for all possible demands."

ALEXANDER ALEKHIN,
annotation of move #10 of his match against H. Wolf, International Tournament at Pistyan, April, 1922:
My Best Games of Chess, 1908–1923

Chapter 1

"Paul, it's the little gestures, the little gestures that count. Very few of us—really, none of us—get the chance to make big differences in how the world works, so we have to try at the immediate, mundane level. Make the little gesture and with conviction. Make the world a better place by increments. By increments!" Waldo has struck his characteristic expansive stance at the Hane Country Club bar, left armpit shoved into the padded edge of the bar top, left hand cradling the back of his bald head. "Yes sir, Snelly, the little gestures. How many do we pass up? The tiny moments God grants us to tease out a small change, a brief incremental change that could have—really should have—momentous effects? And we slouch down in our patented ways, and the moment passes us by because we couldn't see what would ensue." Waldo closes his eyes, as if to imagine history scampering by.

We are waiting for Waldo's wife Hillary to arrive. It is four-forty on Friday afternoon, and, as is his custom, Waldo has left the Hane Tribune early, closed up his publisher's office and gathered me out of the city room for drinks at the club. I am the son Waldo would repudiate, if he had one, the novitiate he wishes to inculcate in the crafty ways of finding a rich wife and living the club life thereafter.

Because he is Hillary's husband, he is the Hane Tribune's publisher, but he knows he has nothing to do with the paper. He merely occupies the publisher's office from 9:30 to 3:30 each day and agrees to meet people those who run the newspaper haven't got time to see. Sometimes he wanders around the city room, trying, he once explained to me, to get the feel of the place, but mostly he reads in the huge corner office and waits for drinking time with Hillary. About twice a year he suggests something to the editors and they agree to look into it. He likes to be introduced as the publisher of the Hane Tribune. He likes to drink tall Gin and Tonics in the late afternoon and Drambuie after dinner. And he likes to get dressed in white flannels and double-breasted blazers and wear shoes with tassels. He loves sporting a white yachting cap.

"You think that would be a good title for a column?"

"What?"

"By Increments. By Increments, by Waldo Turner."

"What about 'Little Gestures'?"

"Not bad either, but you'd have to have something to say. And who has anything to say anymore?"

"Dentists."

"Only minority dentists," Waldo sighs. "Actually, I was reasonably serious. By Increments could be an educational tool for this retirement community and it would shield the rest of the paper from the threat of my intervention."

I nod approval, conscious that, indeed, Waldo had at some time made certain decisions that closed certain doors in order to fling wide open far different ones. He finishes his drink and fires the empty glass about twelve feet along the bar top. The bartender apparently approves, or at least he smiles his deferential, subservient grin, and quickly makes a fresh Gin and Tonic. He carries this back to Waldo, who nods and says nothing. Instead he turns to me again, eyes my partially full glass and says, "Actually, Hilly won't be coming tonight. She's not feeling too well."

I wonder, does this mean dinner is off too? And I begin the tiresome calculation of T.V. dinner versus Kentucky Fried Chicken versus something else.

CHAPTER 1

Waldo says, "I want us to have dinner anyway. We have a few things to discuss."

I can see it coming. We have only one thing to discuss—Pamela Snow, Waldo's candidate for my replication of his life. The Snows reputedly have more money than even Hilly's daddy, Sam Hane, a redoubtable toilet tissue magnate who bought most of Hane County in the 1920s and established the Hane Tribune to provide employment for a few relatives and advertise his basic commodity. Hane worried, apparently, that folks in southwest Florida didn't have much use for "soft as rainwater" toilet tissue. After the land collapse of 1926 the rest of the county fell into his hands, and in return for staving off ruin he had the place named after him: Hane, Florida, in Hane County, Florida. Once Waldo remarked to me, "It's true old Sam Hane owns the name around here, but the Snows own the whole damn alphabet."

Waldo was, and is, no subtle match-maker. He has consistently sought to truss Pamela and me up as a blessed union providing each of us with those essentials we independently lack. In Pamela's case, sanity; in mine, money. Or so he argues. All these machinations terminated about three weeks ago when it became clear that our couplings were inadequate for the mutual depression that centered around them, went with them like a little nimbus of grey something or other. And so I told her it would be wiser—that seemed like the best term at the time—that we both try to establish other avenues beyond boredom. "You're the fourth person to turn down my marriage proposal," Pam said, tears welling up in her eyes—scary bright tears as reflective as the sparkling surface of the bay and then the Gulf of Mexico beyond her shoulders.

Here, I was thinking, the water is clear and the sky gorgeous and the air as caressing as possible. Whence all this sorrow? Be rid of it. Be rid of it. Simply wishing and stating it could make it so.

I had expected the city room to become a regular Waldo prowling ground. I expected to be summoned momentarily to the big publisher's office and harangued or cajoled or ordered to resume this replication of Waldo's life. But, of course, he was, and is too crafty for that. Instead, we went through two regular Fridays of getting smashed on G & T's and watching Hillary eat away the best part of flown-in lobster dinners. And nothing was said, nothing at all despite the obviousness of commenting on Pamela's absence from our festivities. Now, just when I had begun to imagine escape from raillery and domination, Waldo has altered the Friday afternoon ritual and ordered, no doubt, Hillary to stay away. Now comes the pitch, I am certain.

Waldo watches the ball game on the bar television, and when he is midway down his G & T, he sighs a bit and suggests we go to the dining room for an early bird supper—tonight the attachment to the oversize menu announces a special of lamb curry and rice and tomato sauce and vinegaretted string beans, plus a hearts of palm salad.

"I won't beat around the bush," he says, as we dig out our oysters. "Pam's not doing well. She went back up to Tampa on Tuesday and has had treatments since then every day."

"Fifth floor?" I ask quietly. Florida oysters are smaller and juicier. Eating them takes special jaw control, if you want to talk at the same time.

"Yes. Yes, where else? But electrical rather than chemical treatment. She was in a pretty bad way."

"It's not my fault."

Waldo pauses looking at me, but my eyes skitter around him and watch the bartender flailing away with a blue rag at the bar surface where we had been standing. Waldo says, "One of the things that disturbs me about you is the way you use terms like *fault* and *my fault*. You know what that signals to me? A desire to remain immature, to escape, to drift off, to elude even a little interconnection with anything else."

"Anything?"

"Anything and everything."

"We're interconnected," I answer, enjoying the oysters less and less.

CHAPTER 1

"Very funny. Very amusing. Another distancing trick. She'd like to see you, and Hilly and I think—"

"I don't want to see her."

"Why?"

"Because she always misinterprets what I say, what I do, what I think."

"She does or you do?"

"Well, I'm not claiming to be in love with her. Not claiming that 'our relationship' makes the sun come up, the moon rise."

"You don't have much compassion, do you?"

"I'm eating with you, aren't I?"

"Precisely illustrates what I said, doesn't it?"

"You notice how we ask each other questions all the time?"

Two enormous hunks of Crenshaw melon arrive, so ripe that my piece has a layer of goo along the top.

"I have a proposition for you," Waldo says, taking his knife and slivering the melon along the rind and then cutting neat cubes for eating. "Hilly and I want you to visit Pam. You owe her that. You should want to do it of your own accord. But if you don't—for whatever reason—"

"I could give you twenty. But they boil down to one essential: compassion, your favorite term. Remarkable isn't it? Compassion. Why should I deceive her, exploit her?"

"Can I finish?" Waldo continues eating two neat cubes and wiping his mouth with the immense blue napkin. "Let's say you have valid reasons for not visiting the sick, or at least persuasive reasons. That brings me to my proposition. You visit her, You spend some time with her next week, maybe two days with her, or two visits for however long they allow, and in return I'll see to it you get a byline column in the Tribune. That's what you've wanted, isn't it?"

"I don't care that much."

"We'll see. I'll get you a column."

"They won't go for it."

"You let me worry about that."

"Well. Jesus! They won't go for it."

"They don't have to go for it. We, Hilly and I, have to go for it. And we do. We do already. Do you understand?"

"I suppose."

"No. I want you to really understand it, understand the whole process. Arnie and Phil are cracker-jack editors, cracker-jack publishers, the best in this area—top flight. They know the business cold. They can do things, get things done. They know their trade. But that's just what they are, superb trades men in someone else's employ. At the behest of somebody else. Whatever objections they have are ultimately resolvable by someone else, because they don't have controlling capital. It's very simple. They're excellent and replaceable. You could be excellent and replaceable—make a nice life for yourself. Work hard and develop highly expensive replaceability. Or you could think about taking care of Pam and become irreplaceable."

I start to answer, but Waldo holds up his hand, pushes his palm at me. "You're glib enough and I'm tired of hearing your responses, to tell the truth. I want you to reflect a little on what I said. I don't want to address that any more. I want you to think about it. I've thought about your situation. So has Hilly. We make a proposition. Let's talk only about that. Forget the so called 'long-term' if you can, at least for now. What do you say? A visit or two in return for a byline column."

"My byline?"

"Yes, sure." Waldo watches my smile. "Then it's done, isn't it? This melon is delicious, soft, succulent, malleable."

Chapter 2

"How do you feel?" I ask still staring out the window, through the dirty steel netting. On a log at the end of the parking lot an elderly black man has sat down and taken out a small, brown paper bag.

"I feel very, very distracted, but it's nice, you know."

'Yeah," I answer, watching as the fellow drinks from the bag.

"It is, you know. Waking up and thinking, well, where am I and how interesting these lights are and then wondering if I have a name. Have you ever gotten up and not known your own name?" And then . . . some things begin to come back, but sometimes it takes days."

"Eh hehn." It's a little early for muscatel. I decide it's rye or perhaps tawny port in the bag.

"And then they teach you how to make things. I've always like making things, though I hate to sew."

"Does it hurt?"

"What?"

"The treatments, do they sting? I mean I remember seeing movies of people leaping off beds and writhing around holding their temples. Does it hurt?" She regards me strangely. "I don't recall any pain. I don't think it hurts. They wouldn't hurt you, would they?"

"No. I suppose not."

"I only know it's hard sometimes remembering where you are. Some days I think I'm in Connecticut. I spent a lot of time there, I think, in a place like this. And it was colder there."

"I imagine."

"But, anyway, that's not what I wanted to say. What I wanted to say was that I've made something for you. Do you want it?"

"Sure."

"Well, good! But you have to close your eyes and hold your hands out."

"I don't want to hold my hands out."

"Yes, you do. Now close your eyes."

I hear her get off the bed and go over to the bureau. The sound of a light drawer opening. Then something rectangular and cold comes into my hands. (A task, Waldo remarked once, is a task—the merit of the task, the evaluation of the task is always fluid, depending on all kinds of factors. Rescuing the drowning baby and playing peekaboo with the same infant may be the same act, same worth, depending on who does the evaluating. You must remember that when you deal with Pam, and when the world deals with your dealing with Pam. Do you understand?).

"Open your eyes," she says with arch coyness and interest.

It is a small black leather key pouch.

"I made if for you yesterday, when Hillary said you were coming."

"You made it in one day?"

"In one hour," she says but without the pride I had expected.

"It's very nice and I can use it all right. Do you know I'm supposed to get a byline column?"

"You notice how the plastic stitching tucks under there and then you just touch it with a hot soldering iron and it fuses stronger than a knot."

"I'm not sure what kind of a column. Maybe local stuff. Maybe national commentary . . . once in a while."

"It's nice you've got something you're interested in," Pam says getting back on the bed.

CHAPTER 2

I put the key holder in my pocket and go back over to the window. The black man has splayed his feet out in front of the log. White, chalking dust from the parking lot has settled on his shoes.

"I might be here a long time," she says drawing out the *long*. "Dr. Coffee doesn't think I'm coming along fast enough, not nearly fast enough, but I think I'm doing fine. This morning I remembered my mother very clearly and I remembered us clearly too."

"How clearly?"

"Clearly enough. Have you reconsidered? I thought you had, else you wouldn't be here. I remember you said you'd never visit me here again."

"I thought you'd never be here again."

"That's not what you thought—not what you meant."

"Ah, maybe... Anyway, I'm here, aren't I?"

"And have you reconsidered?"

"Let's say I am reconsidering."

"Oh, that's good. That's very good."

Reconsideration seemed the kindest term, since I was visiting her in the first place. Why visit to finish something off and then finish it off only to visit some more? There were attractions, Waldo noted, in a wife who periodically couldn't remember who you were.

"I told Dr. Coffee this morning that you were the first person I ever had an orgasm with. The first and only."

"When did you have that?"

"You remember. You have to, because you asked me what was going on."

"I don't recall."

"Does it hurt?" she says smiling, "I mean the shock treatments?"

"Very funny."

"You can go now, if you want. Is somebody waiting for you in the parking lot?"

"Yes. Why don't you come over and see."

She slowly gets off the bed and we stand at the metal screen and I point out the Negro who has slipped off the log. He rests his back against it, and the brown paper bag has become a kind of wet and grey appendage to his left elbow. His hat is pushed down over his face, and his head is slumped forward, sleeping.

"Is he a friend of yours?"

"No. He's a friend of yours."

"Well, if he is, I don't remember him. At least not yet. If he comes tomorrow maybe I'll remember him then." She pushes back her black hair, cut Egyptian style, caresses her rather long neck. "Would you like a wallet made from the same material?"

"Sure, if it's not too fat a one."

"I'll make it very thin," she says, "very, very thin. And you can have it when you come again."

"That may not be until next week."

"That's okay, as long as you're reconsidering. Then I can keep making it."

"Could you go out for lunch or something, sometime?"

"Dr. Coffee doesn't think so. Not for a while, he says."

"Well, maybe he isn't the last word."

"Yes, the last word," she answers somewhat distractedly. She climbs back up on the high bed, leans back, head against the yellow wall. There is a white track-light just above here left shoulder. In fact, it seems to sit on her shoulder like an owl, a cylindrical owl.

"I should be going. I'll bring you the first column."

"Column? About what?"

"They haven't said yet."

"You're writing a column now?"

"Well, I'm starting pretty soon. You'll get the first one."

"Oh."

"Yes."

"I don't read newspapers much," she says, smiling, then turning to look at the track lamp. "Do you think this," she clinks it with her fingernails, "is part of me or apart from me?"

"Depends on how you sit."

"Well, I think I'll lie down. Could you lie down with me?"

"I don't think so."

"Oh, come on. Just for a minute or two. You could lie right here beside me, and we could talk."

"I think it's against hospital policy."

"Well, goodbye, then. I'll make your wallet for the next visit. You'll see me then." And she nods off, so that in a minute I can stand beside her and listen to very regular deep breathing.

In the parking lot I am tempted to spinout in front of the old Negro flailing up dust enough to cover his whole body, but I realize I only envy his wondrous, un-electrified sleep.

Chapter 3

True to his word, Waldo works his peculiar magic. On Monday Arnold and Phil send a message down that I should meet them in their office foyer, by the coffee machine, a nifty cream and blue Japanese vending machine that Waldo saw in Tokyo and convinced Hillary the paper couldn't do without. Arnold and Phil look a lot alike. Each wears light grey trousers and a short sleeve white dress shirt, narrow dark brown or green ties—it's difficult to tell in the fluorescent light near the machine. Arnold carries a manila folder. Phil holds to cups of coffee.

"Thanks for coming down," Phil says evenly, handing Arnold a cup. "You can get one if you want."

"It's okay. I usually don't drink the stuff."

"Smart boy," Arnold volunteers.

"Yes," Phil answers.

"How long have you been here?" Arnold asks with just a trifle edge in his voice.

"Five months, I guess," I answer, wary now. For some reason I begin to imagine that one of them will fling his coffee in my face.

"You like working here?"

"Sure. Sure."

"Ever think the paper might lack something?"

"Yes, does it ever seem incomplete to you? You know, with a big void somewhere, where it really should have something? Some papers are like that, you know. Some have terrific sports sections or society columns, maybe great arts reviews, and nothing whatsoever in international news. You ever feel the Trib lacks something?"

"Some void you could fill."

This is apparently a routine. I've heard some of the reporters refer to it as the A & P workover. I decide silence is best. No sense prodding the already sensible fury present. Then Waldo's phrase slowly emerges from some self-protective depth. The sign slowly comes up from underwater and it reads "Replaceable." These guys are replaceable. I feel better listening to the routine.

'For a long time now, I've thought," Arnold says across the top of his coffee cup, "that this paper needs a chess column. And Phil and I were just talking about, and we thought, is there somebody here, some newcomer, some fresh blood, some young talent that deserves a break?"

"Deserves a byline," Phil interrupts, "because, after all, chess columns all have bylines and we thought of you."

"I don't know anything about chess."

"What do you know about the city council, about the police department, about firefighting, about any goddam thing? What do you know about any goddam thing?"

Phil seems really angry, but Arnold's voice is suddenly soothing. The old good-guy-bad-guy routine. "New reporters don't know very much, but they learn. You could write a piece on the city council. You can write pieces on the chess world."

"I don't play chess."

"You don't run for city office either."

"You're right," I answer evenly, "and I don't plan to."

"What is that supposed to mean?" Arnold asks.

"Nothing."

"Good. Then it's all settled. Tomorrow by eleven you have a nice fresh chess column for us, one quarter page, for the fill between sports and finance, and then you have another one and another one every fourth day. You got it?"

"How long does this assignment last?"

Phil shrugs. Arnold shrugs. They put their coffee cups down. "Most people like bylines 'till they retire."

"Or die," Arnold adds.

"I see."

"I wonder if you do see," Arnold says. "I wonder if a smart fella like you really does see." He starts down the corridor, *replaceable* gleaming on his back.

Phil says, "You should check the columns elsewhere. It's fairly routine, once you learn the moves, heh, heh." And still laughing he wanders off after Arnold.

On the stairway up I resolve to speak with Waldo, who merely sits Buddha-like, watching a spot to the immediate right of my head.

"This is your idea of a column?"

"A deal is a deal. I delivered a column, didn't I?"

"I don't give a shit about chess. For chrissakes, Waldo, why not let me cover city insurance. It's got to be more interesting."

"I thought about that, when I heard that's what the Bobsie twins had in mind. But I make it a practice to take a few deep breaths and apply a number of telescopes to the picture before I blow something out of the water. There are a few good points."

"Name two."

"One, the task can be routinized, and two, it doesn't require much prose. You can fill the space with those little drawings of the board and the formal game notations."

"Those are supposed to make it attractive to me?"

"Initially I should think it would make it very attractive. Your work while you're learning the silly game can be more or less done for you."

"No deal."

"What does that mean, no deal?"

"It means I tell Pam, it's been fun but no cigar. And I go back to something real."

"You mean the beaches? You're out of shape for that."

"Very funny."

CHAPTER 3

"I contracted for a column with a byline and I delivered."

"No dice."

"And Pam's the only loser then. You get a new career for not seeing her, is that it?"

"Sure. Why not?"

"For one thing there is at least one more attraction to the chess column."

"And that is?"

"Travel. Little out-of-the-way places like Berlin, Paris, Montevideo, Manila, Rome."

There is a soft silence as we savor the names. After a mutual smile, I say softly, "I've always liked Pam."

"She certainly likes you. Needs you. With her, you're, you're—"

"Irreplaceable."

"Precisely," Waldo says looking me right in the eyes. "Now I've got a lunch, and you've got some research." Waldo gets up and puts on his crisp blue blazer. "Try 794.8," Waldo says.

"What?"

"At the library, 794.8, the chess books."

"Most libraries use the Library of Congress system," I add, "but if you haven't been in one since, say, 1957, I suppose the Dewey Decimal system would stick in your mind."

"Why don't you try 794.8?" Waldo says with that supreme assurance that comes tasseled and shining from a clear future of endless decades at the club bar.

Chapter 4

Pam spreads the little metal pieces on the metal tray in front of her. "Of course I know how to play," she says, suddenly interested. "My father taught me when I was four or five. He says I could name the pieces when I was two and could correctly play the pawns at four, but then I could never get the knight moves right. So he kept trying and trying to get me to move the knight correctly, but I wouldn't learn that. I could tell it was very important to him, so I didn't try to do it. I think I could have done it."

"And now you know how to do it."

"Now? Why yes, of course, now. I know all about it. Don't I?" Her voice trails off as if the question weren't quite a question but rather a short-term meditation on the apostrophe in the phrase.

"Yes. Well," I answer, "perhaps we could go through the moves and you demonstrate to me what Daddy taught you so long, long ago."

"I'm not that old."

"Of course not. What is this?"

"Bishop. It moves on the diagonals only. You have two—one for the black diagonals and one for the white diagonals. I bishop pair is very powerful, do you know why?"

But I have begun a quiet, seething meditation. So this is the perfect revenge from A & P How perfect indeed! Spending my

CHAPTER 4

time learning little moves on little diagonals on little black and white boards.

"Do you know why? You can figure it out, can't you?" Her voice sounds like some echoing incantation toward self-improvement, some weird conscience spin-off flailing through the thick, heavy, dusty, hot air in Ward Five of the Tampa Memorial Hospital. To become irreplaceable for her would mean answering such questions forever. Chalking off the weeks, years, decades of answered questions. Yes, the bishop pair is powerful for the obvious reason, the obvious reason—what was it?

Pam was saying, "For the obvious reason that all the squares are covered—sort of, at least—the black and white diagonals are covered."

"What's the point of the game?"

"To capture the king, to checkmate the king, so he has to surrender."

"I know that. I mean what is the point of the game? Why do people play it?"

"My father said it was wonderful to kill a whole afternoon and evening. It made time pass so quickly that almost any rainy day went by lickety split," Pam answers.

"That's why people play it—to kill time?"

"That's why Daddy plays it, I think. But it is a good question. We should ask him. I will ask him when he comes."

"He comes often?"

"Oh, oh yes," Pam says, not convinced of it herself, "whenever Dr. Coffee says he can come, he comes. Unless he's staying out at the ranch."

"Can we go through the moves some more?"

Pam pushes the rooks and the king and queen through their paces. She avoids the knights.

"My book says the knight moves one up and two over or two up and one over," I offer as a lead to a sensitive area.

"Your book?" she asks evidently hurt that I have outside references.

"Learn Chess Fast," I answer. "Waldo got it for me at the library, 794.81R."

"They write books about chess?" she says slowly, evidently impressed.

"Do they ever. Some fellow named Reinfield must have written fifty."

"Reinfield," Pam repeats, ever softer. "Reinfield." The sound intrigues her and I realize the chess lesson is over for the day. She sits back on the bed, begins to fool with the peculiar yellow nubbins of the spread. It's not the hospital spread, I decide. A little redecoration possible for, or by, long-term patients, little markers that the room is more than a way station, a kind of home away from home, is that it? She begins to clap her hands together, eyes lifting over her fingers toward the windows, partially cranked open. Steel netting in front of the jalousie bands.

"You are thinking of rhinestones?" I ask with calculated diffidence. In truth I am fascinated by these little leavings of hers. At some level I maybe envy her them.

"Rhinestones," she says after a while. "I used to wear rhinestones, not many, just one or two on dangling earrings. It was tacky with all that glitter, but I remember the first time I wore them. I remember exactly my father's wonderful guffaw across the dining room. I came down during the dinner with lots of people—probably someone important, someone Daddy wanted to impress. I remember there was candlelight and then I came down the stairs and then there was this wonderful guffaw. It was all so clear, as if it . . ." She seemed to lose the thread. More toying with the yellow nubbins. Then the alluring slithering across the satin or polyester, or whatever it was the spread was made of.

She stops at the edge of the bed, looks at me. "You were the first it happened with, you know."

"Happened?"

"You know. You noticed. You asked, 'What's going on?' when it happened."

"I'm not sure I follow this."

"You were the one. It has only happened with you."

"No one else?"

"Right."

"No one else so good, eh?"

"Maybe. Maybe so," she says looking down at the spread. "Anyway, you knew when you asked, 'What's going on?'"

"Just once?"

"Just once."

"What is going on?" I ask.

"What is going on?" she answers.

Chapter 5

"Where'd you get the technical data?" Waldo asks, evidently pleased.

"There's chess magazines that annotate the games."

"So it's not your prose, then?"

"Maybe not, maybe so. It all passes through the extraordinary prism of my mind."

"Of course!" Waldo says, pretending to applaud. "And you are learning the game."

"Learning the game, Waldo. Learning the game. Pam finds me a good listener, brother confessor. Maybe a well-meaning but ignorant therapist. . . . maybe."

"Let me tell you a thing or two. Actually two. Let me tell you two things this afternoon before we go out for a little dinner and some political talk. Two items of interest to you. Two items to think about through the long, hot Florida night. The lonely Florida night."

Sometimes Waldo begins to embellish on a residual theme, some private vision that been formulating through most of the empty morning at the paper, and he, like Pam, seems overcome by the deliberate texture of the thing, sidetracked by consciousness of whatever it was he was going to say. "Two items. Item one: about marriage—"

CHAPTER 5

"Jesus, Waldo, give me a break. It's the hottest part of the afternoon."

"That's true enough. I've noticed them sweating out there inordinately today. Just how hot is it? Shall we call the radio station for a reading? Okay. Okay. We'll leave item one. Item two: you need to dwell not on the technical stuff so much, but on the human interest side of the game. Personality profiles. Higher reader identification stuff. Gossip. Human interest stuff. Your pieces are competent. Everybody thinks you know the game well. But nobody wants to read the column as it is presently constructed. Except maybe some of the trailer park aficionados."

"Human interest stuff?"

"Precisely. Gossip. Innuendo. Contemplation of the tensions in the matches, that kind of thing. The human side of the game. Have you read this?" Waldo reaches under his desk, pulls out a copy of a book, Reinfield's *The Human Side of Chess*. "Fascinating stuff. Only a few games in the back by way of illustrating personality quirks. They were all nuts. Absolutely bonkers. Every one of them. Wonderful read!" Waldo says proudly. He holds the book up. "I've got a theory."

I accept the book and don't follow up on the offer of a theory. But Waldo is remorseless. "Why don't we take off a bit early this afternoon?"

"Suits me."

Waldo has already stood up, begun the assembly of a letter folder to be put inside the leather attaché case he always carries ceremoniously out of the office, down through the rank and file, to be deposited until the morning on the backseat of Hillary's blue Mercedes. "I've got a theory," he repeats in the leather interior of that car. "It occurs to me that there is a distinctively national component to these champions, or at least a distinctively American style, versus the European one—and I include Russia in that European rubric."

Kentucky Fried Chicken, Arby Roast Beef, McDonalds, Dairy Queen, Dunkin' Donuts whiz by on the Tamiami Trail as we head south to the club. The cement pavement, like the bay on the right, sparkles in a glare that shimmers heat at the air-conditioned chamber of the car. Waldo accelerates, swivels in his specially vented wicker seat on the leather upholstery. "The American champions are much younger. They burn out faster, and they're much loonier. Aggressive, given to all sorts of combinations and hostile actions at the board and away from it. Nearly all religious quacks. Sexually hung-up freaks. Did you know that Paul Morphy, the first American world champion supposedly— I don't think the title was awarded then—ended up his days kneeling naked in a semi-circle of women's shoes?"

"I'd like to try that."

"It's drafty," Waldo answers evenly. "Why not do something on the last days of the American champions? Crib whole sections from Reinfield, if you need to. This fellow Fischer is very much in the American mold. Maybe you could get an interview with him. Where does he live anyway?"

"I dunno."

"Well, maybe I'll make it my business to find out and we'll try to get you to talk to him."

"Not for a while."

"Why not? You afraid?"

"Sure. And I won't be suckered into another absurd possibility argument. I won't."

"Sensitive fellow," Waldo remarks. "Ready for item one?"

"No. Not really."

"Neither am I. It cuts too close to the bone. We need G & Ts for that." "For everything."

"Yes," Waldo laughs, "for everything."

The road to the club from off the trail bisects a large black neighborhood filled with graying tin-roofed shacks, and rusted-out Buicks. Tape recorders stud the tops of the wounded cars. Kids in grey underwear run off and onto the porches that slope down to the littering palm leaves browning in the dirt before the shacks. A few old men in glistening white short-sleeve shirts sit in rocking chairs and move almost imperceptibly on the porches. They pat their foreheads with sand colored handkerchiefs.

Waldo eyes this scene avidly. Every time we come, it is as if the feast of this litter pumps him for the cool, gripping hold of the Gin and Tonic at the bar. He remarks, as he always does, while the Mercedes plumes through the watching envy, "Hmmn, such American choices. Such American choices."

Then the ironwork of the trellised archway to the club grounds looms up, and we are safely in. Harry, the black retainer in a white linen suit, bows enough to bring a smile back to Waldo's temporarily disturbed visage.

"The first few sips, the first few slugs of a G & T have got to be the most refreshing liquid in the history of the planet," Waldo says, sinking more easily, more pleasantly, into the deeper blue shag carpet in the bar. The yachts are mostly out. Grey and white docks stand tranquil and receptive through the polished, floor-to-ceiling glass at the far end of the bar.

"The Americans—young and nuts," Waldo continues, putting both hands now around his glass. The lime half bobs to the surface. He pokes at it with his right thumb. "You need to find a new champion, Snelly. Someone on the way up. Younger and nuttier even than Fischer. Make him the center of your column—become an expert on him. Expertise is the path to fortune in this land. Isn't that so?"

"I thought rich women were," I answer, having finished more than half of my drink. There is a perfect thirst-quenching shuffling of interior props about midway down a good G & T. You need middling gin with a good bite to it, and Schweppes, nothing else, for tonic. And a full half a lime that impedes the drinking even as it shuts the ice away from your lips and speeds the liquidification of your brain.

Waldo orders two more. "Somebody out there just like you, only with chess talent. Do you have any?"

"Why don't you ask me next year at this time?"

"So it's not such a bad long-term arrangement, then?"

"I'll stay through the Interzonals."

"The Interzonals, they sound wonderfully exotic," Waldo remarks contemplating the second drink set before us. "Wonderfully official. The Interzonals. . . . The Interzonals of the mind."

"In Manila."

"The Interzonals in Manila. Very expensive, Very, very expensive."

"Very far away," I add.

"Very lonely," Waldo says softly. "Very lonely."

That's all there is to the negotiation. We adjourn to the dining room for Crenshaw

Mellon, escargot, filet mignon, hearts of palm salad again, and chocolate crepes for dessert, with Waldo's private bottle of Drambuie.

On the second round of that sweet, sad liquid, Hillary joins us. She is a tall, leggy woman, imperially thin with a shock of thick blonde hair that has just the trace of curve as it hits the back of her neck. Very tan, very fit, very shrewd all at once.

"Hilly!" Waldo shouts, standing up so quickly that his legs dump a bit of the table toward my lap. "I didn't think you were coming tonight."

"And so you waited," Hillary says smiling, nodding toward me, as I fight my way to a standing position against the lip of the table. "Please, please. You're having such trouble. Simply give it up on my account," she says half-laughing.

"Hilly, what happened? What are you doing here now?"

"Waiting for dinner, love. I'm starved. Won't you get me some?" Abruptly she puts herself beside Waldo and I slump back into my position/ "How's Pamela?" she says as I readjust my napkin.

"Coming along well, I think."

"Yes. Coffee seems to feel she's making great strides. And for that we thank you, don't we Waldo."

"Of course. Of course," Waldo says. He has swiveled about and is gesturing energetically to the waitress at the far end of the room. "But what happened?"

CHAPTER 5

"Claire bowed out, so Frances called it off. Probably the best thing. I couldn't imagine what we were going to say to each other. Knowing glances, vague references to Jack. The whole depressing, boring affair. I'm glad I'm out of it. And Frances's notion of Thai food is more than a bit pathetic."

"Eh, heh," Waldo agrees.

A tall bourbon and soda arrives, then a plate of potato skins, then four stuffed mushrooms.

"Aren't you boys off to save the Republic tonight?" she says working a fork through one of the skins.

"You shouldn't be so hard on Van Shuten, if that's what you mean," Waldo answers.

Is there a trace of irritation in his voice? I can't quite decide.

"Well, don't let me keep you. After all, the bombs can fall almost anytime now that Waldo's finished his Drambuie. Haven't you darling?"

"Well, I think I'll have one more, to keep you company through the entrée, at least," Waldo says, head cocked to one side.

"Splendid. Well said. I hate to eat alone. And now young Snell why don't you tell me some good chess stories, since your little column is the talk of the town." She smiles, pops one mushroom into her mouth.

Waldo and I watch her precise mastication for the next half hour. Waldo talks about some of the quirkier aspects of some of the champions. He is a fund of anecdotes—a slick litany of personal disintegrations, aberrant behaviors. Hillary seems to be enjoying the recitation, but just before dessert she interrupts Waldo's prized story with a curt, "You're certainly more cogent the second time through, but less interesting."

"Ah, I forgot I mentioned all of this before," Waldo apologizes, smiles weakly.

"Since he has nothing to say," Hillary gestures toward me. "It's just as well and your telling has improved enormously. But you've spent more than enough time with this boring companion. Why don't you hurry to Van Shuten's and tell him doom is not around the corner, but merely across the bay?"

Chapter 6

The group at Van Shuten's consists of a surgeon, a pediatrician, a supermarket owner, three bank vice-presidents, two ministers, one systems analyst from Saturn Inc., in the northwest corner of Hane County, two high school teachers of American history (part-time basketball and soccer coaches respectively) and three older gentlemen whom Van Shuten introduces as friends from a long time ago in the old country. They have Russian sounding names, but in truth I am not clearly focused—as I imagine Waldo is not, too. The gin and wine and Drambuie gives the assemblage, nearly arranged in rows of folding chairs in Van Shuten's large living room, the aura or radiance or fellow feeling that I sometimes get at bars during closing hours, or what I hope it's like in locker rooms after a big victory. We all know instinctively why we're here at this crucial decline of the great republic.

Waldo is introduced as the owner-publisher of the Hane Tribune to the three Russian gentlemen. These fellows are apparently the center of this month's meeting. Waldo adopts a certain distance and a sturdy, nodding patrician air. Can he be grappling for the ability to stand straight, I wonder. This is the third time I have attended one of these meetings and Waldo sees no reason to introduce me once again. I take a seat, naturally enough in the back, let my legs go straight forward under the seat before me, almost touching the neatly polished loafers of the pediatrician.

CHAPTER 6

Van Shuten, short, gnome-like, stands before the group and mentions something about the treasurer's report. One of the ministers stands and reads off cash figures. He remarks that the number of calls to the recorded message is steadily declining, as if people are tiring of the litany of despair. Van Shuten emphasizes that the recording needs more than a weekly change. The group sponsors a telephone message evaluating the current political situation in terms of freedoms lost. There is another report on the continuing attempt to reestablish ROTC at Hane High School, and then another on the campaign to unseat Hane County's long-term and rather suspiciously liberal Congressman who floated to power "During," Van Shuten notes sarcastically, "during the cataclysm of the New Deal and has been sleeping at the socialist switch ever since."

Someone commends Waldo for adding the Buckley, Safire and Buchanan columns to the Tribune but wonders why the Tribune doesn't take a firmer stand against deficit spending. Waldo nods, but doesn't respond—an interesting tactic that clearly nonplusses Van Shuten. After an appropriate or inappropriate silence Van Shuten goes ahead and introduces the three gentlemen who speak briefly about their lives in America as outcasts from their beloved Russia. The three must be beyond seventy-five years of age, but there is clarity and immediacy in their reports of remembered Russia—details of servants, and freedoms and expansivenesses, and blessed safety. Then each finishes with a small hymn to American constitutional guarantees and the continuing threat from the temporary displacers and rapists of Russia, the Soviet Communists. Was life truly over for them in 1917, I wonder? A long time for leftover existence. Being leftover.

I imagine Hillary and the shards of lamb or whatever it was she was chewing as we watched just a while ago. What was she eating? I try to recollect it, but the booze has worked a wonderful relaxation. These old men are really splendid people, filled with a vision of the past that makes the present endurable, is that it? They want to return to their native land. Who would not want to join them? Let's all go back, I think. Especially Waldo and Hillary, surely the sharpest two people I know.

But something is not quite right. I hear hostility in the buzzing air. The nostalgia is gone and eyes are turning toward me. What can be happening? Clearly someone is upset. Someone is very upset. Better listen. Better listen carefully now, but the accents are peculiar—ingratiating but peculiar. Difficult to fix on. One of them is saying something about chess. That's it. Someone is talking about chess. No need to feel hostile about that. But, ah, such an automatic response. A clue there? Maybe I can't last through the Interzonals. Such a long time away.

Van Shuten restates the argument, looking this time at Waldo, who merely turns toward me. Van Shuten says, "So the position is clear enough. Even publishing a column on the game lends a kind of support to Soviet hegemony. I can understand that. The Soviets have put enormous investment into their chess prowess, and we here simply call attention to that achievement. Every other day reminding hapless readers that, after all, the Soviets are masters of this intellectual endeavor. Why should we become the vehicle of publicity of Soviet pre-eminence, is that your position?" Van Shuten turns toward the three gentlemen

"The game seems innocent enough," says one, "but that is the point. It is not innocent to the Soviets. They see it as a wedge into the intellectual aspirations of the rest of the world."

"More than that," the other says, "publicity about the game legitimizes a despicable system that robs the youth of Russia of their own intellectual freedom. Making heroes out of these automatons created by the Soviet chess system."

"More than that, the last says, "it sanctions the whole elitist framework by which Soviet masters lead an elevated life while the masses in Russia continue in their long lines and in their endless suffering."

I am thinking, who is suffering? Let me get this right. The masses of Russia—they are suffering because of my chess column? Can that be it?

"Three powerful arguments," Van Shuten says, "perhaps we can hear from the publisher?"

Waldo slowly gets to his feet. "Good points, but why not hear from the horse's mouth. Maybe not everybody knows it, but Mr. Snell who bylines the column, is actually here tonight. Right back there." Waldo points at me. Waldo's meaty and surprisingly red hand goes up and down gesturing at me.

I start gathering my legs up. It takes an enormously long time to reel them in from under the pediatrician's chair. They are like the old time dental drills, weird springs bobbing back into place under the chairs, despite conscious summonings. And Waldo's menacing hand is like the dentist's light above the group. I struggle to my feet. "Ah, ah," I say, conscious of turning flaming red, "Ah, I'm sorry. I don't quite, ah, I don't quite," I take a deep breath, thinking this is very peculiar. "I don't quite see the issue. Maybe if you could state it again, I could respond a little more coherently, a little more—"

"Chess," Van Shuten interrupts me, "is a Soviet achievement—"

"But Fischer was an American," I interrupt him.

"True enough. But no one would deny Soviet supremacy in the chess world."

"It's a game, a game the Soviets have only recently, very recently, dominated it. Maybe in a while—"

"You're missing the point," Van Shuten says, a little too loud it seems to me.

"You are not thinking deeply about what you are saying," one of the elderly gentlemen says slowly, in a kindly fashion. "It was a game, but the Soviets have transformed it into an instrument of propaganda, a constant reminder to the world of the edge they feel their system has. You have to stop thinking of it as a game."

"There are no games," another says.

"There are no games," I repeat. That seems like good sense. I can begin to relax. "There are no games. There are no games. I didn't want to write the column. I really didn't."

"You didn't?" Van Shuten shouts.

Waldo is back on his feet, four fingers against the back of the chair in front of him.

"You didn't want to write the column? Someone forced you to write the column, is that it?" Van Shuten fairly howls with interest. "Someone told you to do it. Ordered you to do it?"

"Technically," Waldo says firmly, "technically," he repeats louder, "Mr. Snell is correct."

"Who ordered you to write the column?" Van Shuten cuts Waldo off. "Who? Who?"

"Wait a minute," Waldo says, taking his fingers off the chair. "Wait a minute."

Van Shuten stops. The rooms falls silent. Waldo waits, then he says "Wait a minute." We wait. "The decision to initiate the column, the decision to initiate the column," Waldo speaks slowly, doubtless trying to find some way out. "The Tampa Tribune has a chess column. So does the Fort Myers Sun."

"So does the St. Petersburg Times," Van Shuten sneers.

"And the New York Times. And the Daily Worker," someone shouts.

"I understand that, "Waldo says, "The decision was an editorial decision and a circulation decision. We were losing readership in the trailer parks. Isn't it better they should find their chess interests met by the Hane Tribune with its columnists, than by the St. Petersburg Times and with its columnists? Isn't it?" Waldo begins to ride an evidently appreciated point.

"Besides," I add, getting into the loopy swing of things, "the column will have a very American focus. I want to write about younger American masters. People like Fischer who can humiliate the Soviets, the Soviet system, make a mockery of it. Prove it to be stultifying, insulting, to the natural function of the most advanced minds." I wonder what are the natural functions of advanced minds?

"Good point," someone says.

"Fischer was an exception," someone disagrees.

"America is full of Fischers," Waldo says, resonantly. "That's the secret of America, the secret of this great republic!"

The phrase echoes in the long living room, under the slowly revolving bamboo ceiling fans. And before Van Shuten or someone less enthusiastic can react, an elderly black man in a white jacket wheels in a tray of coffees and nineteen tiny, filled brandy snifters. With tacit swiftness the groups stands and moves quickly toward the trays.

Chapter 7

The coffee is strong, stabilizing, but not enough. I swill a snifter. One of the ancient émigrés says to me, "You are not used to political thinking, are you, Mr. Snell?"

"I guess not. I'm sorry."

"Most Americans aren't and that is a tragedy. Most Americans aren't aware of what they have, what their blessings are."

"I've noticed that," I answer swilling another snifter. I try looking beyond the fellow, glazing over my own eyes in an effort to peer through him, but his eyes insist on fixing on mine.

"There are great dangers," he goes on, watching carefully to see the barest flicker of skepticism come into my face. "Grave dangers. These are not good times."

I wonder when were the good times? When was it safe? "My fiancé," I interrupt him. Why bring up Pam here? "My fiancé," I repeat again as if on a trampoline, "feels exactly as you do." For some reason in the slow turn of the gin and Drambuie and wine and now the coffee and brandy, the sound *fee on say* is fascinating. "My *fee on say* feels just as you do. She knows the world immediately around her is full of danger."

"Your fiancé," he repeats apparently equally enchanted by the sounds.

CHAPTER 7

"Yes. Yes, she's hospitalized but coming along well. But she knows rather better than I do just what is wrong out there." I gesture toward the front door.

"Hospitalized?" he says, eyeing me very warily.

"Yes, in Tampa. Acute depression, I think, or something else. Anyway, they have been using electroshock therapy on her. It's helping, I think. She likes waking up afterwards, she says, likes being able to open eyes and wonder where she is and who she is and what is going on. I don't think she's ever wondered what language to speak. Have you had that problem?"

"What?" the fellow says.

"Wondering if you should speak English or some other language."

"I always speak English here."

"Yes. Here. She wonders about here sometimes too. Where is here? All that kind of stuff. Where is here? Has here been here long? You know that kind of crazy questioning."

"I'm afraid I don't."

"Well, I don't suppose I do either. None of us can, I suppose. But it's good we don't have to worry about what language to talk it, isn't it? That could be difficult, couldn't it? My fiancé," I repeat but trail off, looking at the fellow intently now, watching his grey-green eyes as they go back and forth in and around me, trying to guess what sort of flim-flam this is. In reality, of course, it is nothing like charades. I need to know why, all of a sudden, I should have begun referring to Pam in such a fashion. The fellow doesn't seem to be able to answer why I did it.

When I mention it to Waldo later, he is all ears.

"Take it as a sign—the sign that it is, Snelly, and run with it."

"Jesus, Waldo, why put me on the griddle over the chess column?"

"Well, I thought you should have the fun," Waldo says expansively. "I told 'em later that we're going to take on fluoridation. That excited 'em plenty. More than enough to keep your column safe in religious bounds."

"Flouridation? Jesus, Waldo, why do you get mixed up with these nuts?"

"These nuts run this town," Waldo says, apparently convinced. "And they're onto something."

"I don't think that's true," I say after a while. The bay is deliciously dark looking, as Waldo takes me back to the Tribune building, past the little land-filled island studded now with pinkish five bedroom houses that suddenly in the darkness seem natural, yet in symmetrical order with imported cabbage palms in very regular rows.

"Agreed," Waldo returns. "But I admire these people. I admire them. They know what they want. They see things clearly enough to find what they want and they go after it, and after it, and after it. They're the real inheritors of this earth. Something you can't quite understand yet, Snelly. We can't. We aren't the inheritors. We're the savorers, isn't that it? I like to think so. It's not that they're running the town, the county, the whole damn state. It's that they perhaps ought to. They'd know what to do. Regular planners. Committed people. Very committed people and good company when you can get them off fluoridation. Those Russian fellows were a fund of information. One of them was a U-boat commander in Japan at the time of the Revolution. He never went back home. Three years later his family came out through Czechoslovakia on a food train. Think of it. Think of the experience of it. Think of the things they know."

"I don't think they know anything."

"Probably don't. But that doesn't matter. They are on to something. You have to give them that. They don't laze about in the morning. They know why and when the day begins."

I think, but don't say, the day begins at four p.m. with the first, and for that reason the best, G & T.

Waldo pulls into the back parking lot of the Tribune, drives next to my old Fairlane. "You'd better deliver on those American chess whizzes. You better had, and fast," Waldo laughs, "or you'll become the butt of one of their phone messages."

CHAPTER 7

At this hour of the night Hane gets just the smidgeon of chill in the air and a certain dampness on the pavement that suggests more than dew by morning. A kind of clammy preparation. I sit now with the door open, waiting for Waldo to run down his exit speeches, tapping my shoes on the parking lot, trying to make a squishing sound, but not enough moisture has accumulated.

"Let me tell you about marriage," Waldo says behind me. I imagine he is staring straight ahead. At the big revelations Waldo never looks you in the eye. He must be staring straight ahead, watching the empty cement slabs that mark the end of each vacant parking space, or, lifting a bit, watching the still hibiscus plants along the edge of the parking lot. "Let me tell you about marriage," Waldo repeats, certain now to have my attention. But my mind begins to wander.

"There are lots of marriages," Waldo says, "you can begin by trying to find the perfect mate. Is that too stilted a term? The perfect lover and wife, the perfect companion—warm, ingratiating, perceptive, sensual, reassuring. And you can believe you've found her. Really found her."

I push the tips of my shoes deeper into the still, packed dirt. No squishiness.

"But what happens after you've found her? I'll tell you. You discover that what you responded to was a kind of mirage image of what you wanted, having very little to do with the actuality of the woman you're now living with, now committed to. A double disaster. Your fantasy explodes and you have a binding commitment. Not the legal one, but the dream of finding the perfect woman and failing. Enough to cement things for almost a decade, I figure in a case like yours."

"Mine?"

"Guilt makes you go round, Snelly. And not a bad thing. As good as some other motivation, I suppose."

"Horsefeathers."

Waldo laughs. My shoes push harder into the dirt. "You aren't paying attention. I'm talking about making a huge psychic investment and discovering it won't work, and then learning it shouldn't work, and accepting it can't work and then summoning the energy and the fear and the whatever to say, 'okay, now what?' What indeed! The problem is in the beginning."

But the beginning I can think about settles on Pam befuddled look as she asks, softly, sweetly, what day of the week it is.

"Suppose," Waldo goes on, slapping at the steering wheel, "suppose you start with a fundamentally different assumption. Forget calculations of the heart and think about your needs and someone else's. Cost and benefit. Simple optimization, isn't that what they call it. Suppose you start from those premises and evaluate the proposition, as you might any other career move. Suppose you think about what you can and can't live with, and what the rewards and punishments might or might not be. Suppose you get a firm, unclouded look at the future of a partnership. Is that too silly a term? Rich people have been doing it for centuries. Certain cultures do it automatically. Think about the Japanese."

"You think about the Japanese, Waldo."

"What it comes to is very simple, very elemental, and stunningly clear. You can acquire love, can't you? You can acquire companionship. You can acquire whatever it is that makes your little heart go pitty pat. But you can't acquire the other things. You've got to program them in. Plan for them. Scheme for them, weighing cost and benefit. Cost and benefit. Then, instead of guilt, you have a rather firm basis for continuing whatever it is that happens to the—what you kids call—the relationship."

How long has Waldo been rehearsing this? I can see him in the empty silence of his office, making notes on the conversation with Snell. But now, miracle of miracles, it seems I can actually get a squishing sound with my shoes. Rubber soled wonders to deliver me beyond this lecture, beyond brandy, into the dopey arms of the soft Hane nighttime.

"I'm talking about avoiding double disasters. Or compounding them. I'm talking about finding a way to meet each morning with optimism, with a steady sure sense that calculation and appropriateness permeate your life."

"Calculation and appropriateness?"

"Yes. Yes, yes!" Waldo shouts, as if to silence any sarcastic rejoinder.

"Good enough," I say to the darkness. There is a nifty ellipse of light from the lamp twenty feet in front of my Fairlane.

"I don't want you to think this is a private rationale," Waldo says quietly, thoughtfully. "But I want you to pay attention to what I'm saying."

"I do. All the time, I do," I repeat, still watching the ellipse and thinking about nothing in particular, except that it is getting colder.

"Good. Then we have no quarrel. I trust you see the relevance of what I've said."

"Of course."

"Good," Waldo says avuncularly, "then all that remains is for you to find some 100 percent, red-blooded, patriotic, All-American chess players to write about in the best red-white-and-blue prose money can buy."

"Money has bought," I say getting out of the car. It is difficult standing. I ease the door shut.

Waldo leans across the wide leather expanse of the Mercedes' front seat. He bends down, becomes framed in the thick chrome lapping the window on the passenger side. "Paul," he says directly, "Paul, I admire what you're doing. I want you to know that."

"Thank you," I answer. What is it I'm doing?

Chapter 8

Pam says, "They don't have very American names, do they?" She holds my first full human interest column. Not a chessboard in it. Instead, eight nice paragraphs describing five younger American masters and wondering which will be the successor to Fischer.

"It would be better for Van Shuten's group if they were named Joe or Stan or Harry. I agree Yuri and Ivan aren't too patriotic sounding. But which one interests you?"

"Oh, I don't know. There're no pictures. I can't tell without a picture."

"My word pictures don't bring them into focus, is that it?"

"No. No, I wouldn't say that." She spends a few moments rereading the column, maybe reading it for the first time. A lazy woman, I decide. Never really willing to read my column or play through the games. At length she says, "This one, the one in Washington, D.C."

"Why him?"

"I had a wonderful time in Washington once," Pam answers. "And he has a nice name, David M. Spendip. That's pretty American. And he's the youngest."

"That important to you?"

"You're younger than me," she answers, smiling a kind of valium grin, studded with mood elevators.

"Is Dr. Coffee cutting you back?" I ask.

"Yes, can you tell?"

"Yes. A certain belligerence has come back," I answer. "No more long suffering endurance of a hostile and aggressive world. Ready to strike back."

"Yes. Yes," she sighs, half laughing, "ready to strike back at a moment's notice. One moment to the next, ready to strike back."

I take the column back from her. "Well, you picked a good one, the youngest and the one with the best chance to make grandmaster. A possible Fischer all right."

"Body by Fischer," Pam says, slumping back on the bed.

"You know getting pictures is a great idea. Pictures can take up half the column."

"I have a very good camera. In fact, I have two, maybe three," Pam says pulling her legs up on the bed. "Does the crack there," she points to the ceiling, "look like a rabbit?"

"Should it?"

"Don't you remember that wonderful Madeline story about the little girl in the hospital and the crack on the ceiling that had the habit of looking much like a rabbit? It was one of my favorites and ever since I like to lie on these beds and watch for the rabbit. And he's here, maybe for the first time. In two straight lines. In two straight lines."

"What are you saying?"

"The girls in Madeline's school, in two straight lines, always left at half past nine. They broke their bread and brushed their teeth and went to bed and the smallest one was Madeline."

"I see."

"You don't, of course. But it's not terribly important. Just a memory."

"Do you want to come to Washington with me?"

She stops staring at the ceiling, raises to a sitting position on the bed and smiles, then says slow, "With you?"

"Yes."

"With you to Washington D. C.?"

"That's right."

"With you? You want me to come along?"

"Well, that's why I asked you."

"You want me to come along?"

"Of course. Yes."

"That makes me very, very happy. The happiest I've been. Washington?"

"The nation's capital. The same place. To interview Spendip. To get his picture. To fill five columns with mostly pictures and short, witty captions, and none of this heavy, stupid prose." I slap at the clipping.

"Do you think I can?"

"I suppose so. What does Coffee think?"

"He'll want to know what I think."

"And what do you think?" I ask.

"I think I had better go as soon as I can, don't you?"

"I think so."

"It's cold in Washington, isn't it? I had better get some heavier dresses, maybe a wool suit. Do you think that would be best, for interviewing I mean, looking professional and competent and interested? Above all interested in the subject, the other person. That's the key, isn't it? Letting the subject, the interviewee know that it isn't just a job, that really you're really interested in the subject and whatever he wants to discuss. I can do that. I'm always doing that. I'm forever doing that. It's what I'm really good at, don't you know?"

"Sure."

"No. I'm serious. For as long back as I can remember I've been very talented at talking with people, looking them in the eye and letting them know that what they are saying matters to me, has meaning for me—"

"As now, for example."

"Yes," she laughs, "right now notice how pleased I am to stare you straight in the face, and hear that you want me to go to

Washington with you. I'll ask Dr. Coffee tomorrow at the end of our session."

"Good. No sense rushing things."

"What does that mean?"

"Nothing. Except what I said, I guess. No sense rushing into things."

"You want me to ask him now, is that it?"

"Un huh."

"You do. And I'll call him right now."

"Don't. It's not that important."

"Yes. I agree," she lies back down. "It's not that important, probably. What, after all, is important? We used to stay at the Sheraton Carleton, but we only stayed there because we owned it. I think that's why we stayed there."

"You did? Well, we're staying in the Ramada Inn on Rhode Island near 14th street."

"I don't like Ramada Inns."

"Neither do I. But that's where Spendip's living."

"In a Ramada Inn?"

"Yes, with his mother. In a Ramada Inn for the past 14 months, I think."

"How strange. In a Ramada Inn. Maybe it has small apartments, could that be?" She shifts on the bed, pulling her legs up further. She presses her head into the pillow. "When I was a senior our class took a trip to Washington and I was dating a law student at American University. I was supposed to stay with the group, but we were always slipping away and one night after we supposed to be eating at some Indian restaurant in Georgetown, we didn't go. I pretended to be sick, I think."

"A pattern," I say, but she ignores it.

"And so we went to an Italian place and drank a lot of red wine and we got very drunk, I remember, and then the strangest thing happened. We ran up Washington Monument. All the way to the top. Forty-eight stories. Forty-eight series of stairs. It's very tiny up there, do you know that? Barely room for four people to look out the tiny windows. My legs felt like . . . like jelly, aching jelly."

"I don't think we'll do it."

"Why not?" she sighs, closing her eyes.

"I just don't think we'll have the time or the energy," I answer.

"He would," Pam says, pointing to the vague rabbit in the ceiling.

But it seems such an observation invites no comment, deserves none, so we slump in the late afternoon silence. The sunlight sparks off the dust particles above the window sill. I think about cranking the jalousies open, wonder whether a certain cleaner might work on the heavy steel mesh. The last time we fell into such silence I discovered, after a while, that Pam actually was asleep. But such is not the case now. Eventually she says, "Rah Mah Dah," giving equal emphasis to each syllable. The repeats, "Rah Mah Dah."

"A new mantra?"

"Yes. That's exactly what I was thinking. You see it is significant how our minds work in similar ways, isn't it? I was thinking it would make a wonderful mantra, wonderful chant. And you said it before I could, as if you heard me think it. Isn't that something? Doesn't that say something about us?"

"Spen Dip," I answer.

"Spen Dip," she replies, "Spend Dip. Spen Dip. I'm just not getting anything else, are you? Rah Mah Dah was a whole lot better, a whole lot better."

Chapter 9

But the Ramada is hardly better than its surroundings. Litter Kingdom. About one block back from Logan Circle on Rhode Island, the hotel sits like a market at the end of the restored neighborhood. Below it, toward the White House, little town houses have been restored and re-bricked, pottery shops and boutiques have been refurbished, but above it, going toward the Circle there are only burned out shells of buildings, second hand television repair shops, window-smashed liquor stores, unpainted grocery markets, as if the flotsam of 14 Street had simply washed down to the Inn which served as a kind of dam.

Logan Circle is huge, open, and filthy. The statue of the General stands amid beer bottles, and pop top lids, mounds of broken glass and benches flocked with sleeping drunks. The buildings facing the Circle betray 1890s circularities and aspirations, mounting higher and above their narrow foundations like gothic thrusts of would-be elegance, but their interiors are burned out, boarded up, broken through. A glimpse of plumbing pipes here, an empty fireplace there, stripped of its best marble and bricks, naked studs and beams, thick eight by twelve's are clearly visible through the gapping exteriors.

"This must be the shabbiest Ramada Inn of the whole chain," Pam says as we settle into the "Honeymoon" double, a mammoth chocolate carpeted room with a small dining alcove and linoleum-topped dining table, vinyl chairs. There is a small kitchenette complete with dishwasher and refrigerator and stove.

The ceilings are a trifle too low, the lighting highly diffuse from hidden bulbs mounted in a valence above the twin double beds that watch the dining alcove. Did someone imagine a foursome Honeymoon? Light beige drapes. There is a residue film from cleaning rags raked over the Formica night stands.

"Talk about tacky," Pam says, pulling out a chair and sitting at the dining table. "I find this very discouraging."

"We could request another room," I offer.

"I don't think that would help."

"Yes, another life somewhere else. Perhaps on the coast of North Carolina, or . . . or. But what does it matter? I feel better already. I used to think climate and surroundings made a big difference. But of course they don't. You carry into them whatever, isn't that so?"

"If Dr. Coffee says so."

"He does, I think. Although I'm never very clear on what he is saying. Always asking me, did I mean this or that? Was I feeling this or that? Am I clear on this or that? This or that . . . .This or that."

I unpack the two suitcases we had brought. There is a fifth of Jack Daniels wrapped by my undershirts. I pour about an inch into the glass on the nightstand, careful to avoid the strip of paper across the top of the glass. Does the paper signal germ-free sanitation?

"I want some too," Pam says.

"Not a wise idea. This stuff doesn't mix with Librium or Lithium or whatever it is, those little yellow and red things you're taking."

"I know all that, but all the same, I want some." She comes over and takes the glass up, flicking away the paper strap. "I thought they only wrapped toilet seats with these."

I pour another glass. "To Dr. Coffee and his wonderful open-mindedness on this."

"This drink?" she asks.

"This trip. This being together."

She smiles a wide, vacant grin. Her eyes glaze a bit. "Being together," she says slowly.

The track of a vacuum cleaner spreads out at our feet. I can trace the motions of the maid, the parts she skipped, the parts she did twice. I wonder what is underneath the bed, for surely the old wheeled Hoover beater she evidently used could not fit under the edge of these Honeymoon beauties.

"Do you think we should be together now?" I say quietly to Pam, brushing away the thick black hair that shields her wonderfully vulnerable ear.

"Oh, I think so," she answers, setting down the drink.

Down comes the thick corduroy spread, folded five times in a neat, narrow band at the end of bed. Back comes the thick polyester brown blanket. Down comes the tired, evidently worn sheet. The thick, crisp pillows, beneath their slips encased in some sort of crinkly cold material, get stacked up under Pam's head.

"Talk dreamy to me," Pam says, as I undo her clothes and underwear. She has a lovely peach colored and coolly soft skin.

"Dreamy, kid?"

"Yes. You know, real Don Ameche stuff."

"Your breasts are like melons or sea dunes, that kind of stuff?"

"Yes. That's good. Yes. That's it. Very good."

The delicate scallop sculpture of her stomach is fiercely exciting as always.

"Cover me. It's cold in here."

After I am undressed and on top of her, I pull the blanket up, then the corduroy spread. Brown dark warmth surrounds us. I pull it over our heads.

"Now talk dreamy to me."

I begin a slow moaning in her left ear. A slower, rocking exploration.

"Dreamy stuff," I say to her.

"Yea, really dreamy stuff. Oh, dreamy, dreamy."

"A chocolate shag sea," I whisper in her ear and then watch her vacant, grinning face as she brings her legs around my back.

Her hands do a tattoo on my back, delicate palpitation that finds the most erogenous zones, taut niches of flesh above my kidneys. Then her fingers go rubbery, slip off and flop back on the sheet. Her legs settle in as if consciousness has gone somewhere else. Has she passed out? I push a bit of the brown spread back. Track light creeps in from the kitchen. She is smiling, face sideways on the sheet, a little curl of saliva coming out of the top of her mouth.

"Are you all right?" I ask.

"Is anybody?" she answers, suddenly clamping on me again. "Fooled ya!"

"What's happening?" I ask.

"You know. You know," she says slowly flopping back on the sheet. We repeat this game a while, rocking and flopping. Rocking slowly until we both fall asleep.

At dinner in the Ramada's tiny dining room downstairs, overlooking the front entrance, she seems zombie-like, glazed, indifferent. We pick at Salisbury steaks, and thick, soft French fries, side orders of slaw. The dining room is empty. About twelve tables arranged in straight lines. A counter at one end, apparently for cafeteria style breakfast the next morning.

"It was lots better before all this medication," she says.

"It was?"

"Sure," she answers. "You know that. You can tell, too. I'm sure."

"You had more energy," I offer.

"I'm sorry," she returns, pushing her little dish of cole slaw toward me. "Take this as compensation."

"A fair trade?"

"If you think so." We fall to silence, mutual mastication.

Pam says, finally, "I suppose people are upstairs in their own kitchenettes."

"Yes."

"Maybe I should cook for you. Little elegant dinners. Candle-lit dinners in room 412."

"With harpsichord music."

CHAPTER 9

"Yes, with harpsichord music and, and, oh, I don't know. You notice that sometimes I begin a sentence and then it goes away. Just trails off some place like a pennant. I can catch the beginning of it, but then it goes by and I can't catch the end of it—like skywriters or, rather, you know those planes that fly along the beaches with big signs behind them. When they turn, sometimes you can't see entirely what the message is. Do you know that?"

"Hmnn."

"Don't do that. You don't have to do that."

"Sorry."

Just as our coffee arrives a large, matronly woman wearing excessive orange shaded powder and a boy in bluejeans and a grey, white, and red polo shirt come into the dining room. They take a table against the far wall, but after a few minutes the woman negotiates a change, apparently so they don't overlook the lobby. The woman received a tall bourbon, apparently without asking for it, then a shrimp cocktail. The boy puts a small electronic box on the table top and begins punching buttons. She gets a second shrimp cocktail and puts it to one side. After a few moments the boy looks up and smiles at the woman, then pushes the box around for her to look at. She inspects the box and then passes him the shrimp cocktail.

I nod toward them and say to Pam, "Our prey."

"Do you think so?" Pam responds, very interested.

"Yes, indeed. David M. Spendip and friend."

"She looks ferocious and he looks like a child."

"Maybe fourteen. It's hard to tell."

"He looks older, but dresses younger," Pam says staring at them.

The woman looks around, cruises her eyes on us and pauses long enough to issue a little chastisement, then insolently tosses her head back toward the boy. Their Salisbury steaks arrive and a glass red wine for the woman. The boy concentrates on the electronic box, pausing only to show the results periodically.

"We have an eleven o'clock interview in their room, 1210."

"Is that a computer chess kit?"

"Presumably. No sense wasting time with conversation."

"Amazing. He's so cute."

The woman turns around again and returns Pam's stare, but if she had hoped a simple test of will, she had not quite bargained for the Librium advantage. Pam's eyes merely take on a recessive soft glow, as if some internal supports or embarrassment mechanisms had gone to sleep. The woman screws her face up tighter and cocks her head. But nothing seems to break Pam's inert concentration.

Finally the woman says loudly, "Dearie, didn't somebody ever tell you it's impolite to stare!"

The boy at this outburst looks up from his computer. I take hold of Pam's upper arm. She turns toward me, smiling that warm, soft, simple-minded grin. The woman turns back, barks something at the boy who returns to his buttons. I pull Pam up and together we leave.

"You're not helping much," I say as we wait for the elevator.

"I know. I know. But did you see how he was playing with those levers? He's very, very quick, wasn't he?"

"I suppose so."

"Do you think that's what he does all day, plays with that chess machine? I would like that. I could like that a lot."

I contemplate chastising her, but decide nothing positive would come of it. It isn't as if she could be blamed, I decide. "Maybe you can talk to him about it."

"I have a whole list of questions to ask him. I wrote them all out and I'd like to show them to you."

"Sure."

"But if you'd rather ask the questions, that's okay with me. I just want to work as hard for you as I can, and in the best possible way. So that you can see how good I am for you and for your work."

"My work?"

"Yes, working on your column and doing this kind of special research."

"Special research?"

CHAPTER 9

"Yes. I know I can help in lots of ways. You'll see how important and helpful I am. That's what Dr. Coffee says about marriage. About getting married. What I have to do is work. Work very, very hard and show you, sort of unconsciously, how much you depend on my working."

"That's Coffee's idea?"

"Yes. We talk about it all the time. And of course I add things of my own. I know what you like after all. Don't I?"

"Especially in our honeymoon suite."

"Yes, especially there," she says dopily, half-laughing.

Chapter 10

"So, you're the ones. I figured it had ta be you," Mrs. Spendip says at the doorway. Pam and I are right on time. Pam carries a small Sony microcassette recorder. I have a leather folder with copies of my columns in it. "The Hane Tribune?" Mrs. Spendip says. Is there a trace of sneer in her voice, I can't quite decide.

"I sent you some of the earlier columns, and here are some more, if you want copies of them."

"Ah more copies, yeah sure. Maybe on a pearl grey matting, is that it? Incidentally they don't show me much," she answers easily, stepping back so that we can come into what turns out to be a very narrow hall, leading left and right. She takes us to the left. "They show me you can copy whatever you read in *Chess Review*, but they don't show me much. And I see you brought along your space cadet friend."

"What?" Pam says.

"Nothing. Nothin'. You're nearsighted, aren't ya? Maybe you wear contacts, eh?" she says to Pam, who nods.

We're led into a small room dominated by a three-quarter size bed. There is a small table with three chairs. Mrs. Spendip takes the furthest one, and signals us to sit down. "Now why don't ya tell me about this, this Hane Tribune."

"Paid circulation around 63,000. Readership well over two hundred thousand. Some people think it's the best and most conservative paper on the West Coast of Florida."

"Very nice. Conservative, eh? K.K.K., that kind of crap?"

"Pardon?"

"Oh, don't beg my pardon, sweetie. That crap I don't like. Why don't we talk a little substantively? Like five hundred bucks up front, right here on the table."

"The Tribune never pays for interviews."

"Isn't that quaint, positively old world. Special. You and she look a little old world all right—something you might see on the old Danube."

"I'm sorry, but I only wanted to talk with David a bit for some human interest stuff for the column."

"You only wanted to talk to David for a little human interest stuff for your little column in, in, what is it, on the West Coast of Florida?"

"Hane Tribune," Pam offers, working her fingers together on the Formica top of the little table.

"Well, wherever. You know the New Yorker wanted to do a profile, but no money up front, no interview. I told 'em that, and that was the end of it. They never came round again."

I look at her for a moment and then decide, since all was lost anyway, simply to be blunt about the situation. "That was a stupid decision."

"For them, or for me?" she asks, suddenly disengaging from our colloquy. She repeats "For them, or for me?" It seems the phrase interests her, as if the sound of uttering it was soothing.

"For you," I continue, worried that she might not be listening. "You should have paid them to do the profile. Not the other way round. Then you could have billed the hell out of everybody else, since the kid had already been profiled in the New Yorker. It would have been worth a small fortune. Why throw away that kind of publicity for a few lousy bucks?"

"Lousy bucks," she says slowly. "You mean tick-filled deer? You could mean that."

"I mean it was a stupid, silly decision. Cutting your own throat or David's—-"

"Mikey," she interrupts me. "Mikey."

"Okay, Mikey's throat. Right now you need publicity. The more, the better. Otherwise he's just another talented kid who spent too much time at a chessboard . Believe me there are a million of them."

She straightens up, seems jerked out of whatever sphere she had slipped into. "Yeah, that's why you're here, begging for an interview. Because there are a million of them."

"I'm here 'cause I don't know shit about chess and I got this crappy assignment to write a chess column three times a week for the rest of my lousy life, or until I can think of some better way to make a living. That's why I'm here. Since I can't write about the actual chess, I thought, what the hell, I could write about the people who play the stupid game. That way I could disguise my ignorance until I learned something about the game. But I'll tell you something. I don't give a good goddam about learning the moves, the combinations, the openings, the endgames—all that crap. I just want to turn in a few more columns till I can think of something better. Now, if you can help me, I can give your boy, your Mikey, if that is his name, a lot publicity in a remote area of Florida. But if that's not good enough, I can always find some squirrel somewhere in some seedy chess club that's willing to talk about his toilet training and his middle game."

Pam began pressing her head down toward the tabletop. Was she embarrassed by this little tirade? Did she sense something had been left out or was she simply leaving, in another vacancy response to apparent tension? Actually I was feeling better and better, thrashing through my litanies of mild woe. Feeling very good indeed.

Mrs. Spendip was smiling, "Call me Vera. You and I can talk. Why don't you put her on ice for a while," she nods toward Pam.

CHAPTER 10

"She stays, if she wants. Do you want to stay, Pam?"

"I'd like to sit in the other room," Pam says, slowing standing up.

"That's Mikey's room."

"Mikey's?" Pam replies.

"That's his name. He never uses David. And he don't like to be disturbed in his room."

"She won't disturb him, believe me. She doesn't disturb people. She's very quiet."

"Oh yeah," Vera says, "of course she's very quiet. So go ahead, disturb him."

Pam lingers at the turn into the hallway and then waves to me as if departing on a cruise ship.

"Okay, what kind of publicity can Mr. Publicity deliver?"

"You tell me what to say, just tell me and I'll spread it all around south Florida."

"For one thing," she says going to the kitchenette and pouring herself a coffee, "for one thing, I don't mind letting a few of your readers know how hard I've worked getting Mikey ready. And he is ready!"

"Maybe I could run a separate column on you and the mothers of champions."

"Forget that. I'd just like a few people up in Baltimore to know that it ain't the rosiest life trying to get a genius ready for his destiny. I suppose somebody in south Florida knows somebody in Baltimore. That's more than likely, ain't it?"

"His destiny?"

"What else? In six months nobody will beat him. Nobody. Even Fischer couldn't come out of retirement to beat him. And it's not retirement, you know. You read *Chess Review*, right? And about every other month there's a letter from him talking about this or that annotation is full of errors. Mikey spots the errors long before Fischer writes about them. Know what I mean, do ya?"

"Yes."

"The hell you do. I got the distinct impression you don't know squat about chess."

"I told you I didn't."

"That has nothin' to do with it. I'm talking about the Dutch Defense. What Mikey does with the Dutch will make everybody come back to it."

"Sure."

"You know, you're a wise guy. But that's okay. We still haven't reached our agreement, have we? You're right. Two hundred, three hundred thousand readers on the west coast of Florida don't exactly fill my needs. See what I'm saying? So tell me how you're gonna sweeten the deal."

"How about a deep freeze for your cellar?"

"Ah, you're so funny. Why don't you laugh in the elevator on your way out?"

"Okay. Okay. A deal. A very sweet, very easy deal: two tickets to Florida in return for a simultaneous exhibition some place in Hane. Maybe the auditorium or the Y or someplace. Maybe even the big new culture center Van Shuten is building in the bay. And —this is crucial—an exclusive—features and interviews for the Hane Tribune."

"Two tickets?"

"You want four? You have friends? I don't think so."

"I can't live on a ticket."

"Ah, a place to stay then?"

"And meals."

"Like here? A kind of Ramada Inn in Hane, is that it?"

"Something like that."

I think about an offer, and to cover I ask, "You mind me asking a question about this arrangement?" I point to the kitchen dining area.

"What arrangement?"

"The one here. Do you have a thing for Ramada Inns? I imagine you could rent a pretty nice apartment for what this costs."

CHAPTER 10

Vera laughs, sets her coffee down. "Sidney owns a judge in Baltimore," she laughs again, watching me try to make a connection. "And, get this, the judge tells my lawyer 'This is child support.' Got it? Child support! So instead of the cash we get to live here, in this dump, with its lousy thirty percent vacancy rate, in the worst rooms in the place, so nobody will ever want them. But once, can you believe it? The schmuck management actually moved Mikey out for four days from his room into mine. Into here! They carried his chess books in here, for chrissake, so they could move in two Japanese businessmen and soak 'em for that little hole next door. This," she motions to the bed, the Formica nightstands, the mock wood low bureau, "this is child support. It doesn't cost Sidney a dime, since he's partners in this place. But I'm staying. Know why? Let me tell ya why. 'Cause this neighborhood is changing. Ya can see it from the Holiday Inn up. Things are looking ritzier and ritzier. And the prices are going up and the little fag antique shops and the little precious boutiques. Someday even Logan Circle is gonna come back and meanwhile the rates here are gonna double, triple, and I'm gonna be here permanent, until Sidney can't believe how much he's losing every hour I'm in the place. And he's gonna squeal bloody murder, and I'm gonna stick him and stick him until . . . until. Hell, he'll probably sell the place and we'll be back on the street. Yeah, we'll come to Florida. Why not? Mikey likes simultaneous exhibitions. But nothing' blindfolded. I'm with the Russians on that. Nothin' to hurt Mikey's head. Just a simultaneous. Maybe thirty boards. I'll have to talk to him about it. Maybe forty. Talent can't be much down there, right?"

"I'm one of the best around," I say.

She laughs, "Good! We'll go for it."

With things going so well I move into another area. "How about some background on, on Mikey—why do you call him that?"

"Sidney calls him David. Used to call him Mikhail, the Russian. When he was in Junior High, Mikhail because he was always reading Russian chess books—just the annotations. But who can say Mikhail a lot? Mikey's easier, and more American."

"Nobody calls him David?"

"I said, Sidney calls him David."

"What does he want to be called?"

"He wants to study chess books. Some days I call him Davey, especially if Sidney actually sends some cash, which from to time he does. Conscience, heard of it? You probably have, especially with her." She motions toward the other room.

"What does that mean?"

"Such sensitivity. It don't mean a thing. Nothin' nothing. Don't be so nervous. And call me Vera. And what did ya say your name was?"

"Paul Snell."

"And that is Mrs. Snell?"

"No. Not at all."

"I didn't think so. Jesus, what is she on anyway?"

"On?"

"Don't be cute with me. That, I don't like. Just when we were getting' to know each other, you get cute. I don't like that, see? For business reasons I'd like to know whether you're doing the same stuff she is, are ya?"

"You mean macramé, leather wallets, rope-soled sandals?"

"I told you not to be cute, so why don't ya listen to me? Here we are trying to reach an agreement, and I need to have some very clear information who I'm dealing with and whether I should continue to enter these negotiations. So I'm asking a simple, direct question. I'm not taking Mikey into some place that's drug heaven."

I think, is Hane drug heaven? "If you're asking whether I'm doing drugs, the question is insulting. I'm a normal American which means of course I smoke grass, snort cocaine, do hash when I can get it, and have thought about injecting stronger stuff. But I'm no hippie drug freak. I'm a reputable emerging authority on the chess world. You can testify to my expertise. In fact, I'd like to use you as a reference."

Vera merely waves her had at me and says very quietly, "Look, there's something wrong with her."

CHAPTER 10

"There's something wrong with all of us."

She sighs, puts both hands on the table, "When do we get the tickets? And where we gonna stay?"

"I'll have to get authorization from my publisher. That won't be any problem. Yes, there is something wrong with her, and yes she is on something. Librium and some mood elevators, maybe lithium, I don't know. But I'm not on anything, not interested in anything. You should feel safe. And Mikey should feel protected. In good hands. Good regular and boring hands. But even when she's on something, she's a whole lot better than you are, so why don't you shut up about her for a while?" I'm surprised by my sudden sentiment.

"So touchy," Vera says, "so very touchy. I didn't realize you were so connected to her."

"Connected?" I am somewhat puzzled by my own growing irritation.

"Young love," Vera says. "Ya want fresh coffee?"

"No. I want to meet Mikey."

The hallway's narrow, chocolate shag corridor is, in fact, a time warp. Coming into Mikey's room is like coming into another country, another time. Initial obstacle course—stacks of books are in the doorway and against the walls and in the middle of the room. Some stacks are over four feet high. The ones against the wall reach to eye level, a little higher in the corners. In the center of the room, in a space consciously cleared among the stacks are three small typing tables, each one holding a wooden chess board and rather large Stanton-style chess pieces. Mikey sits on a heavily padded desk chair that can swivel and sway. Pam is kneeling beside him, hands on the top of his left thigh, watching him rearrange the pieces on the board in front of him. He quickly shuffles the pieces about and then asks her something. She arches up higher, pressing harder on his thigh, and points to a rook.

"Nah," he says abruptly and quickly moves the queen down, offers a sacrifice, and shows Pam three variations and says, "He resigned."

Pam laughs, wonderfully entranced.

"Mikey," Vera calls from over my shoulder. "Mikey, this is Mr., Mr., what is it again?"

"Snell," Mikey says. "And yes, I'll do it. We'll do it, won't we?" he says holding Pam's hand and pushing the black king over with her index finger. "Lemme show you Feldt versus Alekhine, 1917, a blindfold game. Unbelievable." He drops her hand and begins rearranging the pieces.

"Congratulations on the U.S. Open," I say to Mikey. "You played terrifically!"

He stops rearranging the pieces, looks down at Pam, then at me, then down at Pam. He says loudly, "They shoulda made me a grandmaster!"

Pam instantly applauds.

Chapter 11

"Can you believe it?" Pam shouts when we are back in our room. "My daddy should see those books. Books from everywhere. Maybe the biggest chess library in the world. Maybe bigger than the Library of Congress holdings. He says so anyway. And that's only part of it. There's more in Baltimore."

"There's always more in Baltimore."

"And he knows every game ever played. Every one, every, every one! He let me open a book and start reading off the moves and then would go ahead and recite the rest for me. And he was always right. Always."

"I suppose he cooks, too."

Pam thinks a moment or two—an infuriatingly serious deliberation about my comment. "I don't know. Maybe he does. I'm sure he could, if he put his mind to it. He just knows everything there is to know about chess."

"Maybe we could get him to do the column."

"He says he doesn't like to write. Only to play chess."

"You seem to have gotten along with him splendidly."

"I like him a lot. And I want daddy to meet him. He's very natural and kind of special."

"Ahhh."

"Oh, I see. You are, you actually are, jealous. Oh, that makes me feel very good. Very warm for you. Go on. Be a little more jealous, will you?"

"He has acne."

"Yes, and it's beautiful acne, sculptured acne. I bet his back has the most beautiful pock marks."

"Very good, Pam."

"He's just a boy, Paul. You really shouldn't think about him at all. You know that, don't you? Don't you? You ought to. You really ought to. I like what you think you are feeling. I do like that, but it's not really very true at all. Nothing. Just nothing," she says with a contrition and maternal solicitude that is all but unendurable.

We adjourn to a kitchenette dinner of minute steaks and salad with Ken's Blue Cheese dressing purchased from the Korean-run market on 14th street. I plan a special dessert of Wattie's canned plumbs. But before I serve it, I go back to matters at hand.

"How can he stand living with his mother?" I ask.

"She knows a lot about chess. That's what's important to him. And he is just a child."

"I thought he was almost eighteen."

"He is, but he's much younger than that. He's like a big eighth grader. Such a silly sense of humor. All those puns and scatology."

"Tell me about it."

"Oh, I can't remember, but there was a lot of talk about farting. He really likes to talk about that."

"You must have gotten along famously."

"I think he'd like to see other people, but doesn't know how. He pretends to be totally absorbed in chess, but I bet you could interest him in other people, if he had half a chance. If he could see half a chance, I know he would. Do you think he really will come to Florida?"

"If Waldo will spring for a place for him to stay—mother and son."

"He could stay at our place on the bay."

"I see."

"Daddy and mama are at the ranch most of the time in the winter anyway. So there's a whole house empty and ready for him."

"And meals?"

"Well, I think he'd like to learn to cook, and there's Marisela if he doesn't. She's there through the winter."

"And you'd like to teach him."

"I don't cook. You know that," she points to our dinner plates. "Besides, there are good Morrisons, lots of places to eat."

A siren moans along Rhode Island Avenue. I get up from the table and go over to the Venetian blinds over the window. Cracking a little metallic space I watch a police cruiser soar up the road, litter flying behind it, siren triple blasting as the approach to 14th Street comes up. The back of the cruiser has a caged section. I catch just a glimpse of that as the car twists out of sight on Logan Circle. "I had a friend who lived for a while in New York City. The noise got too him after a while. He told me he'd hear gun shots and screaming late at night or early in the morning around three or four, and after a while he'd hear cries for help. And moaning and he'd wonder what he was supposed to do about it. After a couple of months there, he said he began to resent the disturbance of his sleep. And then, once, when it happened again, and he heard screams and moaning from the street, he opened the window and shouted, 'For chrissakes finish her off, will ya!' Anything so he could get back to sleep." I continue staring up Rhode Island wondering myself why the story is worth repeating. "He said that's when knew he'd have to leave New York. He was becoming a zombie. I wonder what it would be like to be raised in such a place, or in some other city— Baltimore, for example."

I turn back to Pam, but she has pushed aside the plates and put her head down on the table. Wisps of her hair actually have fallen into the residue of steak blood and blue cheese dressing on the plates.

"Are you out?" I ask. But there is no answer. For a brief moment I think she might be dead, and weirdly that prospect has for me a mix of disappointment and liberation. How balance those emotions?

I go back to the table and ease her head away from the plates. She is breathing all right. "Do you want the plums" I ask softly, hesitant to disturb this interesting condition: suspended, vulnerable animation. But there is no answer, and I put the open can back in the refrigerator. I shift Pam to the bed. Her breathing is natural and very regular, apparently she is exhausted. True repose, then? Absolute trust in me? Relaxed with me, then? More likely, simply burned out from the heady encounter with the splendid Mikey Spendip.

I move the phone into the kitchenette, slide the canvas door across the archway and call Waldo. His hello has a four G & T grogginess to it.

"Some progress to report," I begin, wondering what he has in his hand at the other end of the line—a cognac snifter? A Redbook Magazine? His yachting hat?

"Some progress?" he rejoins weakly.

"Yes, we've met the redoubtable Spendip and mother and they are ours."

"Yours?"

"Yes, if you buy the tickets, we get to bring them to Florida and put them up at Pam's house on the bay—"

"Ah, attractive quarters," Waldo says, perking up, "waterfront is so expensive nowadays."

"Spendip will give a simultaneous exhibition some place in Hane and we can sponsor it."

"Sounds as if you've done well."

"You'll buy the tickets?"

"I'll tell Arnold to get right on it," Waldo laughs. "I think you can pick them up, up there. At the Capitol Hilton. You know it?"

"Yes."

"Is there something else?" Waldo says.

So I tell Waldo of my nascent jealousy. There is a thoughtful silence at the other end. Finally Waldo says, rousing himself a bit, I suspect. "Paully, I had a Syrian friend once."

Oh God, not another parable, I think.

"I don't see him much now, haven't seen him in twenty years. Maybe more. I'd have to figure it out. But once when he and I were buddies, I told him I was thinking of marrying a woman a whole lot younger than me. And he said to me, rather casually, but looking right at me, he said, 'Well, you know the young ones want to run and play.' And I thought about that a good deal and decided I'd wait a bit. But I regret that."

There is a silence filled with Waldo's breathing and apparent adjustments—slipping out of his tasseled shoes? Motioning someone to bring another G & T?

"Waldo, Pam's older."

"I know. I know. But that's the point. It's the same thing, if they're older and richer."

"What are you saying?"

"I'm saying two things, two definite things. First, keep your eyes on goals, not diversions and dalliances. You understand? And second, and far more important, if you're going into this with conventional emotions, you've missed everything I've been saying to you. I mean you should, if you're really serious, suggest Pam and this fellow— how old is he anyway?"

"Almost eighteen."

"You suggest that Pam and this 18-year-old go off for a nice long weekend in the Smokey Mountains or up in Gatlinburg or down to Gatlinburg from where you are, and if you're really serious and understand what I've been saying, you'll be dead serious about the suggestion. And you'll feel good about it."

"I see."

"Gin will help," Waldo laughs. "The trouble, Snelly, is that you've still got all kinds of romantic notions about your dream love-life. Just vapor, Snelly. Just vapor. So why not get beyond it, into something that matters? Something that will last, is solid, irreplaceable."

"Maybe I should become a Christian Scientist."

"You are already," Waldo says triumphantly, "that's my point. Do you see it?"

"Hell no."

"Well, you will. And when you do, you'll get free of it. People spend hundreds of dollars an hour for what I'm telling you, incidentally."

"I feel blessed."

"You are, Snelly. You are. So is Pam. And so is young Spendip. What's his mother like?"

"Like you, Waldo. Just like you."

"So we understand each other then?"

"Apparently."

"Good. Then I look forward to a fun week. Simultaneous pleasure. Is that it? Is that the headline? Double your pleasure, simultaneously. Get to watch and get to participate, or get participate and to watch. You got it?"

"Goodnight, Waldo."

"Goodnight, Paul. Sleep tight."

There is a coke machine in the basement, near the metal door to the garage. After I cover Pam with the bedspread, I decide to take the elevator down. Perhaps just boozy advice, whiskey talk from old Waldo, but I am interested in his unforgiving logic.

Mounted in the center of the garage door there is a small thick plate of glass about four inches wide and ten inches high, a little viewer into the parking area. It takes a special key to open or close the metal door. Just before I put my coins in the coke machine a flash of reflected light comes through the glass in the door. I stop and move to the viewer. Through chicken wire reinforcement I can see a bit of the garage. Cars are cramped on each other. I hear, or think I hear, a scratching sound somewhere to the lower right. I press up against the glass and squint. Yes, one, two, three juveniles in scuffed satin jackets are moving quickly around a Mercedes.

CHAPTER 11

Black kids in sneakers and each one carrying a bent coat-hanger. A kind of contest, then? Who gets in first wins the prize? What is the prize? The getting in? How can they drive the car anywhere, since you need another special key to open the overhead door to the outside.

Laughter and scratching on glass. A kind of whirling dance, as they try first one window, then another, circling the car as if it were a predator. Then one of them gets the back passenger door open. Instantly they are all inside, hunched over in the front seat. The engine coughs to life. They rev the accelerator. It takes three efforts, but finally they get the great vehicle backed out and turned into the tiny passage toward the electric overhead door. Will they simply drive through the flimsy aluminum, is that the solution? But no. They ease the car right alongside my door, then move forward until the driver's window is even with the key box to the overhead door. The window comes down and the driver produces the sacred key. Of course! It was probably hanging from the gear shift or in the glove compartment. There'd be no reason to take it inside the building. How simple!

The car eases by my viewing window. The kid next to the driver suddenly sees my face, takes a very quick reading and decides that I am no threat. Merely a puzzled and amused spectator through the glass. As if acknowledging my intentions and capabilities the kid nods and tosses me a bird. I watch his insolent third finger glide past my chicken-coop lens. The overhead door winds up very slowly and then the Mercedes goes screeching up the cement entryway, out of sight. The door slowly comes down. I get my can of cold coke and go back up to the fourth floor. Pam is still asleep. I decide she looks uglier in repose than awake, somehow less vulnerable, attentive, or concerned.

Chapter 12

"Vera is a woman of endless conditions, isn't she?" Waldo says at the bar once again. It is Friday and four-thirty. "On the other hand, she knows clearly enough what she wants and what her little boy can take. Nobody over 1400, she told me. What does that mean, anyway?"

"It means she wants slouch players for Mikey. Rating system. Master starts around 1800, I think. Something like that. Maybe 2000?"

"I thought you were an expert."

"Only to my readers. In our heart of hearts we know what a fraud I am."

"Fraud, Snelly, is a matter of degrees."

"You hold the honorary ones, I suppose."

"Unnecessarily nasty. Why spoil a lovely reunion dinner?"

"Ah yes, the first time Pam has been outside in Hane. I forgot."

"You had best bury that chip on your shoulder. Even a mixed metaphor gets the point across. Enough said?"

"Enough. Enough. Look who we have in the offing."

Pam makes her dreamy way through the long lobby of the club, ascends the turquoise carpeted stairs to the bar and motions for someone out of sight to join her. Sure enough, Mikey trails along, still in jeans and polo shirt.

"The young master himself for dinner then, is it?" Waldo says.

I take a long belt from my G & T. At length they both come to the bar. Waldo gives Pam a kiss on the cheek, then shakes hands with Mikey and wishes him well with the exhibition. Still carrying our drinks we move toward the dining room.

"Do you eat a big meal before a simultaneous?" Waldo asks Mikey.

"Nah, Just a filet and some salad and some ice tea. A lot of tea. An excuse for the bathroom, so I can check variations."

"Well, good! There's a man who knows what he wants," Waldo says pulling a chair out for Pam. "Your mother couldn't make it?"

"She's lookin' over the last minute preparations. She likes to have the room set up just right."

"You don't?" I ask.

"Nah. So long as I can see the boards. So long as they're not too low, so you have to stay bent over, and so long as I can wander around in not too big a circle, and so long as there is a stool every now and then so I can sit down a while, I don't care."

"Only a few conditions, then," Waldo observes.

"Mikey has played almost a hundred simultaneous exhibitions. Six hundred and forty-three victories, twenty-seven draws and only three defeats," Pam says, brushing back wisps of her hair from around her glasses.

"I got a lousy endgame against some Cuban at the Marshall in New York. Actually, it turns out he's a Master. And I think he was juggling the board when I was on the other side, but his notation checked out. I don't keep notations. I haven't got the time. I don't want to give some of these clowns too much time to prepare something."

"And the other two losses?" Waldo says.

"Prepared variations. Very nice wrinkle in the Benoni. I knew I had trouble when everything I played he answered immediately. I think we played the opening in one pass—like ten moves in less than a minute. He just wanted to get to his new wrinkle. I stopped a move short and went on, to let me think about it, but that didn't help. I think he got into MCO on account of it."

"MCO?" Waldo says.

Pam answers, "Modern Chess Openings. You have to know it all, backwards and forwards, if you want to play serious chess nowadays."

"Yeah," Mikey says.

"Well, good luck Mikey," I offer, hoping to get the conversation onto something else.

"It don't matter, one way or the other. But I hate to lose. Just for the record, I hate to lose. I really hate to lose."

Is he talking about something else? Too paranoid an interpretation, I decide. Waldo does the ordering and Pam asks for a Daiquiri.

"I just want to celebrate," she says. "It's been so long since we saw you, Mikey."

"About four weeks. Not so long," Mikey says.

"It seems like ages," Pam answers.

"Are you still at the Ramada? I ask.

"Sure. My old man's too smart to let us get out of there. He's got a great thing going."

Waldo says, "I don't understand."

There is silence. Mikey opens and closes his left hand on the blue table cloth. And finally Pam says, "Well, will you play the white pieces all around?"

"I play it half and half, usually or sometimes we choose hands and let that decide. But I'm gonna try three new twists in the Sicilian. Watch." He brings his little electronic board up on the table top. Pam hurriedly pushes aside her plate. Together they hunch over the board. He shows her some new variation. I understand more than I want to about their whisperings.

Waldo is at a total loss and so he orders another drink. "Hilly's coming later," he says to no one in particular.

"That's good," I answer vacantly. Mikey and Pam do not look up from the electronic board.

"What's next for you?" Waldo says loudly to Mikey, who glances up at him, then turns back to push more buttons. "I mean where do you go from here?"

"California," Mikey says, "then Manila, if I can raise the dough."

"Maybe we can help you there," Waldo says.

Mikey stops in mid analysis, watches Waldo warily. "Like how?"

"Don't you think about that, Mikey," Pam says, "he's very clever you know," she says pointing at Waldo. "Don't worry about that. This really isn't the time. The exhibition starts in an hour."

"Yeah," Mikey agrees. "Lemme show ya the last trick."

Waldo nods to me, as if to say, 'See fella, even these obsessive types stop what they're doing when money is mentioned.'

"Arnold give you space for the feature?" Waldo asks me.

"Sure, and very contritely."

Waldo laughs, but Mikey comes back to the issue. "You gotta way to raise the money?"

"There are ways and ways," Waldo says expansively. "Young Snell here might make you such a celebrity a major news station would pick up the tab. And didn't some millionaire back Fischer once?"

"Just before the Spassky match, but that was different."

Pam says, "Mikey, don't worry. These things have a way, a wonderful way of working out."

"Maybe the paper will pick it up, if you've got a good chance to win," Waldo says.

"I'll win all right," Mikey answers. "Nobody there can beat me, except with a prepared variation."

"Whatever that is," Waldo smiles nodding toward me.

"Nobody can beat me, if everything's even and nothin's been worked out before hand."

"Yes," Pam says.

"Well, I suppose you had best simply plan one tournament at a time. A lot of mediocre talent to be whipped tonight, for example," Waldo continues.

"They're easy."

"Or so it has been arranged," Waldo says. "You have lots of people looking out for you."

"What's that supposed to mean?" Mikey says.

"This little simultaneous," Waldo says, "this little simultaneous isn't exactly the Interzonals, but how would we ever know?"

"What are ya saying?" Mikey asks.

"It's clear enough. I hope you do well," Waldo answers.

"I'll do better than anybody else around here. Better than anyone else you could get to come here."

"Well, I guess we'll see," Waldo says

"That's right," Pam answers, all solicitation. "We'll see in a very few minutes, and then you'll all get your answer all right. Won't they, Mikey?"

What little allegiance have we here, I think? The partially lost leading the maimed? And for what reason?

Hillary saves the day. She comes into the dining room, takes over Waldo's rising antagonisms, and molds them into appropriate assertions of her prerogatives. But that little ritual is lost on Mikey—apparently so, too, on Pam, who merely parrots Mikey's thoughts on his new variations to the Sicilian Defense. Hillary persuades Waldo to remain behind with her when Pam and Mikey and I leave for the exhibition.

Mikey sits in the back seat of Ned Snow's Buick station wagon, a behemoth as long as a freight car. Pam swivels in the front seat to watch him.

"Will it take a long time?" she asks.

Mikey doesn't answer, merely works at his buttons more furiously. So I fill in, "Probably till the wee small hours of the morning. I've heard of some that go on past dawn."

"Not with these wonks," Mikey says.

"Okay, not tonight then."

CHAPTER 12

"We'll all be home early," he says again, apparently about to laugh at his own remark. Then suddenly he is back on the electronic board again, punching in new variations. Through the rear view mirror he looks very young, vulnerable. I can't imagine what opening he can be thrashing through that would make a difference at this point.

Pam says, "I used to swim with a swim club. I mean competitively. I used to dread going out for the meet. I used to get sick to my stomach. I remember I used to think, surely this is not a very nice way to spend your time, feeling this way. And I remember getting so upset just before my race would start. Imagining what it would like on the starting block, leaning over the water. Watching that funny, very blue, too blue pool water and smelling chlorine and thinking it would be pretty cold even after I got in, because the air in the pool room was always so hot anyway."

"Be quiet," Mikey says, pushing more buttons.

"And daddy would always be in the bleachers right near the timer and he would always be better dressed than anybody in the bleachers and I could tell he was just as nervous as I was. And knowing that made it a whole lot easier to go through with the start. Waiting for that gun to go off and thinking, if only they'd press that little pistol right against my temple, I wouldn't ever have to do this again."

"Will ya shut up?" Mikey says louder, but still not looking up from his board.

"But then, after a while I began to think having daddy there wasn't making it so much easier after all. Sometimes I thought it was making it worse. How could that be? But it was. It was! And so I started to think about ways I could ask him not to come, not to be so involved. But did I know any? No, I didn't. Do you?"

"Why not ask him directly and be done with it?" I ask.

"I didn't want to insult him, if you want to know the truth—"

Mikey says, "We don't want to know the truth. We don't want ta. We really don't want ta."

Pam falls silent. I listen to the giant Buick's air-conditioning, and to the little clicking of buttons in the backseat.

"I'm not very competitive," Pam says.

"Well, I am," Mikey says. And with that declaration we glide to a stop in front of the main meeting hall of the Brandon-Mercer Trailer Park.

Chapter 13

No slender operation, this park. Carefully planted pine trees mask the rather shabby aluminum residences. Wide spacious boulevards. Nifty white cement statues of baseball players mark off the corners. The meeting hall looks like a long, low ship—port hole shaped windows spread across the wide Ocala block front façade. Automatic sliding glass doors.

The thirty-six boards have been arranged in a large circle in the cleared main ballroom. The bleachers have been pushed away. Instead, folding chairs have been set up about ten feet behind the circle. It makes little sense, since you cannot see anything from these chairs. Doubtless the audience, what audience there will be, will crowd around the thirty-six players. Inside the circle there are three stools arranged equi-distantly. So this will be the house where Mikey lives, the house that Vera built. His opponents are a motley group, perhaps twenty of them come directly out from under the aluminum shelters hidden in the pine trees. The rest appear much younger. Two clearly are junior high school students. There is a single black man.

At the far end of the room a long table has been set up holding a mammoth silver coffee container and several baskets of potato chips. The Tribune photographer poses Mikey on the third stool. Mikey works his fingers back and forth as if pulling them into proper shape for the big match. Vera and a designated official slip into the circle. Vera motions and the man places a Number 1 sign on the edge of the table below the board. He proceeds to number each table around the circle. Opponents are all in place. Where are the spectators?

As soon as the official announces the start of the exhibition, Mikey hops off his stool and goes directly to Board #1. He holds out his fists and wins the white pieces, makes a move and quickly turns to Board #2.

Waldo says, "You have to have strong legs for these kinds of things."

Pam smiles in a lewd way, as if sharing knowledge of his leg strength, a little joke that I find annoying, but which seems to amuse Waldo greatly.

"When did you get here?" I ask.

"I never miss an opening," Waldo answers. "I don't suppose I upset him very much, did I?"

"I don't think so."

"He may be better, stronger, than he seems," Waldo says.

Mikey has made one circle already and pauses back at the first board. In rapid fire he and his opponent, a slightly balding, red-haired fellow in a bright blue, swan-studded nylon shirt trade moves furiously for about a minute. Then the red-haired fellow tips his chair back, shoves it away from the board and indicates that Mikey should go on. All the prepared moves are over. Has Mikey thrown him a surprise, or did he somehow get off the pattern? Chair pulled back in closer again, the red-haired fellow grips his temples and frowns over the situation. Mikey merely smiles to Pam and mouths silent a rather clear, "No sweat." He bounds along the circle, once or twice getting onto a stool as if to survey the little landscape of his domination. Vera, on the outside of the lineup, follows along, checking the notations and apparently worrying only about one difficulty on either board 17 or 18, I can't quite tell.

In the far corner of the meeting hall there is an alcove of electronic games and a small, low bowling platform table with weighted metal discs for sliding. I try to get Pam interested, but she prefers

CHAPTER 13

first to stand by the circle, as if to offer Gatorade or encouragement to Mikey as he makes his periodic revolution and then, apparently tiring of that service role, Pam slips into one of the folding chairs.

After a while Waldo sits next to her and says loud enough for me to hear. "I can see why there are no spectators. This has got to be the boringest thing imaginable. Snelly!" Waldo shouts at me (I am about half way to the bowling/sliding game). "Snelly, why don't you do some commentary so we can avoid falling asleep?"

"No prepared variations. No opposition. No interest." I say looking back and moving toward one of those peculiar race car driving electronic games. You sit in a special black cockpit and the projected front bumper goes whipping along on the screen in front of your steering wheel, and gradually you learn that obstacles will appear immediately in front of you, and then detonations will occur and you will be tossed burning and exploding into the vicious underbrush of a lower than minimum score.

"Snelly!" Waldo shouts, but I settle into the cockpit, put my legs on the pedals, grasp the wheel and imagine the vehicle starting up. It takes special tokens to initiate the ride and score the game. Apparently these games are for kids, but there are no kids in this trailer park. It is kid-free or so the brochure has advertised it. Do old timers slide into the seat and spin along the day-glo orange highways of the electronically vended universe. Could that be it?

The silence of the room is remarkable. All the sound that drifts into my would-be automotive chamber is the skittering noise of Mikey's sneakers on the polished terrazzo floor. Have they all disappeared? I turn around every now and then to check, but they are in place. The red-haired fellow practically has his forehead on the edge of the board, as if to take the vantage point of his threatened back rank. Mikey has stood for a long time at the board. Some problem perhaps. The electronic windshield before me is more interesting. The screen holds a race track image. At the top of the screen are two side by side racing cars, apparently blocking my way through.

The black plastic seat is comfortable. I lift my knees up, get my feet on the raised edge of the cockpit, slump back a bit. Yes, it may be possible to sleep. Can it be the seat is actually conforming to my back? The top portion of a steering wheel appears on the lower part of the screen, the visual version of the wheel my arms rest on. Yes, a little turning of the real wheel swivels the picture so that one can guide the image on the proper course, if the game were actually to start. But, fortunately, the game doesn't start. Instead, I can hear the sneakered stepping of Mikey's contest. His swift moving about the circle of his challenge. And I slump further back down in the seat, arms sliding down the real steering wheel.

I remember once driving back from New York City, after a night on the town through the winding ribbon of the Saw Mill Parkway, remember concentrating on the white segmented line separating my two lanes of that highway and glancing every now and then either at the leering guard rail that held off the deserted other side from my Ford Fairlane, or at the center studs that marked the miles on the right side of the road. The car was full of people, but they were dozing off. And the air was full of "Music Till Dawn," cascades of Mantovani, or the Hollywood Strings or Carmen Dragon or somebody else who produced music like so much soft flush. And the announcer who specialized in baritone, bedroom tones. Clear, crisp night. No traffic. It must have been three-thirty in the morning.

If I could just keep that white line from moving too far in either direction, I figured I would be all right. But it wasn't easy. It took concentration, and the air was soft, indulgent with swirls of stringy sound and the excess of bourbon was rising through my arms like pleasant paralysis. And the white line kept getting harder and harder to follow. "Flagship American Airlines," droned the announcer and then some other softer, dulcet sounds, as Muffy somebody or other, my date for the evening shifted her weight against my right shoulder. She was sleeping. Beside her another fellow was sleeping, his head on the hopefully sturdy window. In the backseat three more were sleeping, leaning against each other

CHAPTER 13

like so many mutually supportive sea bags. Flat, heavy, syrupy residue of pizza rising, like the bourbon, through the little shuffling-off energy I had left. "I get to make the choices for the next hour," the announcer said, languidly, caressing each syllable, as if to put the sentence to sleep. "And I choose, I choose some early—"

Whamo! The little blue Fairlane careened off the guard rail and sounds like an ax cutting through an oil drum enveloped the car. The arm rest on the door popped into my ribs and glass from the corner vent window rocketed down onto my knees. "Jesus!" Muffy called. The wheel spun out of my hand and suddenly stark in front of us, right smack waiting for me were two racing cars, those ominous arrangements of dots and thundering noise churning all around me.

I hysterically turn the wheel, straighten up in the seat, leap off the electronic pedal, but it's too late. The arc of the wheel on the screen rushes forward right into the bumpers of the slower cars and Kahboom! Electronic, haunting detonations vault up in the black chamber. "Good God!" I shout, but the screen clears and once against the semi-circle of my steering wheel proceeds up the track. A car appears to the right, a sudden road sign to the left. Just in time, I swerve.

Pam leans into the game and laughs, a positive cackle of joy, sounding louder than the hissing, racing sounds.

"What the hell is happening, Pam? What is going on?"

But she merely cackles on, her face now over the wheel and backlit from the electronic screen seems to make her hair electrified, or on fire, sparkling. "I can't see the road." But she goes on laughing and laughing, obviously as delighted as I've ever seen her — thrilled at my confusion and terror.

"Jesus! Turn off the machine," I hear Waldo's barked order somehow over the car drone and Pam's cackle. "Pull the plug!"

And then suddenly everything stops. The screen goes dark. Pam stops laughing. The electronic pedal serves no purpose. I hear sneakers scampering away in the sudden silence.

"Thanks a lot!" Mikey shouts sarcastically and then goes back to his circle.

"What is going on?"

Pam still leans in front of my face. Is she drawing breath from my breath? And then slowly, mechanically she holds a circular token about four inches from my nose. "I got two of these from the custodian. You were asleep, but boy, did you wake up."

"What time is it?"

"Two-thirty, maybe three. I can't remember. I'm out of pills though, so it should be very late."

"Yes, yes. Very late. Too damn late for you. Scared the crap out of me."

"Yes," Pam says smiling and about to cackle again, but I cut her off.

"Why don't you stop breathing on me. Give me a little room."

"You didn't like it, did you?" Pam says, intrigued by the idea of upsetting me, I suspect.

"Is the show over?"

"This one or that one?" Pam pulls upright and points toward Mikey.

"That one. That one."

"Not yet. There's two games left."

"How long have I been asleep?"

"A long, long time. You drool, do you know that? You drool like a baby."

"Chronic sinus condition."

"Oh, I don't think so. I think it's simple regression. You try to curl up in a fetal position and then your drool like a little baby. You look so cute. Therapy would help you overcome your drooling."

"Funny. Why is it taking so long?"

"I don't know. Let's go and see."

Chapter 14

Vera stands like a sentinel beside Board 1, pinching her hands together and watching as if the board were about to catch fire. The rest of the boards are empty, except number 17 where an elderly fellow insists on playing out a long endgame, although he is two pawns down. Mikey has won all the others, but clearly Board # 1 poses some kind of problem. I cannot see why; Mikey has a tremendous material advantage—two knights and his king against only a king and pawn for the red-haired fellow. But Mikey is evidently very upset. He paces back and forth inside his circle. Vera looks severely concerned.

"How long will it take?" I ask her.

She turns toward me, as if my head were on backwards. "What are ya saying?"

"I was just wondering how long it would take for Mikey to finish him off."

"You think he can finish him off?"

"Sure, just take his last pawn and go after him. Two knights ought to be enough even for me to get a mate."

"Hehn!" Vera says. "You write a column! You just knock me out. Ya knock me out."

"Quiet!" Mikey shouts.

"Ready," Board 17 says loudly.

"Just wait," Mikey answers.

"Yeah, ya just wait," Vera echoes. "You took a lousy twenty minutes five moves ago. You just wait till the damn sun comes up."

So it is Mikey's move on Board 1 and he can't quite figure it out, I guess. It seems as if the pawn is there for free. One of the knights can take it off, free and clear, but obviously that possibility holds no interest for Mikey. Can he have actually overlooked it? If he takes it off, what can happen? The red-haired fellow has only his king left. It's not as if taking the pawn would initiate a dramatic combination, allowing other pieces to sweep in on Mikey's king. So what is the problem?

"Mr. Column-writer, Mr. Expert," Vera says, "Mr. Hane Tribune Resident Expert, maybe you should know a thing or two about chess, before you go on writing."

"Quiet!" Mikey says and Vera grabs my arm, steers me back toward the racing cockpit.

"Maybe you'd like to know a thing or two, so you don't seem so ridiculous."

"Nobody has ever complained about my column."

"Good for you. Says a lot about the level of chess around here. Maybe I should tell you a few things so ya don't get hustled someday. You know there're chess hustler in all the big cities. Do ya ever go to the big cities?"

"I was born in New York."

"Terrific. I was thinkin' ya sort of happened by a roadside, maybe in Albany."

"Very tasteless, Vera."

"Very stupid, Mr. Snell. For your information, as a favor to ya, let me tell ya: ya can't win with two knights against a king. That's right. All that material, but ya still can't win. The best ya can do is force the opposing king into a position where ya could mate him, if he had one more move to make."

"I don't understand."

"Ya can get him to a position where if he could move one more time, then ya can pounce on him and win, but if he ain't got nothin' to move except his king and he can't move because you've got all his squares covered, then ya don't win. Ya draw! Got it? Stalemate! So ya hafta to leave him that lousy pawn, so after ya get him into the proper position, then he's got something to move, so you can get him. If a king's all he got, and he can't move it, ya got yourself a draw. A nothin'. A stalemate. A fat nothin'. So the pawn is poisoned. Ya can't take it. Ya take and ya gotta draw. Ya gotta let him keep it, so he can move it when the time comes."

"But he can turn the pawn into a queen by moving it down the board."

"Oh, ya are smart. So that's the little problem. Ya can't take it off the board, but ya can't let it become a queen. Very tough problem. He can keep pushin' it across the board till he queens it, and ga gotta stop that, but ya can't capture the little pawn. And you gotta maneuver his king at the same time, ya gotta do it all in less than fifty moves."

"Why?"

"That's the rule, schmuck. Ya can't mate in 50 moves and no material has been exchanged, ya gotta a draw. 50 moves and draw. Take the pawn and draw."

"Looks like a draw all right."

"It don't. Mikey can do it, but it'll take time. The guy's no schmuck. He's not gonna throw himself on the sword, if you know what I mean."

"Why not take the draw? Mikey's won everything else."

"I don't know why we ever came down here. Mikey doesn't draw. Not in Hane, Florida for God's sake. The one draw is all anyone will remember of the match. Mikey doesn't draw. Mikey wins. Just ask to take the draw, why don't ya? Now I'm goin' back. Mikey needs me now. This is gonna be tough, very, very tough."

"He has won everything else, hasn't he?"

Vera sighs, "Of course, of course. The 17 Board doesn't believe it yet, but that's no problem. Believe me that's no problem, a nothing issue. This," she points at the red-haired fellow, "this is a problem. You gotta see twenty-five moves ahead. Endgame's supposed to be easy—so few pieces on the board—but you gotta see so much ahead. This will be terrific. Mikey does this, he'll be ready for the Interzonals. But he needs my help. And I'm gonna be there for him. Be there, got it?"

I nod deeply, feign appropriate chastisement, but Vera instantly sees through the pose. "You make me sick," she says easily, as if asking for an ashtray.

In the next hour and a half Vera doesn't leave the number 1 Board. She stands first at the right of the red-haired fellow, then his left, then his right again, as if to harass him into blunders. She stares at the board for a few minutes and then smiles at Mikey, who as far as I can tell never looks up from the pieces. He has pulled a stool opposite the board.

Ten feet away number 17 continues his moves, but in a striking bit of demoralizing arrogance, Mikey merely calls out his moves to the player, never once looking up from the serious business of the game at the first board. Vera shifts positions, crowding in closer to Mikey's opponent. For a while Pam takes up the vigil, but it seems she is more interested in trying to get Mikey to smile at her.

Where is Waldo? A wise exit, no doubt, just about the time I woke up. This does seem an absurd enterprise—a total of six people now in a deserted ring of tables and chairs, and no talking beyond a called-out move. I wonder when the fifty move rule begins. Does the opponent designate the beginning, or does a referee later simply go through the score and determine that fifty moves went by without a mate and without a material exchange, and therefore a draw has resulted? More likely, I decide, Mikey is counting furiously trying to draw the net tight around the black king, while at the same stopping the black pawn from queening.

There is a White Tower in the center of downtown Hane, the only place open on the Bayfront at this time in the morning. I think about slipping out to purchase six regular coffees. I can actually imagine holding the floppy box holding the coffees. Probably too much stimulant for Pam. She's usually asleep during this low period of medication. Is that what causes her to stare at Mikey, trying coyly by flouncing her skirt or pushing up her billowy sleeves, to

CHAPTER 14

get him to take notice, to please acknowledge her. Ingratiation and for zero reward—her lot, doubtless Waldo would agree. Her lot: to be ignored—even by the vapid suitors who would not understand the message if they could receive it, would not delight in it, if it were explained to them. Take a seat, Pam, I think. Put in another token.

Two racing car tires, nearly touching, appear at the top of the screen, all right, even though we all are almost a room away from the mechanical cockpit. Two obstacles must have appeared on Mikey's horizon, for he eases off his stool, wanders over to Board 17, stays there, play two moves in rapid succession and waits. Silently number 17 topples his king and shakes Mikey's hand. But Mikey doesn't look at the fellow. Instead, he eases aside the desk of Board 16 and comes out of the circle. He goes over to the mechanical racer, stands in front of it, almost to avoid being seen by us. Number 1 Board makes a move and Vera motions to Mikey, but he doesn't come out from the front of the racing booth.

"Mikey," Vera says softly.

I can hear scuffling behind the racer, but Mikey does not come out.

"Mikey," Vera calls again, questioning, but her tone is strangely indulgent and soft. I sense she is taking up a different role, one she knows all too well. 'Come on, Mikey," she says.

Pam perks up, ever sensitive to upset in the air, attuned to humiliation and retreat. She offers to go over to the cockpit, but Vera waves her off, mutters, "Enh, huh," to her, then smiles apologetically. "Come on, Mikey, we still got a few more moves," Vera says softly again.

The red-haired fellow looks up from the board, swivels around on his seat and looks mildly enthusiastic for the first time in several hours.

"Come on, Mikey," Vera repeats. "Come on."

I can hear sneakers being eased into the front of the racer, mild kicking I suppose.

"Come on, Mikey."

At last a voice from the machine says, quietly, but clearly over the tree frogs in the light lights of the trailer park, "I can't."

"Come on, Mikey. Just a few more moves."

"I can't. You, you offer it, will ya?"

Vera sighs, turns toward the red-haired fellow, then back toward the game section of the ballroom. "You sure?"

No answer, so she repeats, "You sure?"

"I can't do it. I need four extra moves. I can't do it. You offer it, will ya?"

"You sure?"

"Yes."

"Absolutely sure?"

"Yeah, yeah. I can't do it. Takes four more moves, at least, I just can't. I just can't." There is an increasing edge to his voice, and as if to head off any further spiral of feeling, Vera turns back and says. "Okay. Okay. I'll make the offer. I'll make the offer. That's what you want me to do?"

"I can't," Mikey says. "I need four more moves. I haven't got them. I can't. I must have missed something."

Vera sighs again. She looks at the red-haired fellow. Is he a realtor, I wonder? "Looks like ya got your draw," Vera says softly, as if to prevent Mikey from hearing.

"You offering the draw?" he says.

"Yes. Yes, whaddya think?" Vera answers, wearily.

"What is he doing?" the would-be realtor points toward the game section.

"You never mind what he's doin'. Ya takin' the draw or do ya want me to take off the pawn and end everything?"

"You can't take off anything. You can't touch the pieces. You can't offer the draw," the fellow says, still pointing toward the game section, "only he can do that."

"I regular legalist at five o'clock in the morning, and we got a corporate lawyer wants to read the whole contract."

"I know the rules," he persists.

CHAPTER 14

"They all know the rules, don't they?" Vera says to no one in particular. "Especially in the trailer parks. Every way to draw, they know about. They know about 'em all. Specialists in drawing. What they do best in the trailer parks."

"I don't live here," the fellow says.

"You live here, if ya don't live here, ya understand?" Vera says sharply.

"What's that supposed to mean?"

"It means accept the lousy draw. You're lucky."

"When he offers it, maybe I'll accept it. Maybe I can get a queen."

"Good God!" Vera sighs. "Okay. Okay, let's adjudicate it. You pick the ref. and write us when he calls it a draw."

"I want him to offer the draw," the fellow says.

"I'm his second. You want to get legal? I'm his empowered second. I was his second in San Antonio, in Portland, in D.C. I've been his legal second for eight years. He tells me to offer the draw. I'm doin' it. So why don't ya accept it? Ya know the last tie somebody drew with him in a simultaneous? I'll tell ya. Twenty-three months ago. Board 31 in Tulsa, Oklahoma. That right, Mikey?" Vera calls out, "That right?"

There is no answer. Instead, I catch a glimpse of Mikey getting into the cockpit of the racing game.

"A French Defense, wasn't it? Dullest game imaginable. Seventy-nine moves of nothin'. No pizzaz. No strategy. No nothin'. Just step by step into nothin'. Right, Mikey? So look," Vera turns back to the red-haired fellow. "So look, you got a draw against a future world champion, a Grandmaster, for chrissakes. You want me to sign the score sheet?"

"You don't have to sign," Mikey calls out without looking over his shoulder His voice sounds choked. "You don't have to sign. Don't sign. Please don't sign."

"Look, schmuck, what more do you want?" Vera shouts.

"What I want and what's supposed to happen are—"

"Wait!" Pam sudden shouts. She crouches beside the fellow and whispers to him. He shakes his head, but she goes on whispering. He puts his hands on the edge of the board and she continues her hushed whispering, making, apparently a score of arguments. The fellow seems to tap the edge of the board as Pam ticks off her points. Then she straightens up and goes over to the game section, over to the racer. She crouches by Mikey. Vera watches skeptically. I'm beginning to get really tired. I no longer can stifle a yawn and the "realtor" takes up that action, too.

Pam takes a token out of her skirt pocket and hands it to Mikey. They nod at each other. When Pam gets back to the board the racing car starts up. The electronic roar of engine simulation fills the room. Mikey has his hands on the wheel, but doesn't seem interested in steering. He seems to enjoy the crackling booms of collision after collision.

Pam bends down next to the red-haired fellow and he nods. He gets up, goes over to Vera. "I accept the draw." He tries to shake Vera's hand.

"He accepts the draw," Vera says sarcastically. Then abruptly she abandons the sarcasm, almost consciously corrects it. "Okay. That's sportsmanlike. You played a damn fine game. And against Mikey, that's impressive. You're a good player. He won't forget ya."

"Thanks. Thanks," the red-haired fellow says, shaking her hand. "He will be a champion. I'm sure of it."

"Well, if he gets more competition like you, it would help." Vera says with an unbelievable enthusiasm.

What is going on? The fellow leaves. Pam takes my arm, pulls me toward Mikey in the cockpit. Vera hustles along behind us. When we get to the game, Mikey doesn't turn around, doesn't stop clutching the wheel, holding it like a robot. I lean in to see if he's all right. His eyes are fixed on the collision path and the detonations of sound comes regularly as he makes no attempt to void disaster after disaster. Tears are pouring out of his eyes.

Chapter 15

In the sweet foam rubber world of the Snow master bedroom, on the stark trampoline of dizzying pleasure, I can't resist asking, "What did you say to them?"

"Who?"

"Both of them. How did you arrange it?" The tree frogs seem in a frenzy to hold back the sunrise.

"I just told them both the truth," Pam says coyly. She slips out of the straps of her deep lavender nylon nightgown and rises on her pillow, as if to thrust her bare shoulders for inspection. "I just told Mikey that the best way to deal with disappointment was to explode it and explode it and explode it. Just take a little drive and have three hundred accidents, kill yourself a thousand times in this little seat and don't fasten the safety belt. I do that all the time."

"You play that drive game?"

"I don't have to. I told him to take a little drive and face up to it, and maybe fix on the shocks. Shudder with the crashes. I like that a whole lot. I think he did too, did you notice?"

"I noticed he was crying."

"Those were happiness tears," Pam says inching higher on the pillow.

"Sure. Sure."

"They were. I know that. Really were, you know. Maybe Mikey doesn't know that, but they were, you know."

"You're a real specialist of happiness tears."

"Yes. Yes," Pam says absently, wiggling further on the pillow so that her breasts, rather small and neatly symmetrical, come into view. She cups her hands beneath them and with a weird, pursed-lips expression nods toward me. "Oh, take me. Take," she sighs.

"Settling a chess match really turns you on, is that it?"

"Yes. Yes, yes. Take me," Pam says with a half-pout, half-laugh.

"What did you say to the realtor?"

"Not now," Pam says, reaching out to me. We have an awkward semi-embrace. My kiss doesn't quite land on her lips. "Is he really a realtor?" she asks, drawing back.

"I don't know. What did you promise him? These?" I stroke her breasts suddenly covered with goose bumps in the emerging sunlight.

"Ah, I should have, but I promised him something better."

"Yes?"

"Something he wanted desperately," she says kissing me again, pulling me down on top of her. "I promised him immortality."

"Good. Good, by injection or direct purchase?"

"How by injection?" she says, laughing slightly, tugging at the back of my Jockey shorts.

"Shall we try and see?" I ask.

"Yes, by deep injection," Pam says, pushing me upwards after I'm in, so that she can slowly scratch down my arched torso. Then her legs come up. When my head drops in by her ear, she whispers, as if terribly distracted. "I told him you'd write about him in your column."

"Of course! I'd love to, love to—love to," I pant in reply.

Sunlight coasting in over the scrub palms, the cabbage palms of central Florida, enamels the already golden parquet floor of the master bedroom. Sunlight explodes off the aluminum bars of the east window, gilts the edges of the blue curtains, then suffuses the rust-colored chairs and bedspread.

CHAPTER 15

"I always want to stay here," Pam says, "never want to leave here. Once when I was in Connecticut staying there, staying there to . . . to get better—is that the word?"

To get better, I wonder.

"In Connecticut you never saw the sun till late in the morning and then always through trees. You never saw the sky at all. You had to put the sky up there dab by dab, find it someplace else and stick it up there. That's not natural. I knew I wouldn't stay there then."

"What am I supposed to write about the immortal realtor?"

"You have to spend a lot of your time—most of it—looking around for the sky dabs to put up there. Do you see? But here, here, the sky, the sun arrives every morning, just when you first think you might miss it. Why there it is, stark and beautiful and full of energy and softness. And it puts dabs of itself all around you. That's nice. So nice."

"What am I supposed to say about him to make him immortal?"

"Immortality is the bottom left side of page 17," she answers, as if testing the concept. "Mikey will write the column. He's working on it now."

"I can imagine its objectivity."

"He'll get a chance to show some other variations."

"You mean where he went wrong."

"But it will show what a good player the other fellow was too."

"Maybe I should turn the whole column over to him, or maybe to Vera."

"No, you shouldn't do that," Pam answers, supremely wise, motherly in control.

"You and Waldo have a lot in common," I say after a while.

"I've thought that. Daddy thinks that's true, but not for reasons you think."

"I suppose."

The coasting sunlight for a while is distraction enough. I doze off, come to, doze off again. Why would daddy think she's like Waldo. What does daddy know? What does Waldo know?

The bed is low, a beautifully varnished oak frame, holding eight inches of very solid, very expensive foam rubber. And at the foot of the bed beyond our toes disguised now by the rust-colored heavy bedspread, lies the shimmering bay, prickling in diamond colored jets from the surface. To the right in a carefully sea-walled arc Gordon's Key's southern tip comes into the view through the sliding glass doors. Then, more toward the middle are two mangrove islands, curious relics. Beyond them two high-rise buildings on the outer key partition up the horizon. Low, luminously front-lit clouds top the reservoir of shimmering blues and greens. The air appears glisteningly clean. Imagine day after day awakening to this view, I think. Pam is fully asleep now. Day after day. Enough satiety to convince you everything had been suspended, rinsed in this harmless, charged, almost aching pleasantness.

Doubtless old Waldo would shout: here is reason for wealth—to command this high ground, to be delivered to this view each day, every day, day after day. Waldo once explained that wealth was not for accouterments, not for pleasures, but for reassurances—as close, Snelly, as you can come to immortality: to lie each morning and observe this view. On Thursdays perhaps trifling rain, or on Mondays more yachts passing before the mangrove anachronisms than you might like for esthetic or rhythmic reasons, but essentially an unchanging view one hour, one day, one decade to the next. Being able to say, no one stirs this view—that was the answer, Waldo doubtless thought. Was that truly it? What difference did it make? I could, I decide, simply sleep off the issue, sleep through the commentary, sleep around even the harshest meditations.

But of course I could not. Instead, Mikey Spendip came rattling, splintering, crashing at the door. No discretion. Perhaps unaware of what had been and surely would be transpiring again in the room. No. Spendip simply comes clattering through the door. He thrusts a neatly written lined sheet of paper into my hands.

"This enough for your column? If you need more, there's another whole variation I can put in. Really terrific mid-game combination that even I didn't see at the time. She asleep?" Mikey points to Pam, who seems to smile in response to that question.

"We're both asleep," I answer, edging down further in the bed. Spendip's voice doesn't seem to belong with the intense sparkling sunshine. I think of it as a voice more naturally in harmony with fluorescent light.

'Yeah, I can see you're asleep. What dya think of the column?"

"You want me to read it now?"

"Of course. When's your deadline?"

I think about answering that question but decline, hoping to confuse him. He merely sits on the bed and waits for me to read through what he has written: "In an amazingly hard fought contest on the first board, David Spendip missed a complicated winning pattern that it took over twelve hours of intense analysis to find. The classic two knights requires of course that the opponent keep one pawn so that he can move that lowly piece to avoid perfect *zugswang* and thus stalemate."

"What's *zugswang*?" I ask.

Mikey looks incredulous. "You really aren't a chessplayer."

"You guessed it. My secret is out."

"That's unbelievable. Where do ya get off writing a chess column, when you don't even play the game."

"We all have to go to the bathroom sooner or later."

"I don't get it."

"Well, don't worry about it. Just tell me what *zugswang* is."

"It's when you can't move, when you're not directly hurting, but if you move, something terrible happens—checkmate happens."

"A kind of paralysis?"

"Sort of—when you're safe enough, but if you move anything ya lose it, or ya lose your king's safety."

"But of course you have to move."

"Right. That's the point. You put somebody in *zugswang* and then they have to hurt themselves. Unless it's a kind of perfect *zugswang* and they literally can't move without destroying themselves. Then . . . it's stalemate."

"Like living in America."

"Wha dya mean?"

"You're safe till you go outside. You can sit all day in your apartment with shotguns and crossbows across your lap, but if you have to get up and go outside, you're dead."

"I don't think so."

"There're snipers waiting in small boats out there." I point to the glistening bay.

"You got an upset stomach? What dya think of the column?"

"It needs more information about your opponent. What he does, how long he's been playing chess, how he feels about drawing with a potential world champion."

"Who knows anything about him?"

"Well, let's make it up."

"Yeah, he's a furrier in St. Petersburg."

"Very good. You're learning."

Pam turns over. She brings a tan, naked shoulder into Mikey's view, but if that were calculated she must have been disappointed with the response.

"I shoulda won. But nobody could have found the way over the board."

"Not even Fischer."

"I said nobody could have. Only a few people could have found it afterwards. I mean it took more than twelve hours of analysis to come up with it."

"Well, why don't you send it to *Chess Review*?"

"I already did. That's why the flag is up on the mailbox."

"They have a big mailbox, don't they?"

Mikey begins to watch Pam.

"Biggest mailbox on the south shore."

"You gonna run the column?"

"Well, it's better than the one I can write, isn't it? The only question, I guess, is whether you want a byline or not."

"What dya mean?"

CHAPTER 15

"You don't know what I mean? You write newspaper columns and you don't know what a byline is?"

"Okay, okay. Very funny. What dya mean?"

"You want your name as the column's author?"

Mikey thinks a moment and then shakes his head. "I'd have to get paid then."

"Good point. Your mother's son."

"Nah, my father's," Mikey says, standing up. He pulls the shirt-tails of his long sleeve flannel shirt out of his jeans—tribute to the Snow's infinitely powerful air-conditioning system.

"Thanks for the column," I say, slipping down further under the covers. "I'll get the stuff on your opponent."

"Why bother?"

"Waldo will want it. Don't worry, you'll still look good. The headline will talk about your incredible winning streak. How long has it been since you lost a match in a simultaneous?"

"Over two and half years. But I didn't lose. It was just a draw, and I was up way more material."

"Very nice. Now why don't you run along so we can sleep awhile? Later we can all go oyster shucking, if you want."

"I want to work a new variation off the Sicilian, but after that."

"Twelve hours of analysis?" I ask.

"Nah, three at most." Mike says easily. He back steps out of the room—apparently spinning out lines of the Sicilian Defense already. Then he comes back to the door. "You do know what the Sicilian is, don't you?"

"Sure. An overweight woman in a black dress. She gets to kiss Marlon Brando and put a rose in her mouth."

"Very funny," Mikey says again. His eyes linger on Pam's glowing, sunstruck back. As if on cue Pam slowly turns over. Her breasts come out beyond the rust cover, but Mikey has already turned away.

Chapter 16

That afternoon we get to take out the Snow bayrunner, a modest enough inboard driven boat of about twenty-two feet. The plan is to anchor on a sand bar, drink the Martinis Pam has made in the large silver thermos and send Mikey over the side for oysters. As if by direction the afternoon sky is a DeMille production of masses of pink clouds, orange bars of intersection and incredibly blue spears of light. The sun backlights the largest mass of clouds giving them an unbelievable glow. You wait for ignition of fire overhead. The thermos beads up sweat like the tops of our upper lips, but the first Martini is absolute zero chill. It almost clicks against our teeth.

"Did you make it with dry ice?" I ask, aware already of the interior glow to match that overhead.

Pam merely smiles. I can imagine the kick of the drink on top of whatever downer she has been taking this afternoon. Soon enough Mikey is in the water, standing next to the boat and shouting, "I can feel them. They're right below."

"Be careful picking them up," Pam says slowly, then hands Mikey a new aluminum pail and trowel.

"My mask," Mikey says authoritatively, and I hand it to him.

When he is underwater, Pam slumps against the gunwale. "Maybe it's too hot," she says heavily.

CHAPTER 16

"For oysters?"

"For leaving the house. Maybe just too hot."

"Why don't you take a swim?"

Pam nods, apparently turning the idea over. "Is weather very important to you?"

"Very."

"Well," she says, "when I was young. When I was lots younger, I used to think the weather was not terribly important. Although I remember it mostly as very good weather. Good sleeping weather. You could sleep all day, but lately I've come to see how really important weather is. Not that you should think about it. That's precisely the point. You shouldn't have to think about it. What will the weather be today? That's a question you shouldn't have to consider. What will be the weather today?"

Mikey bursts from the surface beside the boat and holds up the pail with about ten crusted oysters in it.

"That's enough," I suggest. But he merely dumps them into the boat, their sharpness nicking up the teak and varnish of the gunwale and deck. "Jesus Christ! Be careful," I shout, but Mikey has already gone back down for more.

"How deep is it here?" I ask, but Pam seems more interested in the weather issue.

"Good sleeping weather. That's the answer, isn't it? Isn't that what it all comes down to? What is the best sleeping weather? Soft rain, dark sky, or something blistering like this," she gestures toward the gleaming bay. "The sun is full of cancer," she says after a moment. "And weather like this is hurtful."

"Do you want to go back?"

"Doesn't everyone?" she answers smiling, feeling her way toward some revelation, I imagine. A revelation that never quite surfaces. Mikey drowns it out with his second pail of oysters. He follows the pail into the boat, lays on the gunwale for a second, realizing he can't swing his feet down on the mess he's made. Pam begins picking up the oysters. I pour myself a second martini. The metal thermos has a wondrous coldness to it.

"I can get as many as you want. Even," Mikey says with full-blown enthusiasm.

"It's enough. More than enough," I answer.

Mikey finally gets all the way in, sits with Pam on the deck and watches as she begins to guide the oyster knife around the rim of the smallest one she can find. I pour her a second drink, which Mikey sips.

"I thought you were in training."

"This is strong," Mikey says, handing it to Pam. But she motions for him to put it down near the engine. "That's too strong."

"Out of strength, wisdom—out of wisdom, kindness," I remark to the unattending bay.

"Out of kindness, inertia," Pam says, revealing the first oyster.

"Out of inertia, nausea," Mikey picks up the game.

"Out of nausea, deterioration," I continue.

"Out of my house," Pam says.

"Out of my window," Mikey says, eating his first oyster.

"Out of my life," I continue.

"Ya gonna use the column?"

"Of course."

"Just like I wrote it?"

"With a little rearrangement. I think you misplaced some of the emphasis."

"Rearrangement?" Mikey says, stopping his eating, giving Pam back the knife. "What emphasis did you give it?"

"I thought I should bring it in line with the headline. About victories and one draw. So I put the draw, the actual game first. Your variation stuff is in the notes."

"You didn't put my winning line in?"

"It's there, but it's in the notes."

"So the game score, the only game score is the draw?"

"In the current column, yes."

"Why don't you run one of the games I won, and then put the analysis of the winning line I missed but discovered afterwards?"

"Well, I thought the actual game, the actual draw was the way to go."

"Why not one of my winning games? Board 13 was nifty short combination, perfect for a short column."

"I can run that in the next column."

"The first column about the exhibition is gonna be the draw, is that right?"

"Well, you wrote the column."

"The first column should be a victory," Pam says, suddenly focusing.

"Yeah, even she says that," Mikey repeats.

"But Waldo wants to give the local angle some play," I answer, aware of an alliance that will spoil the Martini, maybe the afternoon itself. The sky seems too hot all of a sudden.

"It's your column," Pam says—oh for her spaciness to return. Can it be that she will turn harpy in defense of this child, this button-pushing sylph?

"The local issue can be played up for the weekend edition," Pam continues. "The important thing now is for people to see the terrific combinative genius Mikey has."

Has she rehearsed this speech? Has Vera coached her?

Mikey stands up, sulks forward of the engine cover. He flops his arms on the top of the cabin roof. "I wrote the column so people who knew something could see how to win a two knights mate in an actual over-the-board situation. That's valuable. That's a real contribution. It should go first to show that you really understand what was valuable about the exhibition. But if you have to have a sharp, short victory for your lead, then game 13 is okay with me. But it should be one or the other."

"This is ridiculous. We're talking about a miserable chess column on page 17 of a local Florida rag. You make it sound like the National Geographic, or the Book of Genesis."

"It's more important to Mikey than that," Pam says.

"Yeah," Mikey agrees, still staring ahead at the Mangrove islands.

"Why don't I just surrender everything and let you two run my life, my column my sense of reality. You name it."

"Don't personalize," Pam says.

"Yeah," Mikey parrots. "Yeah, don't personalize so much."

"What the hell does that mean?"

"It means we're talking about letting people know about Mikey's genius and you're only thinking about personal control of some trivial issue," Pam says in a flat, therapeutic voice, doubtless mimicked from a thousand sessions with Coffee or whoever.

"I see."

"Yeah," Mikey says again. "You personalize everything."

"We made our point," Pam says with a strange lilt.

"Our point?" I ask.

"We see eye to eye on this issue," Pam says, still carrying forward the strange lilt. "Eye to eye, and toe to toe, and belly to belly and heart to heart, and ear to ear, and nose to nose." She begins a litany.

"Oh no!" Mikey says, turning around. He watches Pam's face radiant now in linguistic extensions to fill the rest of the afternoon. "Oh no," he says softly, shaking his head.

"What is going on?" I ask.

"Can't you see?" Mikey says, "I'll tell ya something. Ha, I'll ask ya something Ya gonna run game 13 or my analysis first?"

"I'm not going to run either first. But both will get run—"

"You're not gonna do it! Ya not gonna do it!" Mikey shouts.

"Limb to limb, mind to mind, mine to mine, mine or mine," Pam says softly then laughs a bit.

"You're not going to do it!" Mikey shouts again.

"No, I'm not going to do it."

"Well, if you're not gonna do it. I don't have to stay here and listen to this all afternoon." Mikey suddenly vaults up on the cabin roof and in a flash dives off into the shallow bay. About twenty feet from the boat he stops swimming, stands and looks back. "See ya! See ya, sure!"

CHAPTER 16

"How well can you swim?" I shout, but he ignores me, plunges back into his head-churning, awkward crawl stroke.

Pam says, "I wonder if he did that to please me, or his mother."

"You, darling," I answer. "Maybe we should go back."

"Back to back and belly to belly. Now my eyes are turning to jelly. This sun is full of cancer, full of hurt, isn't it?" Pam says again.

"You want to run the boat or shall I try?"

"You try. I'll cry. Bye, bye!"

Suddenly Pam is standing on the gunwale, launching off into the bay herself. A hundred yards toward the shore Mike stops and watches her.

"I don't know how to run this fucking boat!" I shout after her, but she seems intent on plowing up the water. There is no answer. She swims on toward Mikey. I sit down in the mucid, baking sunshine and resolve to finish the thermos of Martinis.

Chapter 17

"I'VE NEVER SEEN SUCH a baby, Waldo. It's unreal."

"There, there. Genius has its own rules," Waldo answers benignly from behind his desk. "Think of the columns you've got out of the visit."

"And the headaches."

"Headaches, or heartaches?" Waldo smiles, his best old-lecher smile.

"Don't be stupid."

"Can't help it," Waldo goes on. "Although I can't say I'm entirely unhappy about both of them gone. One in particular was harder to take than the other."

"Yeah, which one?"

"My votes all go for Vera."

"At least she didn't leave me in a boat some place."

"That didn't seem to bother you. Ned Snow wasn't too happy about having to pick it up, but then what else does he have to do? Not like this great paper to watch over?" Waldo smiles again. "No sir, not this great responsibility."

"I don't know how you do it."

"Woodrow Wilson said being President only took four or five hours a day, if you know how to budget your time and organize your help. Now there was a man. And what wonderful love letters, right in the middle of the Mexican crisis. There was a man to admire."

"Did his second wife have money?"

"Did his first?" Waldo answers.

"He was slurring his words and drooling at the end," I continue.

"We can do that in about two hours, if you want," Waldo says.

"Not today."

"Well, why not?"

"Yeah! Why not!"

"Good! Meet you in the garage at four sharp."

"Oh, sharp enough."

At three-thirty Pam calls. Her words are heavy, syrupy out of the receiver. "I was thinking that, thinking that it was, it was . . . I was thinking that it was rather nifty of you to be available now to listen to me. Isn't it?"

"Yes, it is," I answer.

"How's it coming?" she asks, suddenly all attention.

"Coming?"

"You know, what you're working on."

"What am I working on?"

"Aren't you working on me?" she asks with an arched-toe effect visible through the lines.

"At all times."

"That was said very mechanically," she says with a kind of self-congratulatory lilt to her voice.

"Why did you call?"

"I was thinking, thinking that it was. It was . . . It was time to call you. I haven't talked to you. I haven't talked to anyone in fact all day."

"You've been alone at the house?"

"Yes. Isn't that dangerous, leaving little Pamela by herself and with sharp instruments everywhere?"

"And you want me to come?"

"No, I don't," she says immediately, stridently. And hangs up.

At the bar Waldo reviews my recitation of the conversation and says after a while, "Fugue state maybe."

"Fugue state?"

"Sounds like a college football team, doesn't it?" Waldo says. "Maybe not. Doesn't sound good though. Maybe we're going to lose old Pamela."

"What does that mean? Does it mean what I think it means?"

"It means that love is sometimes not enough," Waldo laughs, finishes his G & T and orders two more. "Perhaps a change of scenery. Yes, a change of scenery. I've been boning up lately on the Philippines. Ned's thinking about leasing a yacht out of Kowloon."

"For the Interzonals.?"

"Oh, it could coincide, I suppose. Probably would, if that's a worry."

"A yacht?"

"Yes. Yes, yes. Ned's such a sailor," Waldo laughs again. "A damn fine retrieving sailor. One of the best inboard collectors in the business." Waldo laughs harder now. "Maybe you could abandon it for him, somewhere in Manila bay, within view of Corregidor, old Death March Bataan. The Marcoses are our kind of people, don't you think?"

"Little wretched schemers?"

"Not so little, but schemers," Waldo concurs. "At San Francisco airport Imelda Marcos bought something like $2,000.00 worth of gum. I heard it was because a clerk implied she couldn't or wouldn't pay for a pack, for a single pack."

"I guess that clerk learned his lesson."

"It was a girl, from Daly City, I think. Very fragile little girl, who was most upset about it all."

Waldo turns away from the bar and stares out at the still bay. The afternoon is surprisingly cloudy. Vast pewter billows of clouds flail around over the bush tops of the mangrove islands and the key beyond. "When Dewey came into Manila bay he savaged the Spanish fleet for four hours and took not a single casualty. Decimated their forces and lost not a man. Filipinos don't know who they are, did you know that? They haven't a real concept of who they are. They're always asking themselves, am I Spanish. Should I speak English? Should I speak Tagalog? Should I speak Filipino? Should I go back to my home island, my home tribe, my home away from, that kind of thing?"

"Perhaps electroshock therapy."

"Perhaps," Waldo says with his best cross-cultural anthropologist thoughtfulness. "It was the Americans that screwed them up. Brought in English and cars, and chrome and all that shit." Waldo gestures toward the carefully bumpered and secured yachts riding up and down in the club yacht basin.

"Shit. You call that shit?"

"Yes, Snelly, I do. I call that shit. That's the kind of crap that rots a Filipino soul. You and I can take it. We're used to running water and toilets that flush and kindly prepared French cuisine, aren't we? Heh, aren't we? But the Philippines . . . that most fascinating of all places."

"I see you're going to the Interzonals, too."

"Maybe. Maybe. But let's face it. Little Mikey's got to hustle a whole lot faster than he has been to qualify."

"Well, he puts his time in."

"Time-spending talent is on every street corner, kid," Waldo semi-snarls, moving into his boxing trainer pose. "What he needs is a killer instinct," Waldo declares loudly enough to give the bartender pause in his vigorous swabbing of the stainless steel sink behind the bar. "A killer, guts-on-the-table instinct. Like Dewey. Dewey had it. Had it royally, in spades!"

Sometimes G & Ts work very quickly on Waldo, I think.

"In spades," Waldo continues more quietly. "The ability to identify what needs to be done and then to do it, ruthlessly, efficiently, remorselessly."

"Like the Marcoses?"

"Maybe. Maybe, but I can't be too sure. The stuff you find about the Philippines is written by a lot of émigrés, very bitter stuff, or little radical groups. I wonder if Mikey's really a killer." Waldo muses, drifting. "Ever heard of the NPA? New People's Army—a bunch of Communists in the rural areas? Plenty of killer instinct there. Van Shuten talks about them sometimes."

"I think Mikey will qualify for the Interzonals."

"Probably," Waldo agrees, "but he's not the sort I would bet on. On the hand, I don't suppose I would have bet on Fischer or Morphy either. Let's face it, the kind of Americans who do well at the game have a screw loose. More than a screw, a whole goddam ice tray full of nuts and washers. That's what I think. What do you think?"

Waldo is not interested in my answer, nor, for that matter, am I much interested in formulating one. Instead, we order by tacit agreement another round of drinks. Will we get away from the bar? Some Fridays we stand till eleven eating boiled shrimp with our hands and discussing the 'real realities' as Waldo calls them beneath the apparent realities of—of what, I can't quite remember.

We do order boiled shrimp and interesting red plastic baskets of cole slaw, and then a blue china tureen full of steak fries. Waldo keeps calling for more horseradish. By ten o'clock the shrimp sauce looks more white than red, and it sets the roof of your mouth curdling.

"Cleans out the sinuses," Waldo says smiling and tearing up at the same time. "Look, Snelly, I think you'd better go up to New York for the Zonal Finals, just to give our boy some support."

"I don't think he's that fond of me."

"I know that. I didn't expect you to go alone."

"I see. Adding pimp to columnist as my title, huh?"

"I don't think we're into a situation of sexual congress," Waldo says archly, stumbling along the bar a bit. His blazer sleeve sweeps the tureen along the gleaming varnish. "I do, however, think that some indication that we can be helpful, supportive, would be useful before the Interzonals, and who knows, it may be that—"

"I don't think she's in any shape to go, frankly."

"We're not professionals. Coffee can say that, one way or the other. And that ought to be good enough for us."

CHAPTER 17

"Especially since you don't have to do any of the care involved. You only have to receive the phone calls and make the column fit the space."

"Hmn," Waldo says, breaking open another shrimp. "These things are loaded with cholesterol. No calories, but pure heart debilitation. I can feel them attaching to the walls of my arteries. Can you feel them slithering down the old alimentary canal and then splaying out through the stomach wall and then piling up on the insides of the arteries, reaching out, layer after layer till almost none of your juice can get through, and you begin to get queasy and woozy and the lights start to spin around and the next thing you know, you're on the deck looking up at the stars and some old bat with a parasol, maybe a black woman from out there," Waldo gestures toward the front entrance and beyond, "is giving you mouth-to-mouth resuscitation and Cuban teenagers are slinging you into an ambulance and whisking you out to sea. Out to sea. Jesus." Waldo tilts a little, easing down toward the stools. Will he try to mount one? "Jesus," he moans again. "It'll be good for the paper. Some columns live from the action. Arnie and Phil will eat it up. Our first real correspondent. A scoop on the rest of the world."

"I'll send Vera to you down here."

"No deal," Waldo says, straightening up a bit. "Maybe we shouldn't interfere. Who can say? Maybe we bring the kid bad luck." Waldo seems headed for one of his self-pity spins, and I begin to plot a way back to the immediate pleasures of the bar. "He did, after all, almost lose one here. First time in God knows how long. God knows how long."

"More cole slaw?" I ask.

"No," Waldo answers, sliding further into the depths.

"We could help him," I continue, watching Waldo closely. "But it's Pam who really knows how to reach him, how to bolster him up."

"We need to call his father," Waldo says, stiffening a bit. "A boy needs to talk to his father from time to time."

"Yes, good idea. I'll get working on it tomorrow."

"Tomorrow," Waldo repeats. "And Pam needs to be with him, no matter how you feel about it. Even Hillary agrees to that."

"You talked to Hillary about it?"

"Hillary talked to me. Hilly always talks to me. I'm the one she talks to first. First and foremost."

"Well, then, it's all decided, isn't it? We'll all have a happy time at the Zonal Finals in the big apple. And later we can swim in the East River with some lead water wings and a chain belt."

"Snelly," Waldo says, turning toward me, slowly bringing himself to full height, using his elbow like a crowbar to get the legs firmly in place. "Snelly, Hillary is about the smartest person I know. If you listen to her, if you pay close attention, not only to the things she's saying, then, Snelly, you. . . .you won't, you won't go wrong. Never! You'd better believe me when I tell you these things, and when she tells you these things, too. You better." Waldo has brought two fists together on the top of the bar. He rocks them up and down gently, as if forcing himself to memorize his own statement.

"When did hilly start talking to you? Waldo looks at me, focusing, refocusing his eyes. He attempts to find sarcasm in the question or insult. You can see him examining the question, spreading it out on the drying mats of his mind, looking carefully at the weave, turning the fabric over and softly raking his hand over the invisible fabric to find any out-of-place nubbins. Then his eyes drift past me, out into the beguiling black bay, studded with dock lights and distant glows from nightclubs on the key.

"I don't mean cosmically," I say slowly, trying to find the right phrase to lasso Waldo on shore again. "I mean when today did you talk with her?"

"Who gives a shit?" Waldo says softly.

"Okay. Okay, just trying to make conversation."

"Well, you can't, you know. You really can't so don't try. Do me a favor and don't try. I'm going home." And with that Waldo straightens up again, scribbles his name on a couple of bar chits.

"I'll drive you home, if you want."

CHAPTER 17

"Least you can do," Waldo answers.

I decide to let that pass. We have trouble finding the car in the asphalt parking lot now teeming with other Mercedes. But after a while we locate one that opens with Waldo's key. He slumps back on the thick leather seat and closes his eyes.

"You all right?" I ask, starting the engine.

"Just drive," Waldo sighs.

Black shacks pass easily in the drone of the cool air-conditioned breezes. Somebody once said these mammoth cars were like little mausoleums, air-tight, noise-tight yet resonant with sound, whirring through the endless causeways to unnamed keys in some place or other. Waldo's malaise is contagious.

"Why don't you just leave this fucking burg?" Waldo says at the stoplight to the Trail. Arby's on one corner, Fat Boy's Barbeque on another, Fried Chicken on the third and a nascent Pizza Hut struggling to completion near us.

"Is that a directive or a comment on my prospects here?"

"Who knows?" Waldo says wearily. "If I were you, I'd get the fuck out of here. That's what I'd do, if I were you."

"You want to go to Tampa?" Once, Waldo and I went up for JaiLai—warm beer and constant betting losses were redeemed by the last match. I figured from their skill a doubles pair ought to win easily, but Waldo insisted everything was fixed. So we bet against them. A twenty dollar bill that turned into three hundred dollars at the end of the game.

"No. No, no," Waldo says, "You take me home. Take the car and see Pam. Tell her you're going to New York. Get her to come along. Keep the car. I'll use the Alpha to go in tomorrow. Or maybe I won't go in for a while. Keep the car, long as you want."

"Thanks."

"Sure. Sure, thanks. Thanks." Waldo mutters again. He eases out of his tasseled loafers, brings his knees up against the dashboard. "Good old Waldo," he says, savoring the tones. "You keep the car and drive away to some place over the line. Call me from. . . . from Arkansas."

"Yes, from Earl Butler's Holiday Inn, from the Hob Knob Room of Earl Butler's Holiday Inn."

"Right!" Waldo perks up. "From the Twinkle toes Bar in the Hob Knob Room of Earl Butler's Holiday Inn in downtown Cravenhead."

"With the midnight hot hors oeuvres spread on the black Formica in front of me, Captain Bunky Schmidt hands me the authentic French Provincial telephone at the Twinkle Toes Bar in the Hob Knob Room of Earl Butler's Holiday Inn in downtown, where was it?"

"Fucksville." Waldo says.

We glide into Hillary's long, long driveway to the Gulf. Fireflies have turned out for our arrival. Waldo attempts to shoo them away, when he steps out of the car. Holding his shoes like a present, he steps gingerly toward the iron stairway to his elevated home, hoping apparently not to get any sand spurs on his socks. When he makes it to the steps, he turns back and waves to me. "Bring the car back tomorrow," he shouts in a botched whisper.

"When?"

"Tomorrow afternoon. No, bring it to the paper."

"I thought I could keep it."

"No. Bring it to the paper," Waldo shouts again, "I changed my mind." Then he advances up the circular stairway, still holding his shoes out as if they had contracted some dread odor. Maybe they have.

Pam and Ned Snow are in their pajamas watching Johnny Carson in the family room. Lately I simply let myself in. Ned doesn't turn around when I show up. Pam discretely tucks her legs under her on the chocolate sectional couch.

"I'm going to New York," I say to her, but Ned motions us out of the room.

"Maybe I'll see you there," Pam says when we get to the living room.

"You going too?" I ask.

CHAPTER 17

"Of course. Mikey wanted me to come and I found him place to stay. Didn't Waldo tell you?"

"No."

"The Ryersons are out of town that whole month. We have their apartment on 86th street."

"Waldo knew this?"

"Well, Hillary got the place. Vera was very appreciative."

"I bet."

"Oh," Pam says, registering something perhaps dismay at my reaction.

"Why didn't Waldo tell me? I have his car. He let me have it tonight. Want to go for a ride?"

"Some place special," Pam says slowly.

"Sure. Some place out of the way, maybe some place in Arkansas."

"I was serious."

"Well, so am I. Where do you want to go?"

"I want to go. . . . I want to go. Oh, I don't know. Maybe, maybe. . . . or perhaps. Perhaps . . ."

After a while I say, "Well, maybe it is too late." There is laughter from the family room. Has Ned joined the California fans broken up by late-night witticisms?

"I was thinking of driving out to the beach and watching the stars and thinking all the things we could have done, if we had known each other for a long time and before now. And I was thinking of sitting in the car until sun came up and seeing what it said," Pam says more quickly.

"I have to work tomorrow."

"Of course you do, and I wouldn't interfere with that at all. You know me."

"Is it too late then?"

"It's always too late, isn't it?"

"Can we stop asking each other questions?"

"Can we?"

"What's wrong?"

"Another question."

"Why did you hang up on me?"

"Did I?"

"I see."

"Maybe I should go to bed now. It is late," Pam says, standing up. "We are all staying at the Ryerson place, 504 East 86th street, overlooking Carl Schurz Park. Tenth floor."

"Am I invited?"

"Of course you are, of course you are," Pam says tilting her head and giving me a tiny, gentle kiss on the nose. "Now I have to go to sleep. I need my sleep more than most people. Dr. Coffee says so. It's too bad we didn't go to the beach. This is the best time to see the beach."

"We can still go."

"But it was a silly idea. Daddy wouldn't like it."

"We could still do it. It'll be back to the Fairlane tomorrow."

"I know. I know. We'd better not. Let's just stay paralyzed with lost desire, isn't that fun?" She gives me another kiss on the nose.

Chapter 18

In the city of lost desire you drink, and drink, and drink. So I start with Scotch at the Ryerson mock-sumptuous 86th street condominium. Good Scotch too, smooth and at least older than Mikey Spendip. Not older than Vera, though.

"This is some spread," Vera says taking a little Scotch of her own. The liquor cabinet is a nice bamboo contraption that stands in a hallway linking the dining and living rooms. A hallway bigger than most rooms in Florida. "And this is bamboo is from, guess where? The Philippines!"

Mikey is in the living room, flipping remote control switches to a wall size television screen. Pam must be in the kitchen.

"These Ryersons have some where-with-all!" Vera concludes.

"I'd say you're about right on that," I answer, suddenly happy to join in this communion over wealth with Vera. "You know it's too bad Mikey isn't a basketball genius, or a hockey playing genius. All this could be yours."

"It's already ours and because Mikey's a chess genius. Hey genius!" Vera hollers. "Why don't ya can the box and study the Dutch?"

We come into the living room.

"Takin' a break," Mikey answers.

New York is warm and grey and grey, and grey. Thick billows of exhaust colored air spread out over Carl Schurz Park, like a special fog treatment, or maybe something sprayed down from the mayor's mansion at one end of the park. The walkways down to the river have a slippery dark texture—black linoleum through the tufted grey air. Streetlamps in the park illuminate four inert swings and a sandbox in which two cats squat.

"Every time I come here, I start swilling, the minute I start across the 59th street Bridge."

Vera seems uninterested in this revelation.

"Something about this place sets you drinking," I continue.

"I drink when it's hot," Vera answers, "and when it's too cold and when I'm tired, or when I'm bored, or when I'm ready to drink. Being some place had nothin' to do with it. I hope Mikey can sleep here."

"I used to have a friend here," Pam says from the kitchen pantry entry. "And he was up late night studying and he used to hear people screaming in the streets. Sometimes three or four at night, late, in the wee small hours of the morning. And at first he thought I really ought to go down into the street and see if I can help. Maybe someone is being stabbed to death, or beaten to death, or dragged about in some such way, you know. But after a while he said he'd just go so he resented the noise. It made him furious, all that screaming while he was trying to study or trying to sleep. So once when he heard a terrified scream from a woman somewhere, a block or two away from his apartment, he opened the window and shouted as loud as he could. 'For God's sake, FINISH her off. Finish her off! So we can all get back to sleep.' And after that he said he knew he'd become a real New Yorker."

"Interesting story," I answer," where was he living?"

"Over on Broadway or 8th avenue some place—way over on the other side of the city," Pam says, "Nothing like that would happen over here."

"Or we couldn't hear it, I suppose, through these thermo-panes."

"Or if we heard it, we'd only have ta send the doorman to investigate," Vera laughs.

CHAPTER 18

"But he shouldn't stay in the city for very much longer. He knew that when he wanted the killer just to finish her off. He felt embarrassed about feeling that way. He didn't really want to tell me that, I think."

"But you wheedled it out of him, simply broke his barriers down, is that it?"

"Are you angry with me?" Pam asks.

"I'm always angry in New York and half drunk, but how about we get some dark beer? This area is dark beer heaven, you know."

"We have to eat first."

"We can do both at once."

"No. No. No, I've made a simply splendid meal for our first in the big city. I want us to sit down and to eat it nicely now."

"In the lovely dining room," Vera says "with its lovely candelabra."

"And my lovely spaghetti," Pam continues.

"Mikey don't eat spaghetti," Vera says.

"Yes, I do, ma." Mikey interrupts.

Vera turns toward him, looks coldly at him and then me. "Something is goin' on," she mutters. "He never eats spaghetti."

But nothing is going on. Pam's salad is overdressed, soggy, swimming on small glass plates. And the spaghetti sauce of butter, garlic and canned clams seems scrapped from rusty sauce pans.

"Noodle dishes are very popular in the Philippines," Pam says smiling. But no one pursues that observation.

"Try a different *strand* of conversation," I say.

"What ya using against Smyslov tomorra?" Vera asks Mikey.

"Maybe Alekhine's defense, maybe Philador's. I don't know yet."

"Philador's?" Vera says, "You gotta new wrinkle?"

"Why don't you wait and see?"

"You betta have a new wrinkle, if you're trying Philador's."

"Maybe he'll think I have a new wrinkle and get distracted worrying about it."

"A new wrinkle means a prepared variation, is that right," I ask.

"Yeah," Pam answers. "Mikey's been working on some surprise innovations in the openings."

"I gotta few bombs to throw at Smyslov, but mostly I want ta watch him worrying about when the variation is coming."

"What if he plays a Queen's pawn," Pam says.

"He don't play Queen's pawn," Vera says.

"He might. But I'm better at Queen's pawn defenses and he knows that. Why play to my strength? Unless he has his own prepared variation. Might be a good strategy."

"Would you play the Dutch?" Pam asks.

"Sure. I'd go right back at him. He doesn't want me using the Dutch. He'll want to avoid that. It won't be a Queen's pawn you can bet on it."

"But suppose he tries the English?"

"He won't . Too passive. Too much chance to draw. It's not his style."

"Didn't Lasker do precisely that against Capablanca," Pam goes on, 'in a crucial last game? One he needed to win. So he played a drawing variation and Capablanca couldn't believe it, couldn't believe it and ended up making silly mistakes. Isn't that what happened?"

"Yeah, yeah," Mikey answers, "in St. Petersburg, 1914. But that was the last game of the tournament. This'll be the first. No time for fancy tricks. You play your strength and see whether it's good enough. You try your best shots first, and only later go to the fancy stuff, when your best stuff isn't payin' off. He'll open with the King's pawn."

I say, "You kids seem to know a lot about the game."

"Mikey's teaching me all the time. Here, and through the mail. We have our own correspondence club, don't we, Mikey?"

"Yeah, sure. I wonder how I would answer the English. Invite him into the Dutch. Lemme see how that might work." And with that Mikey picks up his tiny chess set and leaves the table.

CHAPTER 18

After dinner in the Ryerson's oversize bedroom, with its direct view of the park, Pam says, "Wasn't that good of me to introduce the Lasker-Capablanca game. You see how much I've learned already."

"It was terrific of you."

"What's wrong?"

"Nothing. Nothing at all. In fact I was thinking of using your stuff in the column for next Wednesday. Spendip's New York Innovations or something like that."

"Mikey will help you, if it's not too tense a tournament."

"How can it not be tense? The five top players go to Manila."

"We can all go to Manila, anyway."

"You mean as a vacation?"

"No, silly. You have to cover them, don't you? Waldo says you have to cover them."

"So it's Manila, win or lose?"

"Yes, of course."

"And Mikey comes too?"

"Why worry about that? He'll win. He'll have to come."

"And Vera too."

"You shouldn't worry about Vera. Come to bed instead."

"Yes. Why would anyone want to worry about Vera? Lemme take a quick shower first."

"Oh, how thoughtful," Pam says sitting on the khaki comforter on top of the kingsize bed.

In the shower there is still another view of Carl Schurz Park. There is a window in the shower stall with frosted glass up to four inches from the top. Through the unfrosted part you can see across the trees and across the river. At the extreme right there is a brilliant rose-colored Cain's Mayonnaise sign. Then slowly the steam from my shower blocks the view. Just before the Mayonnaise letter runs together I hear, even over the steady drone from the flexible water pic nozzle, several long anguished screams as if someone along the riverside jogging trail has suddenly been waylaid—as if throat cartilage, flesh strips, bone splinters are being clumsily and slowly torn away.

Chapter 19

IT MAY BE I dream about this butchery. I am too dizzy to tell, but at three o'clock by the greenly glowing ship's clock centered above the wall-length set of bureau drawers, I am suddenly awake and sweating. Pam, open mouthed and drooling, has the thick, breath-gulping appearance of the deepest sort of mood-stabilized sleep. Has there been screaming? Neither now nor earlier I realize, after a while. Just the city's presence, a kind of canned agony revealed under unlikely circumstances. You can be skating at Central Park or Rockefeller Center and suddenly in the throbbing, happy music, in the cool rush of breezes and chatter, you'll visualize a face kicked in. No need. The world is, after all, safe, and the doorman, slightly tipsy, half nodding in his golden lit chamber inside the sliding glass doors, stands against all evil.

But still there are voices. I do hear them, from the living room. Hushed, quiet, earnest voices. Have the Ryersons come home? Who's been drinking my liquor, says Papa Ryerson in a great big voice, and who's been squeezing my maid's garlic says Mama Ryerson in the middle-sized voice and who's been pile-driving in my daddy's bed says baby Ryerson, pulling back the covers on Pam and me? No, real voices after all. Real voices and concerned ones. I get out of bed, search for one of Ryerson's silk robes—a splendid Oriental with ties on the inside as well as the outside. The sleeves are too short, but the cloth is so cool and refreshing I can only delight in what sweat is doing to its color. Yes, someone is in the living room, all right. Two lamps are on and I can hear the click of chess pieces.

"You know how I lost before," Mikey says slowly, in a kind of whisper.

"We both know. We went over and over it and over it, Mikey. We both know."

"I kept trying to find a new line, another variation, after Smyslov forked the rook."

"You shouldn't keep thinkin' about that. It was a long time ago," Vera says, also wearing some Ryerson finery, a kimono in flaming orange. For a moment I imagine she is a construction worker, road crew members in charge of day-glo directions of traffic around the culvert in which little Mikey has come to rest. "So long ago, and really only a luck move. Anybody can overlook a knight fork. Alekhine even did you know."

"When?"

"Against Nimzovitch at Margate."

"Really?"

"Yes, sure. It's in the notes."

"You don't think Smyslov's so hot, then?"

"Not so hot as you, Mikey. Not so hot as you. No end game. Simply take him to endgame and wear him down. It'll take time but you can take time. You're young," Vera laughs, then suppresses exuberance. "You know some players you can't devastate—ya can only beat them. Slowly deliberately. Some of the Russians are like that. Even Alekhine couldn't blast Capablanca away. He had to take him to endgame and show him the little deficiencies. That's the difference, and it doesn't come out till endgame."

"I like the middle game better."

"It's more fun, but your genius is in the endgame. That's where you shine."

"You think so?"

"We got the scores to prove it. We got 'em right here," Vera pats two large leather oversize display books.

"What if he plays the English?"

"If you feel strong, answer him pawn to king four and let the sparks fly. You feel cautious, answer pawn to king three and see what invitation he takes up—Queen's Gambit, Nimzo, maybe even the French, and if he commits himself, go to the Dutch. So much for his trickiness. So much for Mr. Smart Guy opening-juggler. Won't make any difference, what he opens. Sooner or later you'll get to endgame and then you'll cream him. Make him squirm all night long. Take your time. Wear him out, chip away at him. Show him you need only a couple of weak squares to break him in half."

"How come I didn't see the fork? It was right there and I never saw it."

"That happens. That happens. You'll never miss another one. That's the important thing."

"How do you know?"

"Where are we sitting now? And why are you sitting here? 'Cause you remember a silly fork that cost you the exchange four years ago, against a much more experienced player. And here ya are running through it again and again. You think that brain of yours will ever let ya overlook a fork again? The imprinting, Mike, the imprinting rules it out. It's circuited out. Believe me. It's circuited out, forever."

"Imprinting," Mikey says, impressed.

"Sure," Vera answers, softening her voice again. "The brain has been designed to foreclose on forks. They don't happen no more. No more, Mikey. No more. And if he plays the Queen's pawn, you stick him with the Dutch. Or whatever you think feels right. Trust yourself. You'll know how you feel out there, when he pushes the wood. You'll get the right feel for what'll work. He's scared to death of you. Your record after that silly fork is better than everybody's and nothing can change that. He knows the fork was the luckiest break he's ever going to get against you. He knows that. You ain't gotta thing to worry about. King's pawn, Queen's pawn, English, Reti, any opening for God's sake. It don't make no difference! See!" And she gives Mikey a very tender hug.

"Think Pop will come up for the opening?"

Vera sighs, "You win the tournament, then your father will be right up there beside you getting his picture in the paper. Nah, he won't come to the opening. He 'works' on Fridays."

"Sometimes he says he's coming."

"Sometimes he says all kinds of things. We had a nickel for every time he says something, we'd own this place."

"You wanta see what I'm thinking about the Dutch?"

"Sure. Sure. But sooner or later you gotta get some sleep. You need your rest."

"We'll sleep late. Let me show you." Mikey quickly rearranges the pieces, proceeding through a standard variation of the Dutch defense, a kind of stonewall formation that invites the white player to attack at the risk of a massive counterattack along either wing.

Mikey goes through several moves, discussing each in low tones and then he shows her his latest variation. Vera makes odd, cooing noises of appreciation—sounds I've never heard before. Sounds I imagine Ostriches make when they are in love.

I decide to go back to bed. Ryerson silk robe is no real defense against the air-conditioning. I begin to feel chilly. Just as I ease the door open, and glimpse a Pam still drooling thickly, her breathing still druggedly uniform, I hear Mike say, "I won't lose to him, will I?"

"You're no loser," Vera answers, steady, implacable, softly unconditional.

Chapter 20

Smyslov plays the King's pawn and Mikey answers with Philador's Defense, a peculiar cramped variation that has only one merit, its general obscurity. There is a little ripple of rumor in the third ballroom of the Roosevelt Hotel when Mikey's move is posted. Prepared variation, everyone seems to agree and Smyslov, a short entirely bald fellow wearing a rather natty Eastern European doubled breasted suit, hunches over the board. Nobody likes walking into a line your opponent has thoroughly explored, knows cold in fact, when you see it for the first time over the board and under severe time constraints of making forty moves in two and a half hours. I don't actually think Mikey has a prepared variation, although he might. I think he is simply banking on Smyslov's nerves about that.

In any event Smyslov elects to take more than a few moments to reexamine in his head the various lines of the Philador. Such reexamination is costly on his time clock. The minutes tick off and Mikey has the pleasure of watching Smyslov fret. Each minute given up now can come back to haunt him when the deadline of forty moves arrives. Mikey's clock won't begin again until Smyslov makes his move and punches Mikey's button starting his clock. After five minutes Mikey elects to get up and walk around There are six other matches going on. Indisputably the best assemblage of

CHAPTER 20

talent New York has seen. No less than six grandmasters, and the rest right at the edge of that consummate ranking.

There is a thick carpeting on the four arranged tiers outside the circle of boards. Spectators will per force step silently. There is even a little press box, filled it seems with foreigners. No English phrases come from the area in any event. Mikey still preserves quintessential American tailoring—jeans and a Puritan Banlon maroon shirt. The two other Americans eschew ties and jackets, too. They are a scruffy lot, indeed, slouching and watching opponents or walking about. The South Americans are better dressed, both in tailored white suits. Ariztobal, the Cuban champion wears a vibrant, soft blue metallic suit, and Calderon, the specially invited Filipino Master, looks barely older than Mikey, but wears a formal, elaborately decorated white Barong shirt.

Mikey comes out of the circle to talk with Vera, but I am not close enough to catch what they are saying. The referee doesn't like this fraternizing and waves Mikey back into his special circumference. Smyslov gives no indication of easing up his mental exertions. It seems he wants to play the entire game before he moves, so that nothing will surprise him. Using the Philador has already paid off then—so challenged him that he has been forced to rethink the current opening repertoire, desperately trying to find the variation he expects Mikey to spring on him.

Pam has taken a seat on the fourth tier. She wears a very smart business suit of grey cord and carries a large stenographer's pad. She looks every bit the chic media representative used to covering dozens of these events. She seems to be recording the moves as they are posted on the various demonstration boards hanging from the ceiling. Suddenly Mikey vaults back to his seat. Smyslov has moved. Mikey responds instantly, moving his piece and punching Smyslov's clock, then watching. Smyslov responds, confident that things so far have gone along his expected route. Mikey moves again, without so much as ten seconds deliberation. Smyslov answers. Mikey in turn moves again, as if to test just how long Smyslov would like to continue this modified form of blitz chess.

Smyslov answers again, and again Mikey makes another move with less than ten seconds deliberation. The referee has fallen behind posting the moves. Then Smyslov pauses—apparently at this point further choices diverge and the possibility of a prepared variation has come to dominate his thinking. Mikey smiles at Pam who holds up her lined tablet, then waves it. Smyslov hunches in over the board again, then makes his move. Instantly Mikey answers it. So it is a prepared variation, after all. Either that or an extraordinary gamble that simply piling the moves on will frighten Smyslov, who now leans back from the board and looks at Mikey, still standing behind his chair.

Then Smyslov moves again. Mikey answers in less than three seconds. Will they turn it into a blitz game? Smyslov rubs his chin and then takes his time writing down the moves on his note card. Mikey sits down. So it will really begin then? Smyslov brings out a knight and Mikey pauses, as if for the first time considering the game. Perhaps it was precisely this point that Smyslov was examining in his lengthy opening deliberation. He does seem happier with the situation, perhaps only relieved that Mikey stopped answering immediately and agreed to join the game.

Vera has moved toward the door. Perhaps she recognizes Mikey's concentration and expects no more moves for a while. I catch up with her in an outer lobby.

"What is going on?"

"Nothin'. Mikey's letting him sweat a bit, I think."

"How?"

"Well, right now it can go either way. Terrific complications and with everything up for grabs, or Mikey can swing it into pure simplification, swap Queens, swap Rooks, and go right straight to endgame. Looks drawish that way, but Mikey has certain chances. Or he can fish around some more, but I think he's just deciding if he sees anything in the complications he hasn't seen before. That happens sometimes over the board. You analyze and analyze a line, and then when you're actually playing it, bam! You see something you never thought of in the analysis sessions. That's what a good second does for you—keeps prompting you to see things you might not have seen, when you're doing analysis. Mikey needs a better second than me. We know that, but we're doing okay for now."

"You expect the endgame then?"

"I expect Mikey to go straight for the win, maybe through simplifying it, maybe through complicating it. I don't worry. None at all. I'm gonna get some coffee. You wanta come along?"

"No, I guess I'll catch what's happening on the other boards."

"All draws for Calderon and the Cuban—what's his name. The Cuban is a big plunger. And Calderon is all technique. Simplify this. Simplify that. Hold on to this, trade for that. Little bits and pieces and never anything flashy. No combinations. No sacrifices. No risks. Just technique. Never made a bad move, never make a great one. The Cuban couldn't be more different. Complicate, complicate, complicate and see what happens when the fires break out. Exciting chess. Maybe not too sound, but exciting. Come on and get some coffee."

But I turn back to the main room. Mikey is still slumped in his chair. His clock is still running. Maybe he wants to be spectacular too. Does he see something? More likely, he's looking for a knight fork on his rook.

The Calderon-Ariztobal match has attracted the most spectators. The bleachers opposite its posting board are packed. It seems Calderon's chair is too large for him. He sits as if at a proper tea, hands resting neatly in his lap, a kind of sylphan composure, almost preadolescent in its languidness and apparent innocence. The world consists of finding just the right move within the strictures of the present position—the best, simplest, least complicating, most reassuring move. Is Calderon's head too small? For a moment he seems a religious figure bobbing slowly to full height in his oversize chair. The Cuban, on the other hand, stands and sits, then stands again, runs his hands through thick mounds of hair. Calderon's equally black hair is firmly cemented slickly in place. Calderon presents a beatific smile, limp hands in his lap. Apparently he is blissed out, or perhaps drugged or at least dismissive of the mobs facing him from the bleachers.

I look around for Pam. She has moved, and then I spot her at the top of the Cuban-Filipino bleachers talking furiously with a fellow in sparkling green stitched Barong shirt. Oh, Mikey, has she thrown you over so early in the match?

Then Mikey's move gets posted. He has opted for simplification, has proposed a massive swap-down of forces. But Smyslov is not just ready for endgame. I don't see how he can avoid the exchanges, and, from Mikey's expression, neither does he. But Smyslov refuses to be crowded.

Pam does not stop her conversation to record Mikey's latest move. She seems fascinated with the fellow, who although dressed Filipino style hardly appears Asian. His ashen coloring and jowly face look almost Slavic. Nor is his age clear—somewhere between twenty-five and forty-five.

Then Ariztobal makes another move which as it gets posted causes a bit of a stir in the crowd. A bishop sacrifice, familiar kingside attack in which the bishop blasts away one of the pawns protecting the king, in the hope of opening avenues that can be traversed by other attacking pieces. Of course if your opponent takes the bishop and survives the onslaught, he has an easy win in endgame, since the bishop is worth quite a bit more than a single pawn. Calderon does not seem pressured. His little head nods as if knew the attack were coming. The tough time will come eight moves hence when it will be clear whether Ariztobal actually has anything. Calderon's response is done with a trifle smile. He captures the bishop, swallows the bait. Immediately Ariztobal proffers another sacrifice. He sends a rook deep into Calderon's territory, leaving it *en prise* vulnerable to capture at any time. For the moment it is poisoned since capture would reveal yet a third sacrifice leading directly to checkmate on the back rank. The fireworks excites the crowd. There is a smattering of applause for the second *en prise* sacrifice. Calderon leans forward. For a moment I think he will actually kneel on the chair to get a little higher perspective on the board.

Smyslov agrees to simplify and he and Mikey trade pieces, first queens, then rooks. So Mikey has taken his mother's advice. The position, when the swapping is done, looks very drawish to me. Even number of pawns and minor pieces on both sides. Perhaps Mikey's king is better positioned toward the center, always more helpful in the endgame, but that hardly seems enough. I watch as Smyslov formally offers Mikey a draw—itself something of a concession for the white player so early in the match, but I can see Mikey shaking his head, getting up and standing by the board as his clock runs.

So the two of them are standing, Ariztobal and Spendip, but with very different prospects. Ironically it is the two youths who are pursuing the defensive, safe, long-term strategies, passive to the end, probing for small weaknesses. Calderon will have to withstand the storm for a sure victory, if he doesn't misstep. Spendip will have to scratch around in a very barren earth for a little coin that might be traded later for something bigger. At least Mikey has escaped all possibility of have his rooks forked. Could that be his reason for simplification?

Pam is still talking with her would-be Filipino suitor, who seems equally caught up in the charm of their conversation. All other eyes are on the Ariztobal-Calderon match, but Pam merely leans in closer to her new acquaintance. At least I assume he is new. I decide to find Vera.

But Vera is nowhere to be found. The coffee shops are relatively empty at three-thirty in the afternoon, and the lobbies are void enough to reveal Vera almost anywhere. I expect her around marble turns, but she does not appear. I settle into one of the deepest leather chairs and begin work on a column discussing the two youngest participants, and Calderon, and their similar opening game approaches to this most important of all championships. I try to work in the human angle. Youth insecurity perhaps, or reliance on longer stamina for longer and longer contests. Opening game jitters perhaps. But the words don't come easily, and there is an abandoned New York Times in a chair opposite mine. Page twenty-three reveals there has been a bombing in Manila. On Roxas Boulevard near the new Cultural Center that has been the first lady Imelda Marcos's biggest passion for the past few years. Not a particularly troublesome bombing. Nobody killed. Some lawn detonated. Humorously local commentators wonder whether the bombing isn't an attempt to hasten the sinking of the Culture Complex into the bay of Manila. Apparently the original pilings aren't adequate to support the first lady's concrete and marble dreams of Luzonian splendor.

Nobody killed. A safe bombing. Nothing to worry about. But somehow the article seems very important news to me. Very important. The good President indicates in attributed comments that the bombing is one more indication that Filipinos aren't yet ready for the lifting of martial law. "Undoubtedly NPA action," he says, scowling and sneering. What is NPA?

When I head back to the main room, I catch a glimpse of Pam and her green cloaked conversationalist, *tete a tete* over butterscotch sundaes in the coffee shop. I wave to them, but only the fellow waves back. Pam seems too caught up in her admiration for his way of spooning ice cream.

Vera is back inside, and very close to Mikey's board. "Just as planned," she says quietly to me.

"I don't see much."

"You don't know Mikey's endgame. He'll open the center, send his king up and see what develops. He can see twenty-five moves ahead in endgame, if he has to."

"That far?"

"Look, I don't wanta argue with ya here. Why don't ya just watch and see what happens?"

I elect to go into the tiers over near the Calder-Ariztobal game. Because the moves are still being posted, I assume Calderon is surviving. The position on the postboard is complicated, but no mate seems imminent. Ariztobal is looking unhappy, still standing up.

After a while Vera comes to sit with me. "Things going just fine," she says, "just fine. Nobody's in time trouble. Mikey's got mobility, control of the center. Something will turn up. He'll make a slip."

"It looks like a draw to me."

"Mikey never begins a tournament with a draw. Never."

I wonder if this is true. Be easy to check, I suppose, but something in Vera's eyes closes the matter.

"Well, at least we have a swell place to go back to," I say with perhaps too much enthusiasm.

"Why don't you just shut up," Vera says swiftly, easily.

Chapter 21

"So who is Mr. Right?" I ask Pam from atop the Ryerson comforter.

"He is wonderful!" Pam says smiling, lilting the *wonderful*. "Do you want to meet him?"

"I suppose I should say if I approve or not. And how old is he?"

"That's the key question. What do you think? Sometimes I think he's as old as every man should be, and sometimes I think he's as charmingly young as Mikey."

"Eh, heh."

"Don't you see, that's an important sign?"

"What is?"

"Your hurt. Your jealousy. Your wonderful jealousy."

"An important sign?"

"Sure. Sure is, you know it really is. Well, you can meet him. In fact, he's invited us all to a wonderful restaurant after the matches tomorrow afternoon."

"He has money, then?"

"No. Do I ever get interested in men with money?" Pam says, laughing. "No. He's a student at Columbia."

"A Filipino?"

"You could tell from the way he dresses. That flashy shirt."

"It's called a barong, and it's rather formal."

"Who told you that?"

"Waldo. Waldo is an expert on the Philippines. Just ask him anything."

"Well, he's just a student."

"A fifty-seven year old student."

"My God! Do you think he's fifty-seven?"

"Oh, at least. Where's this wonderful restaurant, and when you say 'all of us', who do you mean?"

"I mean all of us—Mikey and Vera and you and me and Calderon. He says he's Calderon's second. What does that mean?"

"Why don't you ask him?"

"He said he wouldn't tell me. It was too confidential."

"Really? It means he helps with the analysis after the forty moves are over. He'll play through possible variations with Calderon tonight to make sure they find the strongest way to win. I'm pretty sure the win is there. Too much material. Ariztobal's attack fizzled."

"Who's Mikey's second?"

"Who do you think?"

"Oh, of course! But can she be any real help to him?"

"Nobody can help more. Nobody. That's as clear as it can be."

"The restaurant's Aedile, or something like that, on Broadway and 108th."

"Filipino?"

"No, Cuban I think. He thought that would be especially appropriate after the first match is over tomorrow. Dining on Cuban food." Pam laughs artificially.

"Who is he?"

"He has a wonderful name, really splendid name: Wicksburg Mendoza. He's dying to meet Mikey and Vera. He thinks Mikey's going to be the World Champion soon."

"Over Calderon?"

"He doesn't say, but I hear Calderon doesn't have much passion."

"And Mikey does?"

"Oh, does he ever," Pam says, laughing again, this time with utter sincerity.

"Wicksburg Mendoza, sounds like a kind of soap."

"He says the best sort of things. The most amazing things. Wait till you talk with him."

"I wonder if it's permitted for a second to meet with the opposition?"

"If he likes the opposition," Pam says archly. "If he wants to see the opposition again and again. If he can't live without meeting the opposition. If the opposition is charming beyond his wildest dreams, beyond—"

"Okay. Okay."

After two in the morning I hear voices again. And I'm certain these are not muggings in the streets. Mikey and his mother going through variations. I put on Ryerson's best silk robe and join them.

"He's found it," Vera announces. 'He's found it. In this simplest looking position, an easy win. Five moves out and a win. Smyslov drops at least two pawns, and with absolutely no compensation. So much for your draw, Mr. Columnist. So much for your draw. Want to watch it?"

"Sure."

"Show him, Mikey. Show him slowly, so he can follow it."

Spendip sets up the board exactly as they finished their fortieth moves. "I'm sure Smyslov sealed this." Mikey moves the white king toward the center. "Now watch." He plays a series of easy moves, obvious moves, advancing pawns, bringing his own pieces into the center. 'Now look, what's his move?"

"There isn't a move that I can see. His minor pieces seem chained to defending his pawns and the pawns themselves are blocked. I suggest moving his king back and forth. But Mikey explains, "Once he yields that square there's no way to stop me from coming in. He can't stop my knight from reaching bishop six, and my bishop here, and then the whole pawn chain is vulnerable. Two pawns go at least. Two pawns is an easy win. And there's no way he can avoid the situation. I bet his seconds have been all night sweating on this one."

"Just like you, eh?"

"No sweating here," Vera says celebrating. "Mikey you look at a few other things, if you want, but get the win. Just like I said you would. Take him to endgame and give him a lesson in quiet chess. Noiseless chess. He simply wakes up and discovers his throat has been slit. It's beautiful. You look at a few things, but then you go to bed. You gotta get your rest for the next rounds. Tomorrow is a cake walk, but after that you take on more grandmasters. A week of tough matches."

"I just want to make sure on this one."

"That's the best move. Everything else loses sooner," Vera says. Even Smyslov found the best move, even in this miserable position. Draw, eh? Lot you know, Mr. Columnist."

The next afternoon Vera doesn't get the opportunity to gloat. Smyslov does not show up for the continuation of the match. His second gives Mike the message of resignation. The few fans in the tiers are confused, and Mikey graciously, cockily, goes to the demonstration board and plays out the line he discovered last night. "*Zugswang,*" he announces after six moves on the board. "And the pawn chain goes, at least two pawns." There is tentative, quiet applause.

Calderon takes nearly an hour more, but Ariztobal finally acknowledges that his pyrotechnics have not paid off. In two taxis we go to Aedile.

The place is tiny, a kind of diner, a long green linoleum counter and eight booths. We take the corner circular one. The menus are stapled four by four sheets of typing paper, obviously mimeographed, and more than a little grease-stained.

"Is it safe to eat here?" Vera asks.

"The people here are all very gentle," Wicksburg replies.

"That's not what I meant. I meant has this place been cleared by the Health Department? This place is filthy."

"Not filthy. Ethnic." I answer.

Wicksburg laughs. "And the food is superb. Simple elegant food. The refried beans are the best in New York. Besides, Reyle and I felt we deserved to dine Cuban tonight."

"I don't like refried beans," Vera says.

"It's okay, ma," Mikey adds.

"I think it's a wonderful place, simply wonderful," Pam says, her elevated mood a certain soft balm over the proceedings.

"There. You see, we have one sophisticated voice among us," Wicksburg says, "Moreover, sooner or later you play Ariztobal. Cubans are what they eat. It will help your match. Although, I must say your victory over Smyslov tells me you'll have no trouble this tournament, will he Reyle?"

Calderon, his neck loose in his collar, nods, smiles, turning his head from side to just. Just when I begin to wonder if he can talk, he says in elegant, accented English, "The prettiest endgame in five years."

"You think so?" Mikey says, excited.

Calderon nods again, "You will make grandmaster. You will be the champion someday."

"Yeah," Mikey says, "I don't think he expected a drawing variation."

"He didn't know what to expect. Nobody ever does, playing you." Wicksburg added.

I can see Vera warming up to this place. We order refried beans all around, and black beans and some kind of chicken dish. Moisture hangs in the air, beads up on the dirty plate glass at the front of the shop.

When Pam asks what Manila is like, Wicksburg unleashes a prepared variation. "The future. Manila is like the future, at least the American future. It's what you're coming to—worse and worse distribution of wealth. Language clashes. Guerrilla warfare. Militias committed to change and violence."

"I thought you meant climate," Pam says. "You know the business about the hemisphere is getting warmer."

"Oh, that too," Wicksburg says smoothly re-circuiting his presentation, "but more than that. Fifty years from now a major debate in this city will be what language to speak."

"And what will be the choices?" Vera says, putting down her spoon full of refried beans.

"Basically English and Spanish."

"Not Japanese?" I ask.

Wicksburg looks at me with vague interest or hostility. "I'm quite serious, you know," he says. "What is happening now in Manila is coming here, despite apparent discrepancies in the modernization model between the two societies. Every indication, every social indicator tells us that the rich are getting richer here, living better, living higher and longer, with bigger windows on a wider and wider world—while the poor are living lower, narrower, with less and less. An exact replica of Manila as it is today. With perhaps only twenty-five more years of disintegration intervening. Do you see? So when you visit, you are looking at the future. Try to remember that. Cheap bus Jeepneys, the standard transportation. In another twenty years they will appear in new York as the train systems become largely unaffordable and unrunable."

"You ever seen the Metro in D.C.?" Vera asks sharply.

"In fifty years those arching concrete caverns will be full of vegetable stalls and bicycle cabs."

"Oh really?" Vera continues, "Maybe you shouldn't be eatin' these double fried beans, if that is what you call them."

"Of course I understand no one wants to accept the argument I make. Of course I understand that, but seeing clearly what is going on now in Manila might free New York from some horrible destiny."

"Especially for the folks in a condo overlooking Carl Schurz park," I add.

"Schurz was an interesting figure," Wicksburg says, "something of a radical—a racist, an elitist, but radical all the same, and with a fairly clear view of the next forty years. His predictions about America were very close, very accurate."

"Better than yours, I hope," Vera says, with more good-naturedness than I might have expected.

"True enough, you should regard me, as you doubtless do, like one of those peculiar avatars from a lost civilization on some other side of the world. I a kind of Cassandra from Mars, or the Pacific Basin somewhere. How could as troubled a place as the Philippines be a future marker for anything? Hot, steamy, open, smiling, wide open, beguiling, rancid, fetid, mephitic, all at once, and the future. Quite impossible you might argue. And I would applaud your skepticism, would applaud it. But even our mutual applause will not change a whit what is going to happen."

"Well, what is going to happen?" Vera asks.

"Manila is going to happen. You're going to walk into the future, and if you're lucky, you'll come back here alive to tell everyone about it. But then no one, I trust, will believe you even as you hardly believe me. What is Wicksburg but some quarrelsome something or other, infected with something or other, preaching something or other."

"Oh, I believe you," Pam says.

"Enough to part with the Snow millions?" I ask, "That seems to be what he's asking, aren't you?"

"I'm not prescriptive, unlike some of my friends," Wicksburg nods toward Calderon, who seems a shrunken Rudolf Valentine and quite oblivious to the politics of the conversation. Mikey has him engaged in a chess position. They are both moving pieces furiously. Little brothers. "I don't have prescriptive answers. My task is to delineate lines of eventual development, leaving to others the tactics of the moment."

"It's a battle, then?" Vera says.

"What isn't? Certainly not this little tournament. Can't you feel the heat in the room when the moves are being posted? I can see the mortar fire plumes up in the overhead grillwork. In my country my brothers are dying trying to change things, dying to right things, to deliver to the poor enough to live. They scarcely have the artillery to move even a chair in the tournament room.

Daily they are confronted with lacerating equipment shipped from America to slaughter them like chickens for their legs and wings."

"Here's stuff for you column, Mr. Snell." Vera says.

"You write a column?" Wicksburg asks, all ears and in apparent trepidation.

"Just a chess column."

"For which paper? Where do you write a column?"

I admire the interest he exudes. "Nowhere threatening. The Hane Tribune, Hane, Florida. A retirement county about two hundred thousand strong."

"Syndicated?"

"Ah, that's the nicest thing I've heard since coming to New York."

Pam laughs outright. I dream of redistribution of her wealth. Can this be accomplished without violence? I must consult Waldo on that one. Is it my wealth too? Waldo's?"

"You're just a theoretician, then?" I ask.

"Precisely. And precisely what has been lacking for about fifty years. Praxis. We need people to explain why things have turned out the way they have. Why they will go the way they will. And how it might be intersected."

"Intersected?" Vera asks.

"Interrupted, if you like. Redirected, if you like. Reshaped, if you want. Changed, made better. Made more equal, more compassionate. More just. All the catchy phrases of your liberal groups here."

"You're a liberal then?" Vera says.

"Hardly," Wicksburg answers, 'I'm a bystander."

"Did you have a column in Manila?" I ask.

"My father did. Before September, 1972."

Ah, he has a father. Young enough to have a father. Every boy needs to talk to his father, Waldo says, after four G & Ts. "What happened then?"

"You don't know?"

"No."

"I keep forgetting. Not everyone is afraid of Marcos. Our esteemed President imposed martial law, and that was the end of the free press. My father taught for a while and then he was arrested. For anti-social feelings. Do you have them?"

"I sublimate them," I answer.

"I believe you do."

"He's good at sublimation," Pam offers. Wicksburg laughs.

"And your father's still arrested?"

"Still in jail, yes. Still in jail. The future has a certain immediacy for me, doubtless contributing to my messianism about the Manila-making of the world. At least of the American world."

"I'm sorry," Pam says, suddenly caught, I can tell, by the vision of Wicksburg's father eating old rice in a dismal Filipino dungeon—visitations from rats and trickling water thick with urine and moss. Withering legs and arms.

"Not as sorry as he is, I'm sure. But the conditions are rather better in the last two years. Red Cross visitation. Your government insisted, I understand."

"For Wicks, everything is political. Perhaps a flaw there," Calderon says quietly.

So the little sylph has been listening, doubtless tiring of the litany of deprivation.

"That is the great virtue of Manila. Nothing escapes politicization," Wicksburg continues. "For example, I understand you shall stay at the Manila Hotel."

"That so? A good one?" Vera interrupts.

"MacArthur's headquarters. The best, the oldest, the most charming, the finest indeed," Wicksburg reassures her. "And the most illustrative. If you look out the bayside from the tower of new rooms, you will see the sweep of the harbor, the largest most beautiful harbor imaginable. And right below your dazzled eyes will be the largest, most blue swimming pool, and in the right center of the pool, right in the middle of that chlorined water, will be a bar—a complete bar—with water stools around it. You can swim out and order whatever you like: Planter's punch, Gin and Tonic, Rum and

Collins, Margueritas, whatever you want. Your fondest dreams of tropical paradise will play out magnificently. Your fondest dreams of tropical paradise! Watch the sun rise or set and drink the finest cognac in the water, make conversation with the charming, smiling bartender, just a young fellow fresh in from Cebu or Lord knows where else, but delighted to engage you in conversation. But if you walk to the other side of your room and look out the other picture window, you'll notice not the bay and pool, but the parking lot and Rizal park beyond. But it's the west corner of the parking lot you should pay attention to, for there you'll find several old abandoned school buses. Pay attention to them and to some large, you cannot quite imagine how large from your tenth floor view, cardboard boxes. And you'll notice there are lots of children running around, in and out of the buses and boxes. At first you'll think they're playing and I suppose they are. Splendid idea to play in such contraptions, but sooner or later you'll notice there are people sitting in the buses, older people, and you'll see, if you're very observant a pump handle, a water pump somewhere near the middle of the box clusters. And then, if you're very perceptive, you'll notice clothes lines between some of the boxes, and then perhaps a little fire kept going in the middle of the day. And then if you watch long enough, you'll see some women take the younger children into one of the buses or boxes for a nap. And then after four-thirty or so, some older men turn up and the women will come back out and put pots on the fire and then you can see people sitting down on newspapers and eating whatever it is the women cook. Mostly noodles. Do you like noodles? We gave them to the Chinese I think, who gave them to the Italians or maybe that's apocryphal. And if you still have the stomach for it, get up early in the morning, before the bar on the other side in the deep blue misty perfect water, before the bar opens, before even the oranges and lemons and bits of melon are cut for the day's festivities, and watch the buses. You'll see the men come out and urinate near the embers of the fire. Some of them you'll get to see squat and excrete by the boxes. There seem to be marked off areas, but on what basis won't be clear from the tenth floor. And the windows are sealed so you can't smell anything. And then people start washing up. In buckets. You can see the soap lather on their bodies, and in the pails, and then more water from the pump which will undoubtedly be turned off by ten or so. And then you may realize that, indeed, the buses and the boxes are home, have been home, for these people maybe for ten years. From one side of the hotel to the other. And then you know why on your floor, on each floor there is a martial law guard. He's there looking silly with his big gun and his smiling face and his rather drunken demeanor, at least in the evenings. He's there to make sure the people from the buses and boxes don't get either to the pool or onto the tenth floor. Watch it enough and you'll have to soak a very long time in the marble bath, with its marvelous mahogany built-in drawers, and you'll have to spend a lot of time at the water bar, seated on the stool and ordering and ordering and ordering. But perhaps I labor my point. You'll get to see it here in a short while, short enough, I think."

"MacArthur used the hotel?" Vera says.

Calderon answer, "Of course! He didn't lie." He points to Wicksburg.

"I'm sorry your father's in jail," Pam says, emphasizing *jail* as if it were a comment on the action's legitimacy.

"Of those in jail," Calderon says, "his father has much the best deal. He's too important to torture to death, or mistakenly murder."

"What does important mean?" Vera asks.

"In my Manila it means coming from a powerful family, well connected so that your disappearance would generate lots of questions, lots of comments. Anyone from the buses can be dispatched immediately and will be, for who would miss them? The little box tribe and no one else. But the Mendozas are extended and formerly powerful, presently powerful again perhaps—in the little charade of power exchange that goes on in my country. So no cigarettes put out on the eyelids. No electric shock to the genitals. No water down the nose, down the throat. No beatings on the bottoms of the feet. At least not for now. Perhaps not for another two or three years, but each day the power of the family erodes. Each week Marcos makes inroads on its holding, its allegiances, and so maybe things in a year or two or three will get very much worse for his father. But of course Marcos's power is eroding too, in the silly exchange. But I think this is distressing, ultimately boring talk. We are here to eat Cuban food, enjoy Cuban suffering and continue the tournament. One hopes, one sincerely hopes, that by this time next week we shall be enjoying Russian cuisine." Calderon concludes as if a kind of benediction.

"When did you know Ariztobal's attack wouldn't work?" Vera asks.

"Three moves into it, I had a rather clear sense there wasn't something there. I didn't see all the lines, but I had a clear feeling that there wasn't something in it. Not enough center control. Not enough mobility. I confess there were stronger things he could have done. Wicks fund them later, but even at optimum moves the best would have been a hard-fought draw. Ariztobal has no stomach for such operations."

Calderon's tone is even syllabled, softly benign, almost oracular. His cool explication is almost, but not quite compensation for the steamy heat of Aedile. Evidently too, Mendoza is not entirely pleased at being removed from the discussion. He holds up his water glass, swirls it enough to set the ice clinking and says, doubtless in an effort to get things back off chess, 'I don't suppose we can count on drinking this much longer. Surely this must be among the last times we'll be able to be served this."

"Yeah, why?" Vera asks.

"Safe water is anachronistic. In Manila we haven't had safe water for twenty years."

"How awful," Pam says, "even at the Manila Hotel?"

"You can take your chances," Wicksburg says, "the important thing is that you get used to not having it. Good for sales of orange soda and the like. Any canned or bottled drink. What you are coming to."

"What we are coming to," Calderon interrupts, "is four Russian grandmasters, one right after the other and all in collusion with one another."

"Yeah," Mikey says, "Fischer was absolutely right about them."

"It makes no difference," Vera says. "But now I'd like to leave here. It's too hot, too steamy."

"Of course," Wicksburg answer. "You go across town and we go further up. We should say goodbye here. Let's meet next week, depending on how things go for some Russian food."

"That would be nice," Pam says.

"And in any event, I am certain we shall all meet in Manila," Wicksburg says.

"Four from this tournament will anyway," Calderon says, apparently a good-natured correction of Wicksburg's observation.

Chapter 22

The Russians are rather more difficult than Ariztobbal and Smyslov. The supreme Soviet logicians, Mohrstein and Ivanov are venerable presences long on the grandmaster scene. Draws with them, tedious draws beyond sixty moves each, seem almost obligatory out of politeness. Mikey hardly recognizes his draw for that reason, however. In fact the draw with Ivanov is not a logical consequence, merely a boring one that terminates, after pawn conversions, in perpetual check. Against the younger Russians, Tarlac and Kotov, Mikey is no more successful. On the other hand, neither are they. The draws are more interesting. The one with Kotov comes from a rather explosive new variation of the Sicilian Defense that has a mid-game with a myriad of plausible attacking lines—so many that the variation Mikey employs immediately becomes the subject of enormous analysis in the tournament. The end result is, however, a draw. All that can be salvaged is a sense of respect on the part of the Russians. Mikey, clearly the youngest, least stable of the tournament entrants, just as clearly can play with any of them on the best levels of their game.

Calderon fares far worse. He draws with Mohrstein, loses to Ivanov, Tarlac, and Kotov. Russian cuisine seems out of the question. So as a solution Pam suggests a sushi bar in the west 50's.

Calderon seems quite unmoved by his disasters. "I played a sloppy mid-game against Tarlac, lost an exchange that nobody should have lost. Rather peculiarly I actually felt compelled to make certain moves. Even when I knew, just as I moved the piece, that it was the worst alternative. Maybe Fischer had some justification for taking apart chair, searching every inch of it for para-psychic influences."

"And what about the loss to Kotov?" Vera asks, bits of rice on her chin.

"Let's not talk about it," Wicksburg interrupts.

"We can talk about it. Learn from it," Calderon blandly continues. "I became possessed by the idea that I could, contrary to all the rules, let his knight sit deep on my bishop rank and not suffer any particular consequence And in fact that may have been the case. The loss came elsewhere and without the little painful knight having much to do about it. Perhaps I was too enamored of rewriting the books on the Reti. It was more fun playing Ariztobal."

"Everybody's having fun with Ariztobal," Mikey says.

"Yes, he is my salvation," Calderon remarks, sipping his tea.

"Just the same, to play in Manila, you gotta stay in the top four," Vera says

"Not exactly," Calderon says, "It's a bit of a gray area. My calculations say it will really depend on the point spread among the top four. It may be possible to come in as low as fifth and still merit Federation consideration—perhaps through a qualifying match before Manila."

"Whistlin' in the dark," Vera says.

"Not much of a chance, but a chance. Mathematically possible."

"Better to think about turning around your own score in the next rounds," Wicksburg says.

"It's always better to think that way, but perhaps not my natural style," Calderon says. "If I can turn things around, so much the better, but if drawing is my fate, I can perhaps still play in my homeland."

"Homeland," Wicksburg sighs, with more than a trace of mockery in his voice. "The privilege of carrying Filipino honor before our first family. Ah, that's too weighty a burden for any mere mortal. Perhaps it can be shown that all these years Marcos himself has been a secret grandmaster, secret victor over Fischer, over Karpov, over Atashian himself. Why not? If Marcos can be the most decorated solider of World War II, why not the greatest secret grandmaster in history. It only takes a certain amount of money, certain amount of connections. After all, the Federation must have its soft points. So you see, you shouldn't worry about the homeland's honor. If you don't make it, why there will be our President to fill in and naturally win. Except perhaps for those matches he will have to miss in order to leave the fight against the NPA. That's all the matches. All of them."

Pam says, "I've heard of the NPA, but just what is it?"

"New Peoples Army," Wicksburg replies, "and the . . . the. . , what shall we say?" Wicksburg looks at Calderon, "the hope of the Philippines, the dawn of anew day. The shift of power from one faction another. One old oligarchy to one new one."

"My homeland," Calderon says. He lifts off a piece of cooked shrimp from his sushi mound. Using the chopsticks he scratches away the layer of seasoning on the mound, then puts the shrimp back, finally eats the whole thing in a single mouthful. "You have to beat the Russians in the first forty moves. You'll never do it after that. As soon as the first session is over they help each other endlessly. Every Russian gives advice. I bet the phone bills are terrific. So you have to beat them one on one and that means by the fortieth move."

"Most games are decided by then," Mikey says.

"True enough, but I mean you have to win decisively in the first encounter, almost overwhelmingly. If you're simply ahead, they'll find a way to sacrifice and get perpetual check, or they'll find some obscure combination to an even ending, or they'll find some new way to draw. They don't use seconds, they use thirds and fourths and fifths. It's awesome and illegal, but nobody can stop them."

"I don't think they like each other that much," Pam says. Is there a trace of irritation in her voice? Why should this discussion matter to her in any way? "I watch them quite a bit while you are playing and I don't think they like each other at all. Mohrstein thinks Tarlac is crude. I know it. I know it just from way he looks at him."

"That hardly stops Mohrstein from staying up all night to help Tarlac out."

"I'm not so sure about that. Maybe they don't trust each other."

"You don't need trust for good variations. You only need the variations. You can verify them for yourself."

"Well, I just don't think they help each other that much. Maybe they do have seconds, thirds, fourths, what have you, but I think they worry about their own games first."

"I'm sure you have the clearest perception of what is happening here," Calderon says, a cuff that even Wicksburg moves to reject.

"What she says probably has a great deal of merit. We tend to see these things too rigidly. There may be a lot of inner tensions among them. Stuff we could exploit if we knew how."

"Chess analysis, Wicks, is not political. Not political. Not personal. Not even psychological. Analysis is just analysis. And it is in everyone's interest, despite any petty bickering to pursue it relentlessly, fully, unequivocally. The Russians more than all others know that. And they do it. They do it. No matter what the 'personal' issues are."

"Well, I watch them pretty carefully, and I can tell none of them likes Tarlac," Pam says.

"He is the leader, he's the big winner here, so far. It's logical they don't like him so much," Calderon replies with a smidgeon of obvious condescension.

"Apart from that," Pam continues, "they just don't like him. I can tell. Oh, I can tell, all right. I really can! So I don't know about the variations and everything, but I can tell that they don't like him."

"All right, all right," Calderon sighs, "they don't like him. I don't like him either. Perhaps no one likes him. But if wants to stop

CHAPTER 22

by tonight and help with the analysis, I will welcome him like a brother."

"He won't do it for you," Pam says triumphantly.

Calderon nods and nods. "So I'll have to make do with Wicks, then, is that it?"

Pam has turned away from the conversation, begun to watch the sushi chef, become fascinated by his movements squeezing rice into appropriate oblongs. She seems passive enough, even removed, floating, but I can tell she is actually seething. The heat ripples out from her. I can't believe I've seen her this angry—wordlessly furious.

Does Wicksburg sense this too? He says, "We should go back to work. We do have a lot of work to do, don't we? More than enough for two fellows alone against the Russians. Against Mikey here too for that matter." Wicksburg stands up, gets the bill from the plastic tray at the end of bar and heads toward the front counter.

"You had enough, Pam?" I ask softly, conscious of the double-meaning—trying too late to dispel it with a certain sympathetic tone.

"Yes," she says quickly. "I've had more than enough. More than enough. Too much, in fact, much too much."

"It's okay."

"It's okay, "she mimics. "It's okay. It's okay. You sound like my father."

"I am your father," I answer.

"I want to go home, then, father. I want to go home," Pam says eyes delighting in the possibility.

In the taxi she says, "And I don't mean home to the Ryersons. I mean home, home."

"Something wrong, honey? Vera asks.

"Nothing you can fix," Pam says, looking directly at her.

"Got it," Vera says and turns to the window.

We ride in silence to 86th street and I suggest Pam and I stop for some dark beer at one of the Hofbraus.

"You got it," Vera says again.

I pay the driver and wave him down the street to the apartment building. Pam stands, legs spread against the thick breeze coming down from the IRT exit.

"Anyone okay?" I ask.

She nods and follows me into the closest beerhall, which is strangely empty. We take seats at the elevated bar near the street entrance. I can watch the full length of the room. There are tables beyond the bar, but all are vacant.

"Is it too early or too late?" Pam asks.

"Both. You want to go back to Florida?"

"Yes, I do."

"Right away?"

"Yes, I do."

"Tonight?"

"No. Not tonight. Tomorrow. Tomorrow on a luncheon flight with little bits of smoked salmon, and maybe some crepes. And no conversation about chess."

"No Wicksburg Mendoza."

"No Calderon," Pam answers. "No Vera."

"No Mikey?"

"Mikey is all right. He's all right."

"Don't you think your leaving would upset him?"

"Why? We never talk. All I hear is his talking with her. Going over variations with her. Endlessly clicking around those pieces with her. It makes no difference your being here."

"I knew it made no difference whether I was here, but I thought you made a bit of a difference."

"Hmnn."

I order two dark draught beers. They come with a blue metallic side dish of peanuts. The bartender explains you can put the shells on the floor.

"I just want to go home and see some interesting sky," Pam says. "I look up here but you don't see any sky. You see a lot of grey stuff in the air and you see a lot of specks of silver from planes, but you don't see any sky. No clouds. No cloud formations. I don't like it. I'm not helping Mikey. He's doing fine on his own. She can help him. I can't. I want to go home."

"You want to know what I want?"

"No, I don't. I am going home, do you see that?"

"Sure. I'll call and get the reservations for a luncheon flight. No sense letting any obligations stand before immediate gratifications."

"You think that is what is going on?"

"You don't?"

"I don't know. All I know is that I want to see some decent sky and feel some real heat and look at some interesting people in my own house."

"Well, let's see if we can get Waldo to fly some interesting people in. He knows a swell group of Russian émigrés, who'd do anything for him."

"I just want to be away from here."

"Well, let's go tell them about it. Not exactly smashing here anyway."

"Do you think this irrational," she says as we get to the street.

"A little, but permissible, I suppose."

"I don't want permission for anything I do."

"Well, you don't get it then. If that is what you want. You'll have to stay in your room."

"We used to have another house, on a different part of the bay. I had a pink room. Softest, most soothing pink color. Just coming into the room made you feel better, made you feel delicious. And whole and happy, and . . . and . . . it was a perfect room."

"Because you were eight years old in it."

"Maybe, but maybe it was just a perfect place. It might be that surroundings really are the difference. I talked to Dr. Coffee about that. He thinks it's nonsense."

"From his penthouse, no doubt."

"I don't know where he lives."

"Well, in any event—he lives well, you can be sure. No little Manila cardboard boxes for him. Trust me on that one."

"I don't think where he lives is what I was trying to tell you. I was trying to tell you that I felt so wonderful whenever I came into my pink room. Maybe because it was all mine and I could do whatever I wanted in it, or maybe because the color was so perfect. But the room was like absolution, like benediction, like balm."

"I thought balm was a kind of lens."

"It is. For seeing yourself in. And what you see is not so nice, I guess. Isn't it?"

We make the obligatory nod to the doorman, and then in the elevator I ask, "Do you want to tell them, or do you want me to?"

"I don't care who tells them," Pam answers.

"Okay, you tell them."

"I don't suppose it will make a difference to them."

One thing makes a difference to Vera, however. Her reaction is instantaneous, focused: "That mean we gotta leave here?"

"No. No, no." Pam says quickly. "You can stay as long as you want. The Ryersons are in Portugal."

"Portugal?" Vera says evidently impressed.

"Yes, on the coast of Portugal. In the brilliant Portuguese sunshine, waiting for endless sum—"

"It's because of the draws, isn't it?" Mikey suddenly shouts, standing up from the chessboard. "It's because I can't win after Smyslov, isn't it?"

"No. Absolutely not. The chess has nothing to do with it," Pam lies.

""No. It has everything to do with it. You think I'm just gonna draw my way right out of Manila, don't ya? Well, I'm not. You gotta stay. You gotta! At least till I get another win."

"Who do you play next?" Pam ask, coming right to the point.

"Calderon."

"Maybe this is a good time to go," I suggest. "That way there won't be any divided loyalties."

"Divided loyalties?" Mikey shouts. "Who has divided loyalties?"

CHAPTER 22

"Well, Miss Snow seems to be quite impressed with Mr. Mendoza, Mr. Wicksburg Mendoza, if that is his name."

"Are you?" Mikey asks Pam.

"I want you to win," Pam says.

"Then stay. Stay! At least stay through my next win. You gotta do that."

"Oh, I don't have to do anything," Pam says with an odd lilt to her voice.

"It's the draws, isn't it? I knew. I coulda done better. I shoulda never drawn with Mohrstein. I had chances, but I missed them, didn't I, ma?"

"You missed two good chances, but he missed a lot more."

"I didn't think he had that many chances. Only the bishop move into Bishop six. He shoulda done that, but after that, he didn't have chances."

Vera says, "Maybe you're right."

Pam sits down on the huge floral sofa. "I don't like it here, Mikey. I just don't like it here. I'm not happy here. I want to go back to Florida."

"Well, I don't like it here either. I mean it's not so nice being here from my point of view, but I'm staying. You oughta too." Mikey says plaintively.

"If would be better if there were just a little something pink in this dismal apartment, something spoke of sunsets and golden moments. Golden moments, the way I used to remember them when—"

"Oh no," Mikey says. He sulks across the room, rests up against the thermopane window. "Oh no. You gotta stay. Don't do that on me."

"It's all right, Mikey," I suggest.

"A lot he knows," Vera says.

"Oh no, don't you see what's happening?" Mikey asks.

Pam has begun to rock back and forth gently on the sofa. Retreating by the moment to that inner preserve, inner coralscape that Mikey resents so much. In truth these inward turns hardly upset me at all. Temporary check-out seems almost merciful. It means, for example, that I can delay calling the airlines and arranging for a swift departure.

"Will you stay for a little while?" Mikey asks her again, but she continues to look down at the circular coffee table near the sofa, continues to rock almost indistinguishably back and forth.

"He's got an important match tomorra, a match he can win to get back into the win column. It'll get his score up, and we got this," Vera motions toward Pam, "We got this to contend with."

"There's nothing to contend with," I assure her. "Everything is okay."

"Oii!" Vera says and retreats to her bedroom.

"I'm sure she'll stay till you beat Calderon," I say to Mikey.

"You think so?"

"If you ask her."

"I asked her."

"I don't mean now. I mean later, when she's feeling better."

"I hope she feels better fast," Mikey says. "It was the lousy draws. I knew it."

"She really doesn't care whether you win or not."

"That's what I mean."

"That's not what I mean. Pam likes you whether you win or not. She just likes you and wants to help you."

"Then why isn't she doing it?"

Why indeed? "Why don't you ask her?"

Mikey comes over to the sofa, kneels down and tries to get Pam's attention. She smiles at him, a wonderfully opaque smile. A kind of I-am-a-blind-girl-and-I-don't-see-you-smile, a look that seems to go around him and reassemble itself about twelve feet beyond him.

"Stay for one more game," Mikey says, "I'll win it, I promise. Okay?"

Pam shakes her head.

"Why not?" Mikey shouts. "Why the hell not? Was it the draws? Was it?"

Pam nods—sinister to the end.

"Look, she doesn't know what she's doing."

"She knows all right. I knew it was the draws. I tried hard but I didn't come up with the right combinations. I can't get rid of them but I can make 'em count for me. You understand? Do you?" Mikey takes hold of her shoulders.

But I think Pam is falling asleep. The sleep exit. Splendid device.

Later I tell Waldo on the telephone: "Sweet scene for you, Waldo, the beseeching boy and the good fairy checked out for the evening on a Quaalude special. Nodsville. The beseeching boy prostrate at her feet, imploring, wheedling, searching maniacally for some crumb of consolation and the fairy princess drifting somewhere off of Venus. And good soldier Snell trying to patch things up. It was like your version of marriage, Waldo. It was, sure as I am telling you about it."

"Now, now," Waldo says thoughtfully, "is Pam asleep?"

"Like the proverbial mammoth in the glacier."

"Very clever, but not a good sign."

"Fuck you, Waldo. This is getting a bit more than I need to handle with my little column every week."

"Calm down. It's clear, it's clear."

"What's clear?"

"It's clear that you're upset."

"Fucking A!"

"I don't think we need all the obscenity. Some of us have tender sensibilities."

"Oh, very funny, wildly funny."

"So where are we?" Waldo says.

"Yes, where are we? I suppose I could ship her home, unless, of course, she woke up on the trip down. Say in the baggage car of the Amtrak Silver Meteor or whatever."

"Snelly, you're not helping things with these little extravagances. The thing we have to know is to what extent is something going on that we cannot overcome, or need help for. Do you see what I am saying?"

"You want to talk to Coffee, is that it?"

"That's an idea. I could talk to him and call you back."

"Then I'd have your impressions of what he thinks. That would certainly spirit things along, wouldn't it? Perhaps I could call someone else and give you their impressions of my state of mind."

"Snelly?"

"Yes? Yes?"

"Do you want me to come up?"

"Yes. You come up and I'll go down and we can wave over D.C. someplace."

"Snelly."

"Yes? Yes?"

"Why don't you go out for a while? Sounds as if everything is actually all right there. Now that Pam's asleep and Mikey's in bed, is that right?"

"I suppose."

"And Vera's asleep?"

"I don't know. I don't care. She can be hit by a truck for all I care."

"Well, why don't you go out to one of those splendid 3rd avenue pubs? Have some beer. Relax and try to sort things out. It may be the best thing is simply to make reservations and come back here. You could do worse."

"Mikey wouldn't like that."

"It wouldn't be his first disappointment. Given the priorities, what are your real choices? That's what I want you to focus on. Your real choices. Not the fantasies. Not the little getting-evens, the little vengeances, but the actual, odds-on real choices. Can you find them?"

"I'll ask Pam."

"Vindictiveness is not going to help. Believe me, it's not going to help. There is no immediate crisis, is that correct?"

"I suppose."

"Let me be more precise. Right now, at this very moment is anybody going to jump out the window?"

"I'm interesting in your definition of crisis. No, nobody is near the windows, which don't open in any event. I might throw some people out the window, but nobody as far as I can tell, to the best of my recollection, is going to jump. Not of their own volition. I guarantee it. I'd stake my reputation on it."

"You're a little hard to talk to," Waldo says. "You don't like my idea of going out for a drink?"

"I don't think there's anything to celebrate. I don't like going out to celebrate when things are left hanging fire. Up in the fucking air. So I guess I'll make the plane reservations and drag Pam back to her home. She seems to miss it so. And to hell with Mikey. He'll have to get over it. Just before the one match he ought to win. Everybody says so. Test of his mettle. Maybe that's the way to write it up. Deserted by friends, abandoned by lovers, tossed aside for the cool bay breeze, or maybe the steaming Gulf sun, Mikey Spendip resolved to make the best of his slow start in the Zonal Finals—"

"Snelly, if you get yourself into a lather, it won't help anybody—you, Pam, Mikey, me. It won't help anybody. None of us."

"Perhaps I should try to help. Why should I try to help?"

"You should help yourself first. By calming down. By considering aspects of the problem, facets of it, from all sides. That's the way to take care of yourself and Pam."

"I always take care of Pam."

"I know you do," Waldo agrees, sensing, I think, a little less hysteria in the conversation. I would like to disabuse him of that relaxation, but I am tired of heating things up. As tired as Pam. "A night's sleep will change a lot of things," Waldo goes on. "Some solid rest will clarify what is happening. And to tell the truth, Snelly, sounds like nothing is happening. A lot of energy is being burned off, that's all. Has Pam been taking her dosages?"

I like the sound of *dosages*. Such an interesting word, *dosages*. "I can't keep count, Waldo. Is it fifteen little white ones and four reds per day, or seven, and seven, or twenty and nine. I don't know. She's always popping something in her mouth."

"Well, she just may have gotten behind or ahead on the count. Maybe that's all that has happened. Why don't you come back here? You write the column from here. That's not your first concern. Come home, if you like. The tickets are open, aren't they?"

"Sure. Sure." I begin to nod away from the conversation myself. "Sure, see you tomorrow, or maybe the next day—see you soon."

"Snelly, Paul, I didn't say it was going to be easy, did I?"

What is Waldo talking about?

"Did I?"

"If you want permission from me to feel good about yourself, to feel self-congratulatory, you've got it. Is that what you want, Waldo?"

"I want you to rest up, get a good night's sleep."

"You know what I want, Waldo? Nobody ever asks me what I want. You want to know what I want?"

There is a pause and then Waldo, ever obliging, says, "What do you want, Snelly?"

I think a moment and then say, "I want. I want to liberate the Philippines."

Chapter 23

In the morning it is virtually impossible to awaken Pam. She flops about on the bed as if in some kind of trance. I do manage to get her into a sitting position, but her eyes are half lidded over and she stares mostly at the tops of her knees on the edge of the bed. I can get her to stand but only briefly. With the gentlest pushing she simply folds back into the bed and puts her right arm across her eyes.

"You want some coffee here?"

"Coffee?" she says weakly. "I don't want him."

"To drink. Coffee to drink."

"Eh?"

"Okay, okay."

Mikey meets me in the hallway to the bathroom. "She staying?" he asks with more than usual anxiety.

"She's certainly not leaving till she wakes up. And I doubt she's going to wake up this morning. At least I can't get her up."

"So she's staying, is that it?"

"I guess so."

I think, is that the way you want her? Inert? A zombie in the Ryerson condo?

I have a quick breakfast of cereal with Vera and Mikey, then go back to rousing Pam. By noon there is not much progress. I have a robe around her, but she complains her head hurts, complains the backs of her knees ache, complains that the sunlight (there is none) is too bright. I call the airlines and book us on an evening flight from LaGuardia—a special to Disney World.

But Waldo terminates those plans. He seems much more concerned, "Snelly, I think we are backsliding seriously. Cancel the flight. I think somebody needs to look at her there."

"Well, she seems all right. Not eating, but at least I think I can get her up and around and maybe some movement will stimulate her."

"I think we are beyond that," Waldo says. "You sit tight. Somebody will arrive to help out."

"Who?"

"Probably Ned. Maybe somebody else. Maybe Coffee himself. I can't be sure. Don't take her to the airport. Don't force anything. Just see she doesn't hurt herself."

At one-thirty Mikey and Vera leave. There is a touching scene when Mikey attempts to get Pam to wish him luck. Pam merely rests against the pillow, arms akimbo and smiles archly, that opaque smile.

"You gonna wish me luck?" Mikey says, then repeats, "You gonna wish me luck?"

"Come on, Mike, we can't wait forever. Calderon will start your clock. You gotta believe that. Come on!"

"A little luck?" Mikey takes hold of her hand, but Pam regards him as she might refrigerator repair man, or a ring thief.

"Mikey!" Vera shouts, "tell her you're sorry she's not feeling so good and come on."

"I'm sorry," Mikey says.

"She's wishing you luck in her way," I tell Mikey, who watches me with skepticism and, apparently, hope. It is impossible to say which sentiment predominates in his face. "You're using the Dutch?" I ask.

"Who knows? Today I'm gonna win. Whatever it takes!"

"Betta believe it!" Vera says. "Cakewalk. Mr. Victim himself. Come and massacre me, Calderon. We'll do it too. Bye Pam. Hope ya feel betta."

In the hallway and as she gets on the elevator Vera says, "What's with her anyway?"

But the doors do not await my reply.

At three-thirty the doorman says over the intercom, "Three gentlemen on their way up."

"Who are they?"

"Dr. Gaineway and two others. I don't know. He only said 'Tell Mr. Snell, Dr. Gaineway is coming up.'"

I think momentarily about cleaning up the room. Actually the only things out of place are Ryerson's luscious robe and the morning Times.

Gaineway is brusque, "I have reciprocal arrangements with Dr. Meyer and Belasco at Golden Hill, who have treated Miss Snow before. And you are?

"Paul Snell."

"Can you take me to her, Paul? These are my assistants who will drive Miss Snow to the Hill, if it is necessary."

"The Hill?"

"Golden Hill in New Canaan."

"Golden Hill? I don't understand."

"An institute where Miss Snow has been treated before under Dr. Belasco. Time, Paul, is important in these affairs. Can we go to her?"

"Okay, Phil," I say loudly enough to give everyone pause.

When we are in the hallway, one of the assistants says quietly to me "Dr. Gaineway's first name isn't Phil."

"No kidding," I answer. "He sure looks like a Phil to me."

Gaineway examines Pam's eyes, takes her pulse, looks at the pill bottles on the table. "When has she been taking these?"

"I don't know. She kind of does it by herself."

"How many were in here?"

"I don't know. She takes care of that."

"You have no idea?"

"No. Why would I have any idea?"

"Well, could she have taken a lot of them recently?" Gaineway says with exasperation.

"No. I don't think so. I would have noticed. If anything she's not been taking any at all in the last day or two."

"You don't think so," Gaineway says to himself, bemused, sullen. He goes back to looking into her eyes. "Has she been taking her lithium?"

"I don't know what she takes. She doesn't discuss that much with me."

"She doesn't *discuss* it with you. I suppose it would be too technical."

"Oh, I don't think so. I'm fairly technical. A lot of people say." I watch Gaineway's frustration. Is Pam aware of what is going on?

Gaineway looks at me for a long, long moment. I hear the assistants shuffling around at the end of the bed behind me. It seems Gaineway is taking long breaths, then he reaches for the telephone on the night table. He punches a bevy of numbers and gets passed through to Dr. Coffee. The language is hyper-technical, with Latinate words and occasional glances at me, but the important parts are clear enough. I hear the word "acute" several times and "reaction" and "hospitalization." Then the end of the discussions comes clearly into focus: "I think Mr.," Gaineway pauses, looks at me, "what is your name again?"

"Snell."

"I think Mr. Snell should be replaced. I just don't think he's competent for the position." Gaineway eyes me, as if to say, "sorry". There is a long pause, then still a longer one. Gaineway says, "I see. I see. Mr. Snow indicated quite otherwise. I was under the impression that Mr., ah,.. ah, Snell, that's it. Snell was—I see. I see. But then who is going to sign? No. No. I can rather confidently say she will not be able to. So who is? Ah," Gaineway pauses again. "And where are they? Ah, ah, I see. Not till tonight. When? Ah, I see. I

CHAPTER 23

see. Yes, well, I really think we ought to move on this—the sooner the better. I see. I see."

Suddenly Gaineway hands me the phone. Can it be I will hear for the first time the awesome Dr. Coffee? "Mr. Snell," Coffee says—at least it's not Paul yet. "Would you be free to accompany Miss Snow to Golden Hill? It's about an hour and a half drive. I think under the circumstances someone she knows ought to go with her. Dr. Gaineway thinks hospitalization is important, immediate hospitalization. It's an imposition, but it would be helpful. Additionally, their admissions procedures require someone to sign her in, if she's unable to do so herself. Now I'm sure Mr. Snow will get there very quickly. I'm positive of that," Coffee says with a kind of emphasis that smacks of anger. "But it might be that you would enable her to get checked in immediately."

"How can I sign?"

"As her fiancé and agent for the Snow family, until Mr. Snow could arrive."

"Fiancé?" I ask.

"As the agent, then, for the Snows—if you don't mind."

"I don't see how I can sign anything, frankly."

"It's mostly just a procedural thing so that she can be admitted immediately until Mr. Snow arrives. I'll try to get it waived, under the circumstances. She has been a patient before and Dr. Belasco is a good friend of mine. But as an outside precaution—you might be asked to say you would be responsible for her admission."

"I can't be responsible for anything."

"That's not really the issue. It won't come up, I think. Mr. Snow will be there in time, I'm fairly sure. On the other hand, plane schedules and so forth can't be predicted precisely. Don't worry about the signature aspect. Simply going along with Pam will help. Do you mind doing it?"

"No."

"Good. Can you put Dr. Gaineway back on?"

The conversation with Gaineway takes longer than I imagined it should have, and I am interested in Pam's reaction to all these plottings. For a moment while Gaineway is arguing some point, I think she has begun to have a sense of what is happening. It seems she moves her hand in my direction. I go to the other side of the bed, take hold of her very wet, very limp forearm. She does not move her head. But it seems she is blinking her eyes for a reason. I lean over to stare directly into her dilated pupils. The fingers of my right hand take up hers. "We're going to Connecticut," I whisper. "Do you understand?" Her fingers are almost lifeless, and surprisingly wet. When I try to take my hand away, it seems a little resistance forms from her fingertips. So I take hold again.

"You will need to pack some of her things," Gaineway says.

"Of course."

"I will have a vehicle here shortly. In the meanwhile Mr. Laker will be in charge. Mr. Krimin will do the driving. It should take no more than two hours. I'm going to give her a shot now, to insure that she rests."

Her fingers tighten around mine. "Is that really necessary? She seems rather relaxed right now."

"It will insure she sleeps, gets good rest on the way there." Gaineway fumbles in his bag and brings out a little kit filled with disposable syringes. He measures off the requisite ccs from a clear, rubber capped bottle, deftly fires that amount into Pam's left shoulder. "It's hardly anything serious, just a relaxer. Why don't you start packing?"

I break Pam's weak grip, shake hands with Gaineway who hurries off, and then fish out her small leather travel bag from the closet. Soon enough Pam is packed, strapped on to a nifty, collapsible stretcher with wheels on the bottom. Laker and Krimin carry her out to the elevator and then hit the lever that drops the wheels down. She can be carted out of the building. The ambulance is a Pontiac van, three stools on one side, a thick mattress bed on the other. Krimin and Laker are adroit lifting her from the stretcher to the bed, pulling down more straps, putting a second pillow under head. I take the front stool. Laker sits opposite her, but before we are in heavy traffic, he indicates I should sit in his place, so as to

CHAPTER 23

have a clearer view of Pam's face. I put my right hand on her shoulder. Her eyes are glazing, lids coming down.

For some reason I think of an old Michael Caine movie in which he works a nail into his palm so as to prevent a loss of consciousness, or a surrender to some mind-altering experiment. There is old Caine grinding the nail in, blood like the stigmata coming out of his palm. Don't drift off, Pam, I think, aware of the absurdity of that mental directive. These evil Albanians in their Pontiac van mean to take you to hills beyond reason, beyond consciousness, beyond life itself. Nifty idea. Laker could hardly be less malignant. He looks about twenty years old with bushy greasy hair, and an open, vacant face such as you might see on Boy Scout posters. This is not the devil I decide. But Pam is way ahead of me. She beckons with her dropping eyes. I lean in. She is actually going to speak. Maybe this silly trip is not necessary after all. Expensive, but not necessary.

Pam nods to me. I lean over further, pressing my left ear almost to her mouth.

"Are we in Manila?" she says softly. Laker does not hear, although he surely must be aware she is saying something.

"No. We'll have to settle for New Canaan, though we're not there yet. The new canaan of New Canaan. Do you like that?"

"I like Manila," Pam says, then drops off to sleep.

Chapter 24

Through the Pontiac porthole I get to watch the Triborough Bridge, the Henry Hudson Parkway and the Merit Parkway, ramps of whizzing unhappiness. Like a dirty strip of elastic the roadway extends along the edge of the suburban bliss of Fairfield County, a grim reminder of what supports the lush green lawns inland. Scarred and abandoned railroad stations jump out at the porthole, and then, some place beyond Stamford, the van turns off. Abruptly we are plunged into gorgeous, verdant growth. Heavy oaks and maples overarch the roadway, making a tunnel of fecundity carrying us straight to the happiest of the happy valleys.

Laker says, "We come out about once, maybe twice a week, mostly alcoholics to dry out, but she's a different situation, I take it."

"Not a lush," I answer, surprised that Laker seems anxious to talk. "Maybe nothing's really wrong with her."

Laker shrugs. "I like it out here. Very pretty. The city sucks."

"Agreed, we're from Florida. I could stand to see a bit more sky up here."

"Ah, just look up," Laker says with that peculiar sarcasm of New Yorkers. He should meet Vera.

"Am I going to have to sign something?"

"Tell 'em you won't do it. They don't care. Belasco will admit her on his own."

CHAPTER 24

But the issue never really comes up. At the brick gate to Golden Hill the clerk, already preoccupied with whatever comes over his headphones, merely waves us to the front entrance. There two attendants take the stretcher with Pam on it pausing in the hallway near the desk . . . I fill out a registration slip giving what pertinent details I know about her. When I bog down on "father's occupation," the nurse obligingly pulls out the complete file and fills in the blanks from that record. Pam is truly out now, happily sleeping while she is wheeled around for pulse, blood tests, etc. Then she is silent all the way up the elevator to the third floor, which serves as the gateway to the special "cottages" mounted along the side of the hill.

Pam's cottage is special indeed, equivalent to three large rooms, a family-living-dining room with small kitchenette tucked at one end and a separate bedroom. The bathroom has a bidet in it. Two attendants get Pam up briefly in the transfer to the bedroom, but soon enough she is fast asleep again in this idyllic setting. There is a small wooden porch at the front of the cottage, and I elect to sit there. Apparently Ned Snow is coming and I am to wait for him. I sit in a brilliant red metal chair that rocks on its metal tubular supports.

Down the hill the main lodge extends like a solid white rectangle dropped through the trees. You can see just traces of the black asphalt driveway from the front gate, and then beyond the gate, further down the well-treed slope to the main outskirts of the turnpike industrial area. For a while I imagine I can simply blink industrialism away; refocus so that clean green goes down all the way to the water of the Long Island Sound. But as the sun sets, it seems the industrial base comes into sharper focus. The lines of smoke, the haze of pollution, the sparkle of overhead wires is less escapable.

Once, I hear Pam moan and rush in, but she has only turned over. I think about calling Vera. Perhaps Mikey has completed his forty moves; maybe victory is already his. Perhaps at sweltering, cloudy Aedile they are celebrating a Spendip brilliancy—-Calderon ever the gracious loser? Mendoza already focused on something else? It did seem that Wicksburg's interest in the game was secondary to some larger purpose, perhaps fashion. Could that be it?

About the time hunger begins pulverizing my stomach, lo, two attendants come back with a large wooden tray containing a hot meal for me and a cold one for Pam, "if she wakes up later."

The hot meal, complete with its dome containers, consists of a New England boiled dinner. Is this what they serve all the initiates? Welcome to New England, Puritan land of regained self-composure, Fertile Crescent of self-discipline. The mountain of conscience is about to fall on you—you who have shown lately so little self-maintenance, so little grasp of the elemental realities.

This, is precisely what our marriage will be like. You in drugged sleep. Me on the porch in a red metal chair eating a New England boiled dinner and watching in the distance the Connecticut Turnpike carrying reality on up the line to some ferociously real place, like Bridgeport. I will sit on the porches of the future in the lush drying-out spas of the world watching over your desperate slumber. And in the next cottage will be Waldo tending to his garden and listening to Hillary's directives. The good life, eh?

Ned Snow, when he arrives around nine-thirty, is more than a little apologetic. He is wearing somewhat incongruously (which sets me speculating on just where he was and what he was doing, when he got the "news"), white flannel trousers and a short sleeved blue denim work shirt. Perhaps he was supervising the training of the polo ponies and by his shirt signaling allegiance to common labor while retaining the trousers as emblem of majesty. It is difficult to catch the meaning of his considerably slurred words.

"You're a brick, Paully, a brick for doing this. No reason for you to take up these shamly bursons."

Shamly bursons?

"Poor little Pamy—probably shouldn't have come up here. We rushed things soo much. Terrible to land back in here. She never liked it, you knowsh. Never could stand this place. Don't know why. Hell, the view alone is werth, is werth every sing, don't shu think? And the care here is as good as you can get in Zurich, or wherever else you might want to dry or die in."

Die in?

"Poor little Pamy. A view as good as old Neap, shon't shu think? And now . . . and now . . ." He appears to ponder it, become confused, depressed, then triumphs over such feelings. "Ah, hell! They'll give my Pamy a buzz or two, and in a week she'll be good again, don't shu think?"

"I don't know that she's really in such a bad state."

"Belasco says it's pretty bad, but he's one of the world's greatest crepe hanger. Not to say solicitors for exotic treatments. Zap! Zap! And Pam's swell again, don't shu get it?" Snow slumps down in the identical red metal chair next to mine. "Drugged her, eh?" he sighs.

"Yes, a shot in the van put her out. Maybe she just needs sleep."

"No—checking out for a while. You've not seen it before. She was scared to death to show you. Never want shu to see it. Happens. Happens. Comes over her. Wham! Then it's like the treatments, the session mean nothing. Maybe they don't mean anything anyway. On sing ever worked was a little buzz. You like it here?"

"Do I like it here?"

"Yesh. We can stay here, if you want. Down there," he points to the lodge below, "or we stay in town at the Holiday Inn."

"Stay overnight you mean?"

"Yesh. Yesh. Yes, I mean, if you want to. You probably could get back into the city tonight, but it would be tricky. Better to spend the night. Which place suits you?"

I sense he does not want me to answer the question. "Whichever is better for you."

"Well, to tell the truth, I already got a room at the Holiday Inn. I can't say I like it that much up here." He picks at his fingers a bit. "You can't get a drink up, for example. And after a day of traveling I need—anybody needs a drink, don't shu think?"

"Sure."

"Okay. We'll go back to the Inn. I can get you a room easy." With that Snow turns and goes into the cottage. After a while I follow him in. He is standing beside Pam's bed.

"She was never the apple of my eye," Snow says, regarding her with a blend of exasperation and affection it seems to me. "Not that she ever made trouble. Never did. Not directly anyway. But had a way of getting into fixes, you know what I mean? Accidents. Falling down. Cars. Horses. A way of knowing that when you wanted to count on her, then things would start happening. Things that shouldn't happen and don't normally. Oh, Pamy, Pamy," Snow sighs. "But you, Paullee, you are a brick to carry on for us on this one."

Carry on?

"Shu shouldn't have to do this, but when we weren't here, shu were right there—a brick. I value that. So does Evie. And so, so does Pamy."

"Frankly I'm not convinced there's anything really wrong. Couldn't it simply be that Pam needed some extra sleep and started to get it, when suddenly everybody interfered?"

Snow smiles broadly, point his finger at me. "You go on sinking that way! You do it! She needs that!"

"Or maybe she got off her schedule with the pills Coffee gave her. I never watched over her about those. Maybe I should have."

"Guilt happens when these things come down. But forget it. Guilt out the window. I had an Indian friend once, met him in Delhi, old Delhi, and he was with a Japanese Sumi painter. You know about that? Well this Japanese fellow was a kind of oracle, training lots of avid young Indians in this simple art form. But the guy's English was strange as hell. He had a way of saying 'window' when he didn't like something, didn't approve of something. You'd show him your painting and if he liked it, he'd say 'good, very good,' but if he didn't like it, he'd say 'window.' The Indian fellow told me someone had told the guy if you don't like something, throw it out the window. So he used 'window' as his adjective of disapproval. So guilt, Paullee, is 'window.' Purely 'window.'"

CHAPTER 24

Snow stopped speaking, took up Pam's eel-loose arm. "When she was sleeping as a kid I used to think, how lucky she was. Not a care in the world, dreaming there in her crib, in her bed. Taken care of. No worries. But all the time little fires in the back of her mind. That's what Coffee says, anyway. Little fires and nothing we can do to put them out, change them around. Ah, Pamy, Pamy, papa is here to get you a little buzz, bring you back, sweetheart. Shu think she's hearing me?"

"I doubt it."

"I doubt it, too. Shall we go ahead?" He takes up the phone receiver and tells the front desk to send up the night nurse,

"They'll have somebody stay with her all night?"

"Of course," Snow says, "this is a first class operation. The best. The very best. But you can't get a drink here. I suppose if you brought some in, people might a bad time of it. Shu ever gone on the wagon?"

"No."

"That's a good sign. Shu start going on the wagon and you end up drying out—that's my wisdom for tonight."

We go back to our red chairs. "She always had psychosomatic illnesses," Snow says to the sweetly darkening sky. "In prep school. At Smith. In France. Little, peculiar, unidentifiable slippings. Near appendicitis, near mononucleosis, near hepatitis. Never exactly diagnosable, but so close you had to figure she was either the most learned imitator, or by God she had a strain they hadn't named yet. Maybe that was the case. Maybe that really was the case. She has stuff they haven't identified yet. Haven't named yet. Why not? She's special, isn't she?"

"I think so."

"Not so damn special, as you might consider, I suppose. She's attractive in her way, but no Helen of Troy, if you know what I mean. She picks her clothes really well. She has a sense of style." Snow crosses his white-flannelled legs. "But I suppose you could say the basics are lacking. Nice skin, easy disposition, until, until times like these. And then, even now, not hard on you, is she?"

"Never."

"Right. Never. She's sweet. Sweet disposition. Kind of unfocused but a lot of women are, aren't they?" Snow waits for my reply, but for a moment I don't think one is necessary, but he reminds me a reply is required. "Aren't they?"

"Oh, I guess so."

"Of course. You can't fault her because she's a woman. Wouldn't do, would it?"

"No." I'm right on cue.

Snow looks at me oddly, taps, then pets the wide metal arm rest of his chair, "I remember these things. I remember them. As much redecoration as they do around, and they do. Every time I came something had been redone. They're like the Japanese. Tear this down. Rebuild that. Don't paint it. Throw it away. Put in a new one. Always refurbishing. Yet, these damn chairs are still here. You know why?"

I decide an answer is not required.

"Can you guess?" Snow goes on.

I shake my head.

"Well, I'm not so sure myself, but I have a theory. These chairs are on the outside of the cottages. And the outside is distinctly different from the inside, isn't it? Yes, indeed. They think more about the inside than the outside. Oh, they keep the outside up and all, but it's the inside that really interests them. The furniture inside. Maybe the Board of Directors all interior decorators—or maybe because of what they're doing here anyway, that the inside gets top priority. Inside these cottages has been renovated maybe five times in the last twenty years."

Has Pam been coming here for twenty years?

"Well, anyway the sunsets are good here, aren't they? Did you notice?"

"I guess so." On cue.

The night nurse arrives. Snow shakes her hand lovingly, but it is impossible to tell whether from interest in her or devotion to his daughter's well-being, maybe a lush's bonhomie. In any event we take a rented yellow Plymouth sedan to the Holiday Inn downtown.

The bar is done in seafarer motifs. Nets hang from the high ceiling, and a ship's wheel separates the men's and ladies' rooms. Snow orders two stingers.

"Stingers are the only nighttime drink," he says. "Put you right out, if you manage the right number. That's the trick—enough to put you out, but not enough to really put you out. Know what I mean?"

The glass holding the stinger seems oddly narrower than it ought to be—vulnerable, as if the top cone of brownish icy liquid would snap off its support. Snow drinks his in a single long gulp. I am impressed. He orders two more, but I abandon hope of keeping up. Holiday Inns are not the best places to get loaded in. The carpets are always dark maroon and cigarette machines stand around like sentinels.

"Jesus," Snow says quietly after he takes a sip of the second stinger, "Pam was with me in Nepal, did she tell you? I had an audience with the King of Nepal—roommate last year in college was connected the Royal Family. Anyway we got chance to go there. Pamy and I were kneeling in front of the throne, on very solid wood floors, I can tell you. And, of course the etiquette of the thing is not so clear, heh, heh.I bowed for a long time and so did Pamy and then when I lifted my head up, there was a servant standing right smack in front of us, blocking the view of the King and carrying a tray. Silver tray, it caught the light sometimes so that a little zap-flash appeared on the wall. And on the tray was a pineapple, a whole pineapple. It was a handsome pineapple, but I didn't think it was anything too special. But then the servant knelt down and set the pineapple right in front of me. 'The King wishes you to have the pineapple as a present,' the interpreter who was about twenty feet behind me said. So I bowed again to the King and said 'Thank you very much' about as loud as I thought would be polite. Then I didn't know what I was supposed to do. Should I pick up the pineapple and back out? Was the conference, the audience, or whatever over?

I thought about giving it to Pamy, but she still had her head down. 'I think you can pull your head up, dumpling,' I said to her. But then the interpreter said, 'The King would like you to eat some of the pineapple now so he will know the gift was a good one.' Okay, I thought, eat some of the pineapple. Eat some of the pineapple. How do you eat a whole pineapple when you don't have a knife or a fork, or a napkin, or anything. Just these." Snow holds up his hands. "Well, I can tell you it was rather awkward. I reached for the pineapple, took hold of the top of the things. Prickly and unpleasant and I thought, well maybe I can pull the top off, or maybe there's a way to break it open. Maybe it's been precut somehow so I can easily get a piece. But of course it was solid as a rock, just a perfect, natural pineapple waiting to present me with this problem. And then—I had a vision, I think—a splendid visitation. That's the word, a visitation. I swear I was holding on to that pineapple thinking furiously what the hell was I going to do with it, when suddenly it hit me. Wham! Of course! Pineapples have segments. Anything that's segmented can be pulled apart. So I slowly turned the pineapple around in my fingers and sure enough, right in the middle there's a segment, a nifty little triangle that has been cut a little bit. I could nudge it on either side with my thumbs and break it off and out. So I did that. And the interpreter said,' Don't eat that one,' so I broke off another one and ate the inside right down to the skin. And I broke one off for Pamy and handed to her and she ate it down to the skin. 'Thank the King,' the interpreter said. So I thanked the King, told him how delicious it was. He didn't speak any English, but I repeat it enough and thanked him. And we withdrew, backwards on our knees, all the way backwards. You know what's important about that experience?" Snow finishes the second stinger and orders another. I continue contemplating the two in front of me. "Do you?"

"Not exactly."

"Well, I'll tell you. That was the first and only time in my life when I found out something important under pressure."

CHAPTER 24

I wonder, is this a confession, or an observation about the nature of knowledge in a world filled with hostility.

"Pamy's no good under pressure either," Snow says, quickly drinking half the stinger. "She can do most everything if she has time and she's not pushed. You seem to understand that. And I appreciate it. So does Evelyn. And, God knows, so does Pamy. Little buzzes take the pressure off, I guess. I mean when she's back after treatment, she actually forgets whatever it was that weakens her under pressure. Whatever it is that's holding her back. That's what's helpful about the treatment. Not what Coffee indicates. But that's what's helpful about the treatment. Not what Coffee indicates. But that's what's helpful. Clearing all that garbage away so you can start over and relearn more positive lessons. Ever thought that would be the way to get straightened around? Simple memory purgative. What we carry in here," Snow points to his temple. "Simply blow it all away. Zap! It's gone and everything is bright and polished and new again."

"Glistening."

Snow looks at me tentatively. I regret the adjective. Snow sighs, puts two hands around the stinger. Is Pam awake, watching the night nurse who sits in the wicker chairs in the living-dining room and reads a Cosmopolitan?

"I'm out," Snow says, finishing his drink.

I finish one of mine. He finishes the others. On the 9th floor we go in opposite directions to our rooms.

Chapter 25

Vera says, "We're still working on it. It's gonna be tough. Very tough. That little dandy is tough as nails. Give ya nothin'. Absolutely nothin'. We got a pawn, but Mikey don't see the win yet. We're working on it. There's a couple of lines we haven't looked at. But Mikey needs his sleep too. Maybe I'll stay working on it."

"Does he want to talk to me?" I ask.

"Nah, he's pretty busy."

"Well, tell him Pam's safe and sound. Sleeping now in her own cottage up on the Hill with a terrific view all the way down to the water."

"Hmnn," Vera says.

"I'm not sure when I'll be back."

"Yeah, well so long as we can stay here . . . We're plenty busy here. I'll tell him about Pam. Don't worry about us. Worry about Calderon. He gotta find something a little stronger, or we could be stuck with a draw. I really could use some first class help. Maybe we ought to think about bringing in some talent."

"I got the impression his second isn't too great either." I regret the phrasing almost as soon as I have uttered it.

"Hmnn," Vera says, "you mean Wicksburg?"

"Yes."

"He's not professional, if that's what you mean. But the lines are clear, ya see? And if the win's not there, it's not there. But a pawn's

CHAPTER 25

supposed to win, you know. So I'm still thinking we gotta win, but it's gonna take a lotta work. Right through till the match, I bet. Mikey'll have to sleep, but I'm gonna be analyzing right through, right through. Looks like we could try two or three lines that look promising. That's what the annotators would say, *promising*. We'll have to see. Look, I gotta go back. Anything else you want?"

"No. Maybe I can get back for the finale."

"Let's see what's gonna happen. See ya later."

I watch the 1:00 a.m. weather report. A listless, hatchet-faced hill-billy-looking fellow slowly draws lines on a vast Lucite board depicting the Eastern seaboard of the U.S. I see isobars connecting Ned Snow, doubtless in his stinger-sleep down the hall, tiny Pamela in her own hillside drugged slumber, and in New York Vera and Mikey hunched over the clacking chessboard. That leaves only Snell to watch the scuffed brass chain that controls the squat barrel of light suspended from the ceiling fan over my bed.

The next three days drift past like the soundless Sound in view from Pam's porch. I am aware of Ned Snow's evening patter—tales of exotic places in increasingly slurred tones. Little stories of the exalted in unexalted places. The ministers of Ethiopia who took him hunting someplace in the highlands, the university official in Ceylon, the business partner on the South Island of New Zealand—the slowest, most inertia-drenched place in the universe, Snow claims. On the evening of the second day Pam gets her first buzz.

"She gets really woozy with Pentathol, you notice that?" Snow says in the lounge later that night, after we have safely installed the night nurse. "Says the damnedest things. Once she told me about a skating accident she had when she was thirteen. Hadn't mentioned that literally since it had happened. Never once, and then one belt of Pentathol and out it comes, parading up front like some traumatic material that has to come bursting forth or she'll split into a million pieces."

I have switched to gin and tonics, but Ned is still plowing the stingers under. "Anyway," he says, "she'll feel a lot better now, a whole lot better."

For a while I imagine that he is envious of her. The ultimate stinger: Pentathol and eight-five volts directly to the brain.

"It's what they used to believe about the frontier," Snow says, "you know all those social scientists. That you could go out to the frontier and actually drop back in the evolutionary cycle—start over and reconstruct yourself, learn a new culture, become a new man. Ah, swell concept! But they were really talking about electroshock therapy, weren't they?"

"Perhaps they should have been treated." In truth Pam never seems a new person to me after the treatments, merely a less focused one. The old dreads have merely been disguised or whatever. But Snow will not be denied his metaphor.

"The point is she gets a reprieve and we can help her. After they wipe the slate clean, maybe we can write on it in a way that will keep her from falling backwards again."

"That's a rather tall order."

"A doubt at least," Snow laughs, "but you've got the energy for it, and I've got the wherewithal, don't I?"

I take a long hit from the G & T.

"Isn't that what we're talking about—will and wherewithal? Isn't it?"

I shrug, feeling very much adrift. No, actually sinking.

"You don't want to think about that. I don't blame you. Big job. But all jobs are big. Big. Big."

'Is she actually out, when they do it?"

Snow looks at me strangely. "Of course. Completely out. This isn't the Middle Ages for Chrissakes. What makes you ask a thing like that?"

"I was just worried."

"Well, don't worry about that. Worry about what we can do afterwards to make things better for Pamy. Worry about that, right?"

"Sure."

CHAPTER 25

"Good. Now when we go to Manila, I want things there to be well taken care of—all of which means you and I have got to talk some about what's necessary for Pamy. Are you interested in discussing that? Are you?"

"Of course."

"I thought so," Snow says rather resoundingly. The bartender, who is reading a paperback near the glasses filled with small olives or onions or cherries, looks up. "We need to have extensive consultation with Coffee, if he won't come along with us."

"He was thinking of coming?"

"Well, he's a big sailor. Likes that a lot. Probably he was thinking about it, but I suppose he won't come along. But we need to have a much clearer idea of what Pam is supposed to take, and when, and how much. You want another?"

Snow orders for both of us. "Manila's one of the best places in the world. Everybody speaks English. And you can get anything you want. Anything!" Snow emphasizes the word and nudges me in the shoulder. "Hot, gloriously decadent place. Great buys for leather and clothing, if you want. 'Course I'm more interested in the politics of the place."

"Really?"

"For business reasons. Group of us were going into shrimp farming, were dealing with the Lopez family."

"What happened?"

"That's the great thing about the Philippines. Nobody is quite sure, or at least nobody is telling us. Apparently the elder Lopez got arrested and his family holdings confiscated, although I understand he is safe enough under a kind of modified house arrest. He's got enough connections to make a stink, if anything drastic were done to him. Shame, too, since we were about to put the whole package together and then Bam! Everybody we've been dealing with is suddenly incommunicado. Mostly in jail, I guess. Only goes to show we had lousy intelligence about the place. Working through a French group. Had no idea all of it was going to unravel so damn fast. My share going to be in Pamy's name. It was going to be hers."

"Her own shrimp farm," I remark as Snow finishes his stinger, "sort of a nice thing to drop at a party."

"In Cebu," Snow says, "another island not too far from Manila. Beautiful island—fantastic beaches. Incredible food and dirt cheap. You can get a ferry down from Manila. Yeah, Pamy would have liked it. When I go, I'll try to say hello to Lopez, if they'll let me."

"You don't have connections at the palace?"

"Eh? No. Nothing. Just a tourist. I wouldn't mind having some connections. You have any?"

"What do you think?"

Snow laughs and orders another. When it comes, he holds it up and says, "Well, you'll see a new Pamy in the morning. We all will. To the new Pamy. Slate wiped clean. All that old infestation, all that old capacity shut off. Maybe if we're lucky, purged and ready. Ready to show that after all, her old man ain't such a bully. That her mother isn't such a harpy and that her, her Mr. Snell still about, still solid, dependable, concerned and everyday growing on the job."

"Cheers," I answer.

"I'm serious," he says, "Evelyn and I appreciate your willingness to stay here with Pamy. I feel confident leaving things in your hands for a few days. I think you care for my daughter and that makes me feel pretty damn good. 'Course these have a way of helping too!"

The hill-billy weather man can write temperature backwards from the opposite side of the Lucite map. An impressive feat. Perhaps he should work on Pam.

The morning after a buzz, as Ned would say, is always the most disturbing part for the onlooker, the most fertile part for the patient. For a moment I am not quite sure Pam actually recognizes me. She smiled all right, and sits up in bed, watches me carefully, as if I were about to take a fuse out of the television.

"Do we know who we are this morning?" I ask.

"Do we?" she answers, lilting her voice with a familiar excitement. The game, how she loves the game.

CHAPTER 25

"Yes, Cleopatra, do we know who we are and where we are going and why?"

"I know a few things, but maybe those aren't the things I know."

"Well, let's start with what you know"

"I know someone named Mikey. He must be young, eh?"

"Oh, very young. Just a child."

"With very strong legs," she says smiling more broadly.

"If you say so."

"And competitive, very competitive about something or other."

"A game perhaps?"

"Yes, a game. That's it. I know now of a game of. . . .of."

"He beat Calderon."

"I knew he would."

"Did you?"

"Well, I just said it, didn't I?"

"Not easily. Something like seventy-five moves and the most tangled endgame imaginable. But he kept declining the draw and eventually Calderon, the technician's technician, made a silly blunder. In fact Calderon's having a terrible tournament."

"Is he?"

"So Mendoza says." But it seems the name does not interest her. I am encouraged.

She slumps back into the pillow. "And you're Paul, aren't you?"

"Yes, ma'am and a little worried about you."

"Why?"

"Well, you kind of went to sleep on me a few days ago and I began to think maybe you weren't going to wake up much. That made me a little sad."

"It did?"

"Yes, ma'am. Several things occurred to me at the time. You want to know them all?"

"No, just the nice things."

"They were all nice, I suppose. But why don't you tell me about Paul."

"Loyal and exasperated," Pam says. "But soon enough going to take me away from all this."

"That I wouldn't mind. I hate the damn red chairs outside. I hate the view of the Sound. I hate the nifty food and the prompt attendants. And I hate the nights in the Holiday Inn. You're supposed to have everything you could want, isn't that so. So I spend nights at a Holiday Inn and drive a rented Plymouth to visit you and find out if you remember me. Not the high life I was promised, is it? But do you want to know the absolutely worst thing about it?"

"Yes. Yes, I do."

"Okay, what is it?"

"That you feel you have to do it, or that you want to do it, and that you can't stop doing it."

"Exactly!"

"Oh, I know what you mean. I always feel that way about everything I do. Everything. And then I'm always discovering that it really makes no difference to any of the people I thought I had to do it for. Once, I felt I had to have cloth napkins. We always use cloth napkins. I was having my mother over for lunch. So I spent all morning hunting for the perfect cloth napkins. I knew the cloth napkin market in Hane like nobody's business. And I finally found the perfect cloth napkins and I bought the perfect ceramic holders. And I put two beautiful, really splendid napkins with their really terrific little holders on the card table I used at my efficiency apartment for entertaining. It was the first time I was having my mother to my place. I suppose I was nervous. Anyway, I had these really splendid cloth napkins and then I served the luncheon."

"Pate and quiche?" I ask.

"No, some fried chicken I had made the night before and some potato salad I made with a recipe using limes. It was delicious, but the next day it was really sour. And my mother looked at the napkins and said, 'My God, Pamela, you are extravagant. You're on your own; get rid of these pretentious touches.' She refused to take the napkin out of its holder. And so you see, it really didn't make much difference. I'm always doing that. Preparing for expectations nobody really has. Except you, of course."

"Of course. Are you saying I shouldn't worry about you?"

"Dream about me. Hold me tight," she laughs, "but don't worry about me. Nothing to worry about here, is there? I've been here before. You said red chairs. Red metal chairs?"

"Exactly. Outside and overlooking Long Island Sound, if you lift your eyes beyond Stamford's skyline, or is it Bridgeport?"

"Oh yes, I have been here too many times already."

"I got the impression your father has been here too. Is that right?"

"My father?"

"Old Ned Snow. Do you know the name?"

"Can you describe him?" she smiles.

"Genial fellow. Maybe drinks too much. Lots of energy. Calculated dresser—the rich but tacky look. Like a drugstore magnate, or somebody with too many lumber yards."

"He's been here. A kind of family retreat. So has my mother."

"Ah, old home, eh?"

"I don't think so. But you'll take me away won't you?"

"Whenever Belasco says so."

"Belasco," she says, repeating the name. "A kind of fruit?"

"Maybe. I can't say for sure."

"What is for sure in this life?"

"Mikey's having a good run. He beat Sorowak with a prepared variation off the Philador, the one I kept waiting for against Smyslov. He saved it for the toughest match. Blew him right away in thirty-two moves. He'd get a brilliancy prize if they still gave 'em out."

"Philador?" Pam says thoughtfully. "Why does that name make me tired?""

"Probably because it's boring. Nor to worry about it. I'll keep watch over Mikey. He's doing okay without us."

"He needed us?"

"He thought he did, but I'd have to say Vera can cover for you very, very well."

"Ah," Pam says, slipping down further into the bed. "Vera, a name I don't like for some reason."

"Not to worry. I'll take care of her. You tired now?"

"Very sleepy. Weepy and sleeping, as if everything weren't as new as I thought it was. This is a pretty place, and you tell me there are red metal chairs outside. Not a nice trick, was it?"

"I'm sorry."

"Oh I know you are. But maybe if I get a chance to dream a bit more, when I wake up, we'll be away from here in some place special. Some place where it doesn't seem quite so . . . so . . . so thick."

"A thin place?"

"Yes, with thin people. And thin food."

"And thin thoughts about everything."

"Especially thin thoughts."

"Where would that be?" I ask.

"You know," Pam says, chuckling. "You know perfectly well."

"Ah, yes I do. And it looks like Mikey is going to get us all there. Mikey and Ned."

"Now you rest, ma'am. I'll sit in the outside red chair and watch the bustle of the colony here on the slopes overlooking the Long Island Sound. And if we're near the Sound, then how can we avoid being so?"

"Yes. Yes, how can we avoid being so?" she answers.

In the soft New Canaan breeze, in the softer New Canaan sunlight, lulled in the metallic rocking, I think, sound is also a chess term. A sound move, a sound opening, a sound variation. But to repeat the word is to lose its comprehensibility. The sound of sound, if repeated, is unsound. Sounding sound unsounds the sounder. A new mantra for drying out. I should rush this information to Belasco, to Coffee, to Gaineway, shouldn't I? I should call up Vera and share this splendid insight.

Soon enough we shall be away from this place, this placid, vacant, verdant interlude beyond Bridgeport's greater reality. By such

CHAPTER 25

sentiments Manila has got to be salvation itself. Nothing suburban in Manila. Only greater reality, i.e., tropics and poverty. 50 million people, 7000 islands—what more could you want? Cultural mix? Chinese, Malay, Spanish, American, Muslim, Catholic, Tribal, etc., etc.

Yes, Mikey was going to do it. The salient fact as the tournament progresses was, of course that Mikey has yet to lose. The opening rounds weren't impressive, except in that fact. No losses. Now in the closing of the tournament his wins against Calderon, Sorowak and Ivanov began to pile the points onto the half point accumulations. And unlike the opposition Mikey had no zeros to be factored in.

A draw most likely would result against Mohrstein—even God would draw with Mohrstein. But Kotov was certainly more vulnerable to endgame silliness. Mikey's score accumulation then should leave him in the top four, perhaps in the top two. Only Tarlac was having a "better" tournament, and even Tarlac despite the string of victories had dropped one wild, speculative game to Ariztobal, of all people. The Cuban had stumbled, so the rumor went, into a marvelously fecund variation of the Sicilian and had traded kingside pawns for a would-be attack that might, under other circumstances, have been easily fended off, except that Tarlac was racing down the opposite side of board, going for broke on the Queen side Alas, his pawn conversions could exist only in the notes, for his King fell before the pawns could get to the magic last rank

Against the other Americans Mikey would certainly do no worse than draw. And if he got lucky or terribly aggressive, he might even push Tarlac for the top position. Before that happened however, Tarlac's Russian compatriots might begin to pad his score with easy wins.

And weren't we all looking forward to the change—the salvation of Manila? Longing to get away from here. What, after all, was here? A procession of pills and crises, meals out and meals in, red metallic rocking and lush green of somebody else's lawn. Down in the valley, in the main lodge who was to say the less happy resident were not, even smashing their soft, addled heads into the foamy walls of innumerable rooms as they strove to brush away the lint, the spiders, the dragons, the great leering scorpions of the gin-filled sky? Be gone, America. The place is ultimately a glacial nest for creatures dead before they are born. Shove it, America. We're off to Luzon.

Chapter 26

Waldo had explained, "You're the advance agent, Snelly, the point man. You go in under the heaviest fire and take out the most dangerous natives. Clear the land for Mikey, Vera, Pam, Ned, Evelyn, Hilly and maybe me, if I can get the time."

"They may need you at the paper," I had replied.

Waldo grinned that great, cheesy grin that signals irony's triumph over embarrassment.

And now, as the point man, I am confronted at Manila International Airport with pointed fingers. Hands decorate the chain link fence coming out of customs. Fingers beckon from beyond the chicken wire enclosure at the end of the concrete escape way. Index fingers curl at me and Spanish accented English bellows around the concrete overheads. "Taxi? Taxi? Ride into town? See Manila. Tour the hot spots. Want something Special? Want a girl? Nice girl. Wanta boy? Nice boy. Want two monkeys? Two nice monkeys. See Makati! Corregidor! Hotel? Hotel?"

I had expected a hotel caravan, a special bus for the exclusive residents of the Manila Hotel, and undoubtedly there probably was such a bus, but it surely was not evident. Nor were there the familiar bank of telephones linking you, despite culture, to the real world of elevators and little mints on your pillow.

Instead, an amazing array of taxis and drivers, each one more grimy than the last, more rusted than the one before, more grasping and implacable. A regular gauntlet. No sense trying to run it. So I surrender about midway down the line to a fellow who already has both hands on my two suitcases.

"Hotel?" he shouts.

"Yes, the Manila."

"Hah! The best!" He leads me out of the line into an ancient dark blue Datsun. Miraculously the suitcases fit in the trunk. The air is peculiarly hot, grey, smoky, muggy. The driver wears a red bandana and pale blue Bermuda shorts, leather sandals. His eyes are not visible through the dark glasses. "First time in Manila?" he says in strange colloquial English.

"Yes."

"How long?"

"A month. I'm here for the chess tournament."

It seems that information silences him. The terrain is flat, dusty and tropical with a vengeance. Royal and cabbage palms spring up everywhere. And as we come to Roxas Boulevard the sudden expanse of the bay is startling. Vaster than the Long Island Sound, more still, more shimmering. It seems as big as a universe, slate grey but gleaming. When the boulevard turns we almost come even with the water, so that I can see plants coming up to the edge of the concrete, plants and sea grasses, as if we had driven into the center of the Everglades. If you looked only at that vegetation and the bay gleaming beyond, it would seem you were alone on the planet. Of course the Datsun rattle, the exhaust fumes, disabuse that concept. It takes no more than a swivel to the right to catch a glimpse of the road grid through the shattering urban sprawl of Metro Manila. But for a moment along the boulevard there are perhaps deliberately spaced bursts of silence, an alternative reality. Magellan must have been dazzled when he sailed into the place four centuries before.

"I suppose the bay is polluted?" I ask the driver, but he merely fiddles with his tape player, until the cool sounds of Jimmy Buffet emerge.

"Lotta pollution," he finally says.

CHAPTER 26

We cruise along the bayfront, past the Philippine Cultural Center where the tournament will be held, past the U.S. Embassy and then past the Manila Hotel itself. We continue up the boulevard and I begin to worry about those stories I had heard about Manila cabbies.

"Isn't that the hotel?" I shout over the edge of the narrow seat.

"Is it?" he replies.

"Yes, I'm sure of it."

"Where did you say you were going?"

"The Manila Hotel. That's it back there."

"Oh, hey man, I'm sorry, Joe. I thought you said the Manya Hotel."

The driver continues in the direction we are headed until he comes to the third turn-off, then he executes a slow U-turn. We start an equally slow return. When we get near the hotel, he does not take the obvious main entrance. Instead, he pulls into a back parking lot and begins a slow drive around the parked cars. "I'm trying to find the front," he says, laughing. The meter continues to run.

"Try over there," I direct him toward a narrow roadway that culminates in a dead end. We reverse and continue the exploration of the lot. I think about telling him to stop at once, but instead I slump back and wait a bit. Finally he "finds" his way to the front entrance.

The hotel's air conditioning is its first signal achievement. The lobby is enormous with a ceiling easily seventy feet up, but still the place is as cool as a meat locker. The carpet is thick, spongy, the pillars plated in a soft reddish wood. A long mahogany registry marks off the right side of the lobby. On the left there are series of grouped leather chairs, and beyond, against the far wall, a bar area. A woman, tanned, rather tall and wearing a long Sari-like gown greets me at the porter's assignment desk. She leads me to the Registry and then to my room, explaining that she is my supervisor for the stay and any problems should be referred to her.

"How about the armed guard by the elevator on this floor?" I ask, wishing to confirm Mendoza's little sermon.

"Ah, you should not worry about him. It is part of Martial Law. The President has seen to it that there is no chance of disturbance or theft of our guests."

"One on every floor?"

"Yes."

"They don't get drunk and start shooting for fun?"

She looks at me for a moment and then says with casual certainty, "If he does, I'm sure you'll find it interesting."

I wonder if I should tip her—seems too imperious for a tip.

"You are attached to the suite for the Spendips. We can open this door if you'd like."

"Not till they come."

"I see. Will there be anything else?"

"I don't think so. Do I have a view of the bay?"

"Certainly." She goes to the beige drapes and pulls them back. The gleaming, endless lake comes into view. Undoubtedly, too, the pool is below. "If you want to use the pool, simply get robes from the Captain at the front desk on your floor. Our guests are required to wear the robes. It guarantees no interlopers use the hotel facilities."

"Of course. Are these walls teak?"

"Teak and Mahogany. And the baths are done in marble from the mountains in the north. If there is anything you need, please call me." She glides out of the room, easing the door shut.

I go over to the window and look down at the huge, kidney-shaped pool. Sure enough, there is a bar in the center with stools mounted in the water. But there is no back window overlooking the parking lot. You'd have to cross the hall and go into a back room. So Mendoza is guilty of a little expansion—for what reason? Impact? Rhetorical flourish? Embellishments to increase commitment?

The room is enormous. Two mammoth double beds with enough space between them for a third. And the appointments display disdain for cost-cutting. The woods alone are expensive, the hand carvings on them, the filigree work, and the lattice attachments must have doubled the original investment. And the room, like the lobby, is cold. There is a teak pitcher of ice water. I pour a glass. It tastes of chlorine. I flop on one of the beds, bounce up and down. A long way from Hane.

An hour later there is a knock on the door. Was the water drugged, I wonder? I struggle off the delicious envelopment of bed and get to the door. Is the guard with his 45 special or whatever waiting to blow my head off?"

"Yes?"

"Message," an obviously young voice says.

A set-up I think. Why is there no peep-hole? "Just a minute." Doesn't the killer always say "message" or "telegram" and then the hapless victim opens the door and the two goons rush in for the fatal pistol whipping, or worse yet, the summary hurling out the window to the drained pool below. But it's too absurd. I open the door.

An urchin dressed in a grey T-shirt, frayed jeans shorts and sneakers that have toe holes, hands me a business card and says, "He would like to see you in the lobby, if that is convenient. He will be there for another two hours."

I look at the card: "Silberio Garcia-Lopez, Architect, Playwright." It says and lists a Manila address. At the top of the card, written in light blue ink is "Welcome! I am a friend of W. Mendoza."

"He's in the lobby now?"

"At the lobby bar," the boy says, looking expectantly.

"Ah, just a minute." I fish out a peso and drop it into his hand. He doesn't thank me. "Tell Mr. Garcia-Lopez I'll be down in about ten minutes, will you?" But the boy has already vaulted toward the elevators. The armed guard stands about twenty feet from my doorway, as if recording the entire scene. I quickly close the door.

Mendoza, the guardian angel, has appointed our initiating ambassador. I decide it is a thoughtful act. Doubtless someone to make sure we understand the realities of the current political situation. Someone to recruit the Snow holdings to the cause of equal distribution of wealth in the Philippines. At least he's interested in us, I decide. And besides, one can use a guardian angel in Manila.

Alas, Garcia-Lopez is perhaps too angelic, too ethereal. He is a much older fellow, but the taut complexion of an inveterate cortisone user. Tan, bulgy, and more than a little decadent look. He wears a powder blue, well-tailored suit and holds a cigarette holder out with the panache worthy of Roosevelt or Oscar Wilde. Beefy elegance and perhaps alcoholic. A bubbling clear drink (with a lime segment) sits on his hexagonal mahogany table. The boy, who had been waiting by the elevator, leads me to him.

"I'm sorry to keep you waiting," I say.

"On the contrary, you are all-American prompt. A Filipino would have heard my offer of two hours and then come down in two and half. I would have been here still, of course."

"I'm Paul Snell."

"Silberio Garcia. The Lopez is just a formality. My mother's name. I am Garcia. Mr. Mendoza wrote me about you, and about the Spendips."

"I bet he did."

Garcia laughs. "In any event, I felt it was my duty, since I am looking after Mr. Mendoza in a manner of speaking—which is to say I am financing a great deal of his deeper look at the Western world—I felt the least I could do was come by and tell you and the Spendips that I am delighted to be your host in these islands. Someone you can call, if you make the mistake—which now that I've told you, I'm sure you won't—of taking a Green Archer Cab."

"A Green Archer Cab?"

"Yes, that's the name, I believe. Embossed on the side. And with an illustrative shaft." As he says the words, Garcia's eyes sparkle. "I do not recommend using the company."

"Why?"

"Oh, they have the habit of taking foreigners out of town and killing them, or so I hear."

"Well, thanks for that bit of pregnant advice."

CHAPTER 26

"Pregnant indeed. A very distasteful sound," Garcia laughs again.

I join in the laughter and he seems very interested in the depth and commitment of my mirth. "The Spendips are not here yet, I take it?"

"That's right."

"No reason to arrive I suppose, since our own champion is still struggling to make the final cut, so to speak."

As Calderon had predicted he made the final five and was allowed to play a qualifying round against Mohrstein who came in just ahead of him.

"Are they still at it in Baguio?"

"Yes, indeed. The twentieth, or two hundredth, or two thousandth draw. The papers aren't even covering it anymore. And when these papers stop covering a chess match, you know it is boring. Under Martial Law that's about the only sort of safe news. But I suppose we should not get onto politics, at least not is in such a public and, what shall I say, administratively-inclined place. Better to talk at some intimate music spa, say, the Pensione Filipina, some evening, if you'd like. Do you want someone to show you the sights? Someone to initiate you into the darkest secrets of the least Asian East?"

"I don't know."

"An utterly safe and beguiling answer. How about a drink?" Garcia gets two more G & Ts and a side order of peanuts.

After a peculiar silence, Garcia says, "Mr. Mendoza mentioned you might be traveling with a young woman, a Pamela Snow, whose father had some dealings with a great uncle of mine at some time, about some thing. But nothing came of it—like so many projects here. Is she coming?"

"I think so, and perhaps her parents, from Hong Kong aboard a boat."

"One does not take a boat from Hong Kong," Garcia laughs. "So you are without feminine companionships, a lack easily remedied here in Manila I assure you, especially for such a handsome chap."

I am aware of a certain threat in Garcia's compliment and become despite myself warier. I watch his eyes, which engage mine for perhaps too long, it seems. "In any event I can show you some of the loveliest or some of the most vile spots in which one can overcome—what shall we say—separation?"

"Thank you. I don't acutely feel separation much. Miss Snow and I were rather close for a month in Connecticut and then three more weeks in Florida. She's not well. I more or less lived in as a kind of nurse."

"Splendid attachment, splendid. And not be trifled with. Certainly not by some of the less seamy exemplars of our metro area. So it shall be cultural activities, or are you a sportsman? We could catch a cockfight, does that appeal?"

"I really need to scout out the match situation, the Cultural Center or whatever."

"Ah, yes, Imelda's little sinking banquet hall. They're going to play there, are they?"

"At the Little Theater."

"Not at the Folk Culture Coliseum? How disappointing! But I suppose one would have trouble attracting ten thousand Filipinos in the heat of the day to the Coliseum for a chess match—although chess is played here widely. Do you play?"

"No, not really. I just write about it."

"Splendid arrangement. We all need to write about things we have no intention of mastering. I never write about architecture, for example, about which I know more than anyone else here. More even that the fair Locksin who designed those little abominations in the bay. Instead, I write about loneliness in Detroit's black quarter, or getting seasick in Stockholm, two of my best plays, incidentally. I have something of a reputation, not that you would, or should, know it. Here, for example, is a rather striking article about

CHAPTER 26

me." Without wasting a motion Garcia fetches a black sheepskin briefcase from beside his chair and pulls out a magazine which been folded back. He pulls the pages into a full double truck and there is a picture of Garcia clad only in a skimpy string jock strap, standing in the garden of a house which overlooks most of Manila. There are alabaster statues at various levels of the garden. Garcia in the picture seems to be talking to the photographer, or someone reading the magazine. The title extending across both pages is clear, simple: "Genius in a G-String."

"I wrote my Stockholm play when I was living in New York on a Guggenheim. It was produced, as you say, so engagingly 'off-off Broadway.' The reviews were not favorable, as you might imagine from the simpletons who pass for critics in your country. There's more on the over leafs, if you're interested. Striking picture, don't you think?"

"Yes." I turn the page and this time Garcia is wearing a long sarong without a shirt. He is sitting on a rattan couch and apparently looking through the playbills of his performances in Europe and America.

"Eighteen plays there," he points to the table on which the playbills appear.

"Rather impressive, in addition to your architecture work."

"Yes, of course, but, frankly, one's architecture assignments grow rather thin in Imelda's Manila. I'm on the outs with the palace, if you hadn't guessed."

"I'm sorry."

"Heh! Yes, it was the wrong guess, several, no, too many years ago. It's as if Haydn spurned Esterhazy. Where would he be if that had come to pass?"

"I don't understand."

"Well and good. A strained analogy anyway, and no matter. You doubtless think I'm self-obsessed. I try to wear as few clothes as possible at my home," Garcia says gathering up the magazine and putting it back into the briefcase. "But why don't you tell me about yourself? Wicksburg says you're a writer who would find me very simpatico. Does he have it wrong?"

"I'm a short-term columnist. Chess column, about which I know nothing. But I am able to convince the front editors it makes no difference."

"You are too modest. How would get such a job, except on your considerable talent?"

"Imagine," I answer.

"You excite me," Garcia says, laughing. "I'm imagining a fantastic scene of despicable perversity. Compromising photographs. Perhaps Boy Scouts in various stages of undress."

"You spent too long in New York. The paper's owner is a kind of foster father."

"Is that how they say it nowadays?"

"Not quite. You need to meet Waldo to realize the absurdity of your picture."

"But what is the connection then?"

"Mutual exploitation of the helpless, the aimless, the soulless, but wealthy women of the world." I am surprised to hear myself say, "The matching of care, compassion and compensation all at once."

"Then I could qualify for ravishment, couldn't I?" Garcia laughs. "It would only be a matter of dress."

"Why not? Find something appropriate to wear, and I promise to send Waldo out to exploit you."

"I was looking for something younger," Garcia says, with the exactitude of a trader about to get down to essentials. In fierce deflection I ask, "Is Mr. Mendoza here in Manila, or in the Philippines elsewhere?"

"A stunning riposte! And I accept it," Garcia raises his glass and drinks in celebration of this detour of the conversation. "No. He is not here, not anywhere on these islands, I think though perhaps he could be, if the immigration authorities perform in their usual fashion. Mr. Mendoza is more than a little *persona non grata* hereabouts." "So who does Calderon have as a second then?"

CHAPTER 26

"That is a bone of contention, I am afraid. You have touched on a sensitive nerve, indeed. Presently there are two helping him, if that is the word, in Baguio. What help they can give is somewhat problematic, I am afraid."

"Drawing with Mohrstein is no small accomplishment."

'Drawing is what Calderon and Mohrstein do best. And how they have not disappointed us!" Garcia says. "The quality of the advice is not helping on the Filipino side I am afraid, but I am only a partial wood-pusher, a tyro at best, in the game. Sometimes I share its passions, however."

"So you could second."

"Or you?" Garcia answers, "For all the help we'd be. But you really bring up a problem that I need to discuss with you in far greater depth and after the Spendips arrive. For they could be helpful to us too."

"Us?"

"Oh yes, us; this is Asia, Mr. Snell. And one always speaks for a group here. No one is alone, ever. Not ever." Garcia puts down his cigarette holder, and folds his hands on the table as if to signal the end of today's audience.

Chapter 27

In the next two days I inspect the Little Theater, describe it in dull detail for two columns and prepare the background for a trip to Baguio to see if Calderon can indeed qualify for the Interzonal. Then, just after I have made plane reservations, news comes that at long last Calderon has achieved victory. On the 79th move Mohrstein resigned the 23rd game, eight over the original fifteen games planned to determine the final member of the Interzonal Match.

How can it be Mohrstein lost an endgame? Apparently the heat, the long strain of playing endless matches with as relentless—and far younger—a drawing master as himself. Maybe Filipino food. Who can say what caused the great misstep by the misstepless one, I speculated in one final column on the match. One thing seems certain, Calderon must be exhausted by the ordeal. He can hardly be in good condition to play the Interzonal, which will begin in a few days.

"My theory," Garcia says over a luncheon of noodles, "is that the referee knocked over the Russian's King with his sleeve and all participants agreed anything was better than continuing their essay in boredom. On the other hand, I suppose Dr. Mohrstein will not have a happy time of it back in Kiev or wherever they send old, lame drawing masters."

""I'm sure he'll stay here as a second for the other Russians."

"Ah, of course. You are correct as usual. And when will the Spendips arrive and Miss Snow?"

"Tomorrow. I received a fax from Ned Snow this morning. They are coming together, Pam and the Spendips. I will meet them."

"I insist on your using my car and driver. Better yet I will drive them myself. Then they won't have to run through that mob of cabbies outside of customs. I insist on it—unless, of course, there will be some members of the press about." Garcia suddenly turns thoughtful.

"I suspect there will be reporters. Vera likes that."

"Vera?"

"Mikey's mother."

"Reporters. Well, in that case, I shall not appear. And, in truth, you would be better advised not to use my car. I'm sorry to be such an, such an Indian-giver—is that the term?"

"Yes, that's the term. Why should a little publicity be troublesome?"

"I'm not much in favor now at the palace. You would do well not to be seen with me, associated with me. It could lead to, what should we say, hassles—is that the current American term?"

"Yes."

"Well, there you have it. I am sorry to be taking away with this hand what I offered with the other, but such is the situation in our happy land." Garcia laughs. "Even chess has become political, given the state of fear now. Give the corruptions running riot everywhere. Ah, such decadence as Rome only dreamed of. Once you are safely here, then you must come to my house for dinner. There will be no reporters there. And you can see my gardens which are more than a wonder, even in Manila. And I have a cook who can, with proper lubrication, reach inspired heights. Even Wicksburg agrees with that. And afterwards we could frolic. You and Miss Snow, the Spendips, and even Calderon, if you wanted."

"You know him?"

"Through Wicksburg, of course. And I have made a small contribution to the development of his rather boring genius."

"Logicians sometimes don't produce very exciting games."

"Discretely put. In point of fact, I find Calderon almost as boring as his chess. He always poses somewhere between a guru and a retardate, daring you to find out which. As if both personalities were vying to get out of that svelte, little body. Such passivity. According to Wick the little fellow actually believes he's in tune with some ethereal chess mind beyond the chaos of our sad world. That might account for the peculiar way he has of looking through you, at some greater reality. It's more than a bit disconcerting. A boring disconcertion. Wick is positively animation itself, next to him. Shall we go and see him?"

"Calderon?"

"Of course. He's here in Manila now. Do you want to see him?"

"Why?"

"To discuss upcoming events. To get the latest gossip on the Russians."

"So he does have some fascination for you?"

"More than this lunch, I confess . . ." Garcia says.

"I see."

"Always taking things so personally, Mr. Snell. You should be beyond that, I think. Yes, Calderon bores me, but I can think of several reasons why you and I should see him. And why the Spendips should see him after they get here."

"Several reasons?"

"Well, one at least, although I will let him speak for himself on that. In the meanwhile what do you have more important for this afternoon? To wander the boulevards in this heat?"

"Actually I could use the interview with him for my column."

"It's done then," Garcia says, pointing at me with the spoon with which he has eaten his lunch. "His very modest pensione—a political judgment on your own posh living situation—is a short ride from here. I propose we take local transport since the area is one in which leaving your own vehicle might be a losing proposition. My Manila is full of losing propositions."

CHAPTER 27

The Jeepney drops us off before a two-story building of flimsy reddish wood without any identifying sign. On the second floor in a front corner small room, Calderon sits at a rattan desk. There are two single beds with sagging mattresses and maroon bedspreads behind him.

"We should have taken you to lunch," Garcia says. "It would have made things more interesting."

"I'm sorry too," I add.

"How is Mikey? Calderon says.

"Same as ever. Maybe sharper," I reply.

"I've noticed an interesting thing—lately the Russians talk more and more about him, and with increasing awe. The Fischer phenomenon. It used to be, they said, any good Russian could beat him, and now they wonder if Atashian is up to the challenge, should it come. I really think they feel nobody can beat him. Even Mohrstein concedes that he's 'very strong.' And they regard him as an artist—the first step to deification. If he wins the Interzonal I predict he will devour Atashian—especially since the Russian seconds think there's no way to stop Mikey."

"Should I write that in the column?"

"Why not?" Calderon says, "I'm not political and neither is Mikey, is he?"

"Political?"

"Yes, filled with passion for vengeance in the world—something like that."

"What he wants to know is how much Mikey subscribes to the Cold War," Garcia interprets.

"I don't think Mikey's heard of it."

"Admirable," Calderon comments in a detached way. "So run the column and let the world think what it will about our attitudes toward the Soviet colossus."

"Mikey does hate Russian chess players. He thinks they cheat. He sees them as the enemy, I suppose."

"Yes, but probably no more than he sees me as the enemy," Calderon adds. "And they are the enemy, after all, as indeed I am. Especially now."

"How did you get the win? I haven't seen the score of the game. Actually, if you have one, I'll do a column on it."

Calderon open his desk, takes a neat Xerox of the score sheet out and hands it to me. "I'm not sure myself. I think his seconds got tired, or wilted in the heat. I became aware in the second session of the game, after a night of consultation that he wasn't playing the best variation of what surely could have been a drawn endgame. A series of less than accurate moves. Nothing you could point to and say, 'this was a mistake'—just a string of bad moves, each one correctible of itself, but eventually putting him in a very difficult position. Unnecessarily weakening a pawn chain, keeping the King too long out of the action. It was rather sloppy. And by the time I think he knew there was more trouble than anyone imagined, he was really tired of playing, tired of the game. I think with proper attention it could have drawn, but it would have required Herculean attention. The kind Mohrstein routinely gives, but maybe he got sick of playing draw after draw after draw in the heat. They kept the hall too hot really—way too hot. But it did not bother me nearly as much as it bothered him. He's too much of sportsman to say so, of course. It might be the hall is jinxed."

"How could Mikey have played it differently?" I ask.

Calderon thought a bit. "I suppose he would not have played it in the first place. Queen's Gambit Decline is not his favorite response. And if he does play it, he hopes for an early exchange variation. I can't imagine him getting into such a position. Mohrstein loves open, drab positions where one only has to be logical to survive. Certainly Mikey instinctively would never have made the endgame missteps. Even asleep, he would never have weakened his dark squares so much of made such vulnerable pawn chains. On the other hand, who knows what anybody would do in this heat after twenty-two draws, day after day of no particular prospects."

"Was that your strategy?"

"With Wicks away, I didn't identify a strategy. I play the board each day. He's forever complaining about that."

"What will you do for seconds now?"

At the question Calderon looks at Garcia, then pauses, finally says, "I don't know. I guess I will keep using Avincula and Teves, but they aren't much help."

"Could Wicks come over?"

"Too risky," Garcia says, "moreover, it has yet to be demonstrated that he would be all that much help."

"Wicks is a good second," Calderon says.

"About on a par with Avincula and Teves," Garcia adds.

"So what will happen?"

Calderon says nothing, and after a while Garcia speaks," Well, why don't we all wait a while and perhaps something will turn up."

"I doubt it," Calderon says.

"Yes, so do I, but hope, as the poet noted, springs eternal, or at least through the end of the week and the Spendips arrival." Garcia says.

"You want Mikey to be a second?" I laugh.

"Splendid idea!" Garcia shouts. "Out Russianing the Russians. A collaboration aimed at shutting them out of the top spot. Worth discussing."

"I doubt Mikey's much interested in cooperating with anyone," I answer, "and Vera would be very interested in the illegalities of it, even under Filipino law."

"Let's not bring in the law," Garcia says. "I was jesting, as I'm sure you know."

"Mikey has to be nobody's second," Calderon says. "We could scarcely help him as his second."

"One needs a second for other than chess reasons, wouldn't you say, Reyle? Garcia asks, but Calderon does not reply.

"You mean psychological support?" I ask.

"All kinds of support, don't you agree, Reyle?" Garcia persists.

"I need someone who can help me do tough endgame analysis, since all my games seem to go at least two sessions. That's what I need. Perhaps that is all I need."

"But no one is so atomized, so separated from others," Garcia continues. "No one. No one ought to be, nor can anyone really be. This is fundamental. Or at least that is the notion we are playing with lately, isn't it Mr. Snell?"

"I don't know."

"I take it you have been almost inseparable from the Spendips and Miss Snow."

"I'm not either's second."

"Just a term," Garcia laughs. "Just a phrase from the annotators who don't know a thing of what is going on here."

"What is going on here?" I ask, conscious that some game is being played between Reyle and Garcia.

"Armed guards in the street. That is what is going on here. Opening this morning's newspaper, and I use that term, very, very loosely to describe the little absurdities that our fair President puts on the streets each day. Looking at that newspaper I find, amazing to behold, not a shred of news in it. Or, some little anti-American snippet. Drunk GIs in Subic or some such thing, and weather from all over the world reported in luxurious detail, an ad for a few of the foreigner's supermarkets in Makati, but news? Not a chance! Commentary? Not a chance! What is going on here? What is?"

"Instead," Calderon says, "we have that splendid casino in the bay, that wonderful sinking Cultural Center where with newsmen like yourself the best of the chess universe gather to find out who gets thrashed by Atashian."

"And Imelda, the great Imelda, turns up on shopping sprees in Paris, in Closters, in Melbourne, always purchasing to remind the world that she is the wife of the great President and one of the richest creatures in history. Meanwhile the drunken guards wander the streets and over there," Garcia gestures away from the bay, "Over there the suffering continues. The starving continues. It's all supremely depressing, isn't it Reyle? Mr. Snell, do you suppose young Spendip has any idea what life is really like here?"

CHAPTER 27

"Mikey?"

"Yes," Garcia says, "Mikey, the little genius."

"I doubt it, unless the news has made its way into chess annotations."

"That it has not." Calderon says.

"Precisely," Garcia continues, "anything like the real news never gets into print here. Any kind of print. How would Mikey know? This is the only observation to be made. It would hardly be his fault for not understanding our situation, wouldn't it, Reyle?"

But Calderon does not answer, merely pushes the score sheet at me. "You can have it if you want."

"Could you put a check by the moves that seemed less than adequate for me?"

Calderon seems excited by that request. He makes several little asterisks, carefully wrought, by six of the endgame moves.

"I'll explain to my readers that these were the questionable moves identified by you. I wouldn't say directly why they were bad ones. Instead, I'll invite my readers to make the analysis you evidently did about them."

"Better to inform them what is happening here," Garcia says, "so Mikey will find out—Mikey and all the others. Better yet, let me show you. Come, Mr. Snell, I'll take you around Manila. A short cook's tour designed to soften up your stomach for a balut later."

"Balut?"

"The staple of the underclass here, you ought to try one."

"What is it?"

"Better you should not know till after you have eaten one."

"No way."

"Ah, such endearing slang. Let's leave Mr. Calderon to his preparations. Opening surprises, isn't that the name of the game, Reyle? Opening surprises? You must win in the first fifteen moves or you don't win at all, isn't that it?"

Calderon doesn't smile, doesn't indicate any appreciation for Garcia's banter. Instead, he stares at the door and nods as if to give us benediction for our departure.

Chapter 28

"Sometimes I don't think he's really Filipino," Garcia says in the Jeepney. "Sometimes he hasn't even the flesh of a Japanese, those bananas of Asia."

"Yellow on the outside, white on the inside?"

"Ah, you have heard the phrase before. A favorite here in the Metro area."

The mid-afternoon heat is overwhelming, the fumes along Taft Avenue dense, pungent, vaguely nauseating. We enter a line of Jeepneys. Their front hoods are festooned with chrome horses, the sides of their paneling are awhirl with Day-Glo paint.

"The cheapest way to go," Garcia shouts, waving to some of the younger boys in the back of the Jeepney before us. "Twenty centavos depending on how you bargain, or at least that's what it was when I rode these things. I bet they paid nothing." He waves again at the boys.

We bog down in traffic and spend close to twenty minutes moving no more than a hundred feet. At length even Garcia finds the delay intolerable. He jumps off, pausing only for a bit to bid the boys goodbye and wish them luck. I follow and we pick our way across traffic onto a dirt lane that tracks the back of giant mall and weaves eventually into an area without vehicles, without paving, without shops, without most everything except human beings who spill out on to the paths and lanes as if the tin shanties behind

CHAPTER 28

them were in fact factories for their assembly. There is thick mud everywhere.

"You know that fellow who brought you the message? He lives here with his family. Let me introduce you, though I don't see him about."

Garcia leads me across a muddy roadway, through a block of solid humanity, all dressed in shorts and T-shirts and shoeless. They flow around us, dark skinned, sharp-eyed. Garcia strolls among them an improbable figure in his cream Barong shirt and powder blue slacks. My shoes have slopped over in the mud. There is a line of wooden, tin-roofed shacks, each with a window on either side of the low front door. There are no panes of glass, no screens in any of the windows. The air seems alive with the buzzing of mosquitoes and the constant sliding around of crowds first on one side, then on the other, of us. When we draw parallel with the shacks the scent of urine and excrement comes in sharply. Garcia draws a handkerchief out of his pocket and blows his nose. Some of the shacks have a doorsill, but most simply welcome the mud from the streets in. The urine stench grows almost overwhelming. "Raul lives right here." Garcia makes a ceremony of knocking on the edge of the doorless opening. Immediately four little girls, two small boys appear in the doorway and then an older woman wearing khaki shorts and a green, sweat-stained T-shirt looks over their heads.

"Oh Master," she says, "Please come in."

I have trouble disengaging my right foot from the suctioning mud. The dirt on the floor inside is dryer at least. The woman pushes two folding chairs toward us. There is a small brick fireplace in one corner of the hut and a much older woman is hunched over a pot suspended over the blaze.

"A little bit of Macbeth here in old Metro Manila," Garcia says to me, "would you believe it?" He turns and chats with the woman in Tagalog, then looks back at me, "Raul is still down in Mabini hustling," he says. "Would you like some tea? I think you would.

Yes, you would. Are you comfortable?" Garcia asks with cynical solicitousness.

Two of the little girls have closed in on me. They are wearing only grey underpants. Their hands are caked with mud from the outside, but their eyes in the semi-darkness seem to cackle contemplating me.

"What do they want?" I ask Garcia.

"You've got it all wrong. It's what do you want. That's what they're after. Can't you tell? They learn here really early." Garcia laughs. He turns back to his chat with the woman. Two older boys come into the hut and slink along the wall watching. The whole place is no bigger than fifteen feet square. The older woman near the fire hands me a thick ceramic cup full of dark tea. Garcia takes his and thanks her extravagantly. The tea is luke-warm and the smell of urine dominates its aroma.

One of the girls pulls at my Gant Madras shirt purchased with such expectations of Southeast Asia, at the Hane Mall.

"Am I supposed to give it to them?"

"Ah, conscience pang, is it?" Garcia laughs. "Only if they agree to take off their underpants and bend over. Go ahead, ask them."

"Good God!"

"Some people," Garcia says, "Americans especially, find it difficult to 'take' Manila. How are you doing, Mr. Snell? Want to stay for dinner?"

Garcia shouts at the older boys who sprint out of the shack. In a minute they return with a third fellow carrying a basket. The boy comes over to Garcia, who flips back the burlap covering of the basket and begins to inspect what looks like eggs in the dim light. He put his hands on them to test their temperature apparently. Finally he selects one, gives the boy two pesos, flips a few more to the boys who brought the vendor in.

"Here you are, Snell, your first balut. They're quite good and very potent, very helpful, as you can see. "Garcia motions to the children. "Very potent, at least the natives argue so."

"How do I eat it?"

CHAPTER 28

"Just break off some of the shell and start eating. But if you want my advice, you'll take the first bite without looking at it. Look at it later, after you tasted some. It really is delicious. Although its virility aspects are somewhat exaggerated. I speak from experience." Garcia laughs.

"And if I'm not hungry?"

"You surely will disappoint the many spectators who want to watch the big American eat his first balut. On the other hand, I can explain that these younger Americans are afraid to eat anything but white bread and peanut butter."

"You seem to enjoy this."

"These are, as the saying goes, my people."

"Is that why they call you Master?"

"Raul and some other occasionally live at my house, and I have given the family money from time to time. They feel a strong sense of obligation. The term doesn't imply what it does in English, merely an endearment, a formality of status. Now stop delaying and provide us all the sport we came for."

I glance at the kids who, indeed, have moved closer to watch.

"I'm telling you not to look at it," Garcia says.

I crack the egg around the top by striking it softly on the edge of the folding chair. Without looking down I peel pieces back.

"You have an inch peeled away?" Garcia asks.

"Yes, I guess."

"All right then, simply carry it to your mouth. Watch them and chomp down on it. The taste I think will be familiar."

"You sure I shouldn't look at it?"

"That is my advice, having taken countless visitors through this ritual, but never, I must say, here. Just remember it's a staple of their meager diet. One of their delicacies and not, repeat not, to be thrown up."

"You're not making this any easier."

"I tell you what. If you'd prefer you can avoid eating the egg and instead you could live here for the duration of the tournament.

I could set it up, with a very low hotel rate. You'd save hundreds. Is it a deal?"

I plunge the top of the egg deep into my mouth and close teeth around the exposed portion. It is soft, vaguely fuzzy, and in the chewing I am aware of small, clicking sounds, as if it were brittle in spots. It tastes very much like chicken, and is, in fact, rather delicious.

"Nicely done Mr. Snell. You seem to be enjoying it."

With the last swallow it occurs to me what the balut is. I have a momentary gagging reaction which I stifle by coughing. The kids begin to smile. Of course! A fertilized egg, a chicken embryo.

"How close was it till birth?"

"Ah, perceptive of you. Very close. As close as possible. Some feathers even and a soft beak—did you taste it?"

"I suppose if one eats a grown up chicken, an embryonic one should make no difference."

"A very Western reaction. Rational to the end, even as you turn blue-green with bile and nausea."

"I am not nauseated."

"Of course, you merely coughed because of the air-conditioning in here."

I break a few more bits of shell off and then proceed to eat the rest of the balut. The kids seem far less interested now that I have succeeded.

"I should have known you would be the outdoorsy type. I suppose you can tell me you've caught and cooked your own squirrels or rabbits or what other creatures in habit your place of birth. Actually I find outdoorsy types very enticing."

"I was born in New York City."

"Rats then."

"Are we through here?"

"I suppose we are. Leave-taking is always a little awkward. Do you have coins with you?"

"Some."

"Well, let's start distributing them. Are you impressed with where they live? Where most Filipinos live? Altogether here—one big happy family on boards at night. Notice the blankets stacked over there and the boards against the wall. And maybe if they're lucky, if Master comes every now and then, why baluts twice a week. The rest of the time, rice and noodles, noodles and rice. They could live for a year on what you're paying per day in the Manila Hotel. And the baths there I understand are made of marble. Imelda, the ultimate Imelda, thought international tourist trade would improve the standard of living of her precious Manila constituency. Ha!"

Garcia begins distributing pesos. "Try to restrict your giving to those inside the house. Out there is simply no end. And we'll have to sprint to the Jeepney. Hopefully the older fellows will help us get there."

"Are we going to be mobbed?"

"Shouldn't we be?" Garcia laughs. He bows to the woman, pats the grandmother on the back and then breaks for the door, so that he is actually running a bit when he goes through. I follow him, and, as Garcia had hoped, the older boys push and shove off the crowd, moving us toward the waiting Jeepney.

Chapter 29

THE POOL BAR CLOSES at about 11:30 p.m. I get to watch the bartender slip out of his black trousers, get into a bathing suit and wade back to the terrace. For the last hour there have been no patrons—at least none visible from my room. I have played through the final Calderon-Mohrstein game and found it as boring as Garcia indicated. Only in the very last when the board opens up, does it seem that adventure might be possible. But it is not exactly clear to me why Mohrstein resigned. I cover this ignorance in the column by simply declaring: "Acknowledging the clearly lost position, Mohrstein gave up," as the annotation for the final 79th move.

The night over the bay is powerfully black, broken only by lights from some of the parked freighters several thousand yards out from the shore. And there is immense silence in the room. I can't even hear the fan moving the indisputably cool air into the room. I wonder if Pam really will come with Mikey and Vera. Why would she pass up the yacht? Did Ned really know what she would do when he wrote? Does he now?

For almost three weeks after we got back to Florida Pam and I lived in the bayfront house, an arrangement that Ned more or less sanctioned, since it left him free to go to Bimini with Evelyn. And I was rigorous in making sure Pam's daily quotient of pills was carefully maintained. Three times a week I drove her to Tampa for further outpatient interviews with Coffee. He encouraged her to

CHAPTER 29

get married, or so she reported every time we took the Tamiami Trail back to Hane. If we took I-80 she never said much, but if we took the Trail she was fairly bubbling with conversation. I do not understand the silencing effect of the federal highway system. Perhaps the tacky spectacle of the Trail with irrevocable bits of Americana loosened her tongue. Maybe in the debris of that roadway she herself felt like one more piece adrift and looking for some adhesive surface. There was Snell, open, unsmooth, made for the sticking effect. On I-80 the Mercedes droned on from one health center to another. At the bayfront Pam began to cook some. Mostly Creole food. How domestic we became.

I made breakfast, little modest affairs of English muffins and hot Ceylon tea, although Coffee favored no stimulants at all for her. Sometimes I made an omelets while she slept upstairs. And then I went off to work, but only half days or so, since, increasingly, my column has become the only contribution I make to the paper. Doubtless Arnie and Phil would have preferred I occupy a desk, look busy, but lately they have given up pretending I am a "regular" employee.

Irreplaceability, doubtless Waldo would note, has its prerogatives. One develops such talents as one has, and some of us are better at making omelets than others, and for the right people. Domestic irreplaceability was shattered by Ned and Evelyn's return from the islands. I actually moved back to my apartment and we all went through the charade of inviting me to dinner to eat with the family, to make light conversation and then discretely to kiss Pam goodnight around eleven o'clock, since, as Evelyn explained, Dr. Coffee wanted Pam to get as much sleep as possible. After a week Pam suggested that either they or she should move to the ranch east of Hane, so as to end the silliness. But before that issue was resolved, Waldo decided I should be the advance man in the Philippines.

Does the bartender, after drying off, go home to a dirt shack such as Garcia so pointedly displayed to me? By what trick does one work in the Manila Hotel amid the marble and mahogany and then return home to dirt floors and board beds? Does passion for self-betterment provide the lubrication across the divide? Here on the tenth floor, in the cool air-conditioning, here watching the closed pool bar and listening for, but not hearing, the motions of the precisely chilled air, here with a view beyond the breakwater to the very multinational emblems of the far, far world in the center of the bay, I grieve for the starving masses of the Filipinos. I have never felt such immensely comfortable compassion, immense soft sadness. How to tame it?

Only with a special American hamburger sent up by room service. It comes on its own white clothed table and with its own pewter covering dish. There are chips, and bits of pineapple and cantaloupe set near the neat scoop of cole slaw, and adjacent split half-sour pickle. The fellow who brings the burger wears sandals and the hotel uniform. There is mud caked into his skin around his bony ankles.

"Say, how many people live at your house?" I ask, all tenderness and deep feeling.

"I live alone," he answers skeptically.

"Good. Do you have brothers and sisters?"

"Two brothers. They work for Metro Manila Maintenance," And then he is gone.

I can't say my leave taking was filled with angst for Pam. We sat on the tram at the Tampa International Airport and when I turned to kiss her, it appeared she was asleep. Keeping the pills strictly on a schedule has turned her into something of a zombie, I think. Anyway, Ned drove her back but on the trip up he was not clear who she was coming with. Transpacific with Vera and Mikey might have been more than she, or they, could take. On the other hand, if she comes by boat, do we have to continue the charade that I am the dutifully chaste suitor who keeps respectful distance the lovely, odd lady with her parents?

Ned knows the absurdity of this. Does Evelyn? What does Evelyn think? Ah, there is the enigma. She remains a cipher indeed,

CHAPTER 29

for Pam never talks of her. And all I have ever said to her barely extends beyond inquiries at the dinner table.

Maybe Pam will come with Vera and Mikey. Vera could be the least concerned, and therefore the most efficient, dispenser of medicine for Pam. And if Pam threatened to come unglued then who better to deal with the little piranhas of the medical profession than Vera herself?

Mikey's father did come for the tournament close in New York. And there was a picture in the Times of him shaking his son's hand. Vera refused to occupy the same frame, and so her pictures with Mikey came below the father/son one. I was in Connecticut during the reunion but learned later from Vera that "It was hardly memorable. He got what he wanted. Maybe it'll be good for ten more wills in Baltimore, or maybe some malpractice suits, whatever he does, when he ain't shuffling real estate."

"Does it upset Mikey's play?"

"Nah. Mikey's tougher than that, tougher than all of us. He don't give in to things like that."

Was Mikey tough? How would we know?"

For the column I decided that Mikey and Tarlac had the best chance to become the challenger to Atashian, although Calderon's performance in Baguio clearly signaled he was formidable beyond previous recognition. To outdraw the drawing master, wear him down and finally, eight games beyond the limit, get the victory, took great concentration, great mental and physical reserves. Would they be used up for the festivities at the Little Theater in the cultural Center? Would my readers care?

Then there were the other finalists, the venerable Brazilian Dr. Ernesto Levy, the other Russians Ivanov and the Ukrainian Petroff who qualified by merit of being the previous challenger. A six man roundelay until someone emerged with the requisite points and all for the honor of facing Atashian, who simply hadn't lost a game in the previous 18 months, despite a record number of entries in Soviet and East European tournaments.

Only Mikey looked like the strongest candidate. Tarlac had a better record, and clearly had unusual combinative gifts, but for that very reason would probably be vulnerable to Atashian's relentless style of play. And hadn't even he lost the thread with Ariztobal? One could not imagine Mikey doing that. Only Mikey had the staying power and the imagination to give Atashian real competition. Unless, of course, Calderon discovered some place a bit of artistry to go with his newly won stamina. But gurus aren't supposed to be creative. They are only supposed to sit in exemplary fashion, only supposed to *be*. Clearly Calderon could *be* staring through you at the next tier of consciousness. But creative? Not likely, Only Mikey then.

"Let's face it," Waldo had said once, "the kid's straight out of the Morphy/Fischer mold. A brat, manic, obsessed, scheming, and absolutely brilliant over the board. So damn defocused that once he drops the mania of the game, he'll split into a zillion pieces, but while he's on the ride, we'd better go along. It's going to be a humdinger."

Waldo's tireless fashioning of reality. What, after all, did Waldo know about chess? What does he know? So far as I can tell, almost nothing, even less than me, but he has fashioned Mikey into an important chess personage, begun to toy with that reality of Mikey so as to get through the long early mornings, is that it?

More likely, Mikey has become Waldo's property in that he alone is Waldo's contribution to the Hane Tribune. Naturally the kid must grow in importance as the sole product of Waldo's less than prolific newspaper mind. But if Mikey is Waldo's fashioning, what then is Snell? It's easier to go to bed than play with that nasty thought.

About 4:30 a.m. I am awakened by noises from the next suite.

"How about this! Don't this make the Ramada Inn look shabby! And cool, so much cooler than outside, and look at this," Vera has gone into the bathroom.

"Can I get something to eat?" Mikey says.

"Why not? This is a class hotel. Class, why not?"

CHAPTER 29

"You can't," I shout through the thin fire door, which is still locked.

"Eh?" Mikey answers.

"You can't. Room service closes at two o'clock."

"That you, Paul?" Mikey says.

"No, it's Tarlac. I'm up here setting up electronic mind controls."

Suddenly Vera is pushing at the door, kicking at it apparently. "They said connecting suites, but this connection is stuck. You get it open from your side?"

"No. It requires a key. We'll have to wait for the morning. Is Pam with you?"

"Whadya think?" Vera says.

There seems to be no correct answer.

"No," Mikey explains, "she's still in Hong Kong."

"Nah, they left there already," Vera corrects him.

"Well, she's not with us," Mikey says.

"You sure we can't get something from Room Service?" Vera says.

"Yeah, I'm positive. I tried the first night or maybe the second."

"So what are we supposed to do? The Thai flight was delayed and they had no food. We missed supper. Lunch was pretty small, too."

"I think the coffee shop opens around 6:00 a.m., maybe Room Service too."

"Two hours? So let's unpack. Make the time go by. Come on, Mikey."

"Calderon won, didn't he?" Mikey says.

"Yes, I've got the score right here. I'm going to use it in a column. You want to see it?"

"Do I ever! Shove it under the door won't you?"

"Why not meet in the hall. We're right next door."

I hear the door open. I put on the hotel robe and meet Mikey outside. He is wearing jeans and a polo shirt. He holds his hand up for the sheet, but I shake it, just to test him.

Still holding my hand, Mikey asks, "How did Mohrstein lose?"

"Very slowly."

"That figures. What I'm interesting in is how he fouled up the endgame in the second session. I've seen the moves for the first session."

"Calderon has put marks by the moves he thought were inadequate in the endgame."

"Great!" with that Mikey goes back into his room.

I go back and sit on my bed, but by now I'm wide awake. I open the curtains and watch the bay. Still black, but subtle shifts become apparent. The tanker lights still interrupt the darkness but occasionally I get the feeling that by glancing from left to right, by avoiding concentration on those lights, I can actually begin to make out the full shapes of the ships. In another fifteen minutes I notice further changes. The sky at the horizon is lightening, the plates overhead seem to be turning dark grey. I can hear Mikey playing through the moves in the next suite. Doubtless Vera is beside him, making her own notations. I move to the fire door to listen.

"He shouldn'ta done it, should he?"

"No," Vera agrees.

"It don't make a lot of sense, does it? I mean it's not a natural move, not a logical one. Mohrstein couldn't have made it, could he?"

"It's a weak move, but it doesn't seem to be a bad one, anyway," Vera says slowly, waiting for directions.

"Nah," Mikey goes on, "it simply doesn't have a point. Why would he do it? It wastes a whole tempo and for nothing. Just weakens the position. I don't follow it."

"Maybe he saw something that really isn't there. That happens," Vera says.

"There's nothing there. Anybody could tell that in a minute, in a second. I don't understand why he did it."

"Well, it was after a long match, you know, been playing and playing and playing and I hear he doesn't like heat and there wasn't a real air-conditioner up there. That's what I hear. Just a kind of cooler to recirculate the same air."

"Still, Mohrstein doesn't play moves like that," Mikey says.

"I'm gonna get some sleep," Vera says.

"And the next moves aren't any better. It's like he was drugged."

"Well, don't you get drugged playing Calderon? " Vera answers. "Now I'm gonna sleep. When you want breakfast, call for it will ya?"

"Sure. Sure."

"Goodnight, Mikey."

I go back to the bed and for the next few minutes I can hear Mikey playing and replaying Mohrstein's moves, but then I drift off myself.

Abruptly there is knocking on the door. I stagger over to open it. What time is it? Mikey waits in the hall. He is carrying the chess board, holding it out from himself, since a game is clearly set up on it.

"Sorry to bother you but I want ya to look at this."

"I was asleep."

"Well, she's asleep, so I can't go over it with her." Mikey says, coming into the room. "Won't take long. Just look at a few of these moves. Watch." He makes a series of about eight moves. Not much is on the board.

"I don't understand."

"Watch the moves again. You see how each move Mohrstein makes seems to follow no pattern at all. No plan. Mohrstein doesn't play that way! It almost seems he moves from one side of the board to the other, and each time Calderon builds toward the center. It's like he's inviting him to bust him wide open."

"Mohrstein was tired. He was sick of playing endless draws. The heat did bother him. Calderon admits that."

"He does?"

"Yes."

"Well, watch the sequence one more time. See if you see something in it." Mikey rearranges the pieces and runs through the moves again. "You see? After the fourth move then suddenly Mohrstein wakes up and starts playing this game again. It's like he's playing some other game and then, all of a sudden, he starts playing this game. But by then, it's too late. The logical thing would be to liquidate the Queen side pawns, swap them off. Clear that area and then concentrate on holding the center. That would be logical, if you were still playing for a draw."

"Maybe he thought he could win."

"Maybe, but watch. Calderon offers to liquidate the Queen side, proposes the exchanges and what does Mohrstein do, he leaves the pawns *en prise* and plays a pawn on the King side. So Calderon pushes forward and locks the Queen side pawns in, makes two of them backward and vulnerable. Then Calderon builds toward the center and Mohrstein proposes liquidating the King side pawns, pushes 'em up for exchange, but Calderon ignores that and so what happens? Mohrstein pushes them forward, spreading them out, making them vulnerable. It's like he's saying, 'Ya want some targets? Here are some easy pawn targets.' Then all of a sudden both players start maneuvering to break through in the center."

"Suppose Mohrstein could have broken through sooner?"

"He couldn't. He lost at least three tempi doing nothing. Nothing. Just fooling around. I don't understand it."

"He's hardly the first grandmaster to look silly. Petroff once missed a three move mate, I hear."

"Mohrstein's not Petroff, never played like Petroff. He'd never make mistakes like these. It's impossible."

"Try playing twenty-two draws in this heat for six weeks and see how good your concentration is."

"You don't understand. Ever hear of Schlecter?"

"Maybe."

"He's the most famous drawing master in the game, in the history of the game."

"Good for him."

"I'm serious. He drew with everybody. On any given day he could always draw. He always played for draws and he nearly always got 'em. If you were in a round where you needed a point and you had to play Schlecter, you might as well shoot yourself. The point is he never came out with gambits, with combinations, with complications. He never came out looking for a win. If you had a game in front of you, a scoresheet, but it was unsigned and you didn't know who the players were, if you played through the game and there were fireworks in it, you'd be certain it wasn't a Schlecter game. You understand? A certain style of play automatically meant it wasn't Schlecter Do you see?"

"Yes, yes."

"So some people say Mohrstein is ten times more predictable than Schlecter ever was. Ten times more dependable. You put anybody who knows anything about the game, you put them down in front of this board and you play these moves, one thing will be certain—they'll tell you Mohrstein didn't play these moves."

"So they'd be wrong."

"Right, they'd be wrong. That's what you have to say. But I'm telling you it's impossible. These moves a 1200 rater wouldn't make."

"They don't look that bad to me. Even Calderon said they didn't look that bad."

"They don't look bad, but they don't look like Mohrstein either."

"Maybe it wasn't Mohrstein. Maybe it was a double. Maybe Mohrstein's really in Zurich hustling computer chips."

"I don't think so," Mikey says with disarming acceptance of the possibility.

"I'm going back to bed."

"You do that. But I'm tellin' you Mohrstein couldn't have played these moves."

"Why don't you talk it over with Calderon? Or maybe Mohrstein himself. He's still around, functioning as a general Soviet second, I'd bet."

"I heard he went back in disgrace."

"Calderon says he's still around."

"Okay. Okay," Mikey says, apparently happy for some reason with the discussion. "But I got some ideas. I got some ideas."

The grey plates of the sky have become a nice pewter color. I pull the drapes and resolve to sleep till noon.

Chapter 30

I actually sleep till one o'clock. Air-conditioning does it every time. There are no yachts on the horizon, none in the bay. Just the boiling sunshine and down below at the pool, eight happy souls dragging their legs in the cool, chlorined water while they sip Planter's Punches, Rum Collins, whatever. But then I notice three people in robes next to the building, on an elevated portion of the terrace. They are huddle over a chessboard. The hoods of their robes are up, so it is impossible to tell who they might be, but on the other hand, who else would be huddled over a chessboard at poolside?

I knock on the fire door and call out, but clearly Mikey and Vera are not in. Who is the third hooded figure then? I am too high up to tell what they are playing through, but my guess is it's the Mohrstein-Calderon game. Who might the third commentator be? Could Vera have struck up an acquaintance so soon? They arrange and rearrange the pieces. Better to be at the bar for a morning, or early afternoon, Bloody Mary.

I take a quick shower, get a new robe from the front desk on the floor and arrive at poolside. The three are turned away from me, like white-robed monks playing dice on a table I can't see from the terrace level. For a brief moment it occurs to me that it might not be Mikey and Vera. The voices dispel all doubt.

"The important thing, Mikey, is not why he played so lousy—the important thing is to figure out why he," she points at the third figure, "played so good." She laughs at her own cleverness.

Mikey and Calderon sit upright. Their hoods flop back off their heads.

"Still struggling with that game?" I ask.

"Yeah, even Reyle doesn't know what happened to Mohrstein. Only, he's not complaining about it," Mikey says.

"He's got the right attitude," Vera says.

"Good morning, Mr. Snell," Reyle says, standing.

"Please call me Paul and please don't stand up."

"Yeah," Vera says.

"They are peculiar, improper moves," Calderon says thoughtfully.

"Well, ya still need to analyze other stuff," Vera says. "You spent too much time on this game already."

"She is right, Mikey," Calderon says. "Better we should look at what Petroff has done to revitalize the Caro-Kahn."

"I know that already."

"Even his most recent games?"

"The one he played last week, the ones he played last night, the ones he's gonna play tomorrow, next week. I know them all. Lousy line, interesting complications but a lousy line."

"I see," Calderon says. "Well then, maybe we can take a break and see the rest of Manila."

"Yeah," Vera says, "I hear the Central Market has all kinds of good buys."

"Indeed," Calderon answers. "When Mr. Garcia brings the car."

"Garcia? Coming here?" I ask.

"In about ten minutes or so. He's consented to drive us around," Calderon answers.

"He certainly takes Mendoza's requests seriously," I add.

"Does he?" Reyle asks, looking at me with a search for significance I find disconcerting.

"Come on, Mikey, we'll get dressed," Vera says standing up.

Mikey begins to put the pieces away inside the folding board.

"Do you want to come to?" Calderon asks.

"Probably not. I haven't had any sun since I got here. And there are parts of Manila I'd just as soon not see again."

"What does that mean?" Vera says.

"There's a lot of poverty here," Calderon answers evenly.

"Poverty don't bother me," Vera says. "Don't bother Mikey none either. We know what that's like, don't we, Mikey? We got a father, an ex-husband who's a damn expert on poverty. He knows all there is to know about it, don't he, Mikey?"

Mikey says nothing, keeps putting chess pieces into the board.

"The good prices at the Central Market come right out of that poverty," Reyle says to Vera.

"I don't care where they come from, so long as I end up with 'em," Vera says laughing. And with that she and Mikey start off the terrace. "Meet you in the front lobby in fifteen minutes, okay?"

"Of course," Calderon replies.

"Maybe he had an upset stomach. The water's pretty bad here. Is that right?" Mikey calls out to Reyle.

"You mean Mohrstein?"

"Yeah. Yeah."

"Well, maybe we should ask him." Calderon says.

Mikey nods, then runs to catch up with Vera.

"Garcia's tour is a little rough," I say, "they might not be too happy."

Calderon says, "It remains to be seen, if we wish to keep them happy. Actually, Mr. Garcia might not come along. He'd prefer, I know, to have lunch with you. Is that possible?"

"He'd rather stay here with me?"

"Oh, I think so. He has a few things to discuss with you—besides enjoying your company."

"I bet. I'm not looking to be propositioned."

"I don't think that's what he has in mind."

"If he wants to stay at poolside, that's okay with me. I want some sun."

"I'm sure that will be fine with him. You ought to be careful of our sunshine. Despite the clouds around, this is the most potent time of the day. No Filipino would sunbathe now."

"Okay, okay. I'll stay out only a little while," I answer, arranging a deck chair so that I can stretch out and stare up at the raging sunlight.

"I'll send Silberio out to you, if he wants to have lunch."

I nod, flop on the chair, open the robe and immediately I can feel the sweat rising. Indeed the sun is ferociously hot. I turn on my side, watch the bay for a while. I strain to see if a large white yacht has entered, but the bay is so enormous Pam could have arrived utterly unnoticed. After more time in such a mucid fire I drop out of the robe and dive into the pool. Much warmer than I expect. I swim in six swift pulls to the only vacant stool at the bar. A fortyish, red-haired woman turns to watch my ascent.

"You're a good swimmer" she says.

"Thanks," I motion the bar tender toward the tureen of Bloody Marys.

"Where you from?"

"Florida."

"No kidding! I used to live in Florida, but I thought it was too hot, so I came to Manila to cool off. I always come here to cool off, heh, heh," she says drinking her gin and tonic.

"Whereabouts in Florida?" I ask.

"I ought to say Palm Beach, shouldn't I? That would help, wouldn't it? Where'd you learn to swim?"

"Lake Erie."

"Lake Erie? No kidding! I used to live near Lake Erie in Buffalo. That where you're from?"

"No." the Bloody Mary arrives. I stir the drink with the piece of celery stalk.

"Okay, okay. You have your little secrets and I'll have mine. That's what Manila's all about, isn't it? Your little secrets, my little secrets. But I'll tell you something—from the way you swim, I'd say my secrets are more interesting. You're a little too healthy."

"Not really. I'm as decadent as they come."

"Ha, heh. Not with that body, dearie. Are you some kind of athlete?"

"Well, actually, I'm here with a professional trampoline group."

"I thought so. A trampoline group, eh? What the hell does that mean—a trampoline group?"

"The Flying Octavios, heard of us?"

"Sure, dearie, sure. You finish your act with dogs, right?"

"For some audiences."

"Hey, I like you. You can swim out to my stool any time."

I am aware of a powder blue blur on the terrace. I turn to look and see Garcia waving his arms. "Gotta go," I say.

"He part of your act?" she says, adjusting three brass bracelets further up her long freckled wrist.

"He catches the dogs as they come off the sheet," I say and finish the Bloody Mary.

I decide to wade back. The Bloody Mary has a nice kick to it. The water suddenly seems a fascinating swirling blue. It takes a while to get out of the pool. Garcia has settled himself in adjacent deck chair, but he is clearly unhappy in the sunlight.

"Lemme dry off and then we can move into the shade," I say, using my robe as a towel.

"Yes, that would be nice. I like a tan but lately it seems nothing but cancer and liver spots."

"Can we get lunch or breakfast out here?"

"Yes," Garcia answers, "if we go over there to the umbrella terrace. They have rather good lunches actually. A splendid avocado and shrimp salad, I remember. Although, in fact, I don't come here too often."

"Ideologically unsound?"

"Financially too, don't you think?"

"I suppose. Lately I don't worry about that stuff much."

"Splendid arrangement. You must tell me how you set it up. In fact, Mr. Snell, despite the disparity in our ages, I have the decided feeling you could teach me a great deal," Garcia says.

"About chess?"

"About hustling," Garcia says with some bitterness.

"Is this how you start the day in Manila, with a little insult?"

"Oh, I didn't not mean any insult. Far from it. In point of fact I am touched with more than a little bit of awe. I really believe you have a great deal to teach me. Much I can learn from."

"I bet."

"I am not being the least cynical."

"Maybe there's something you could teach me first." I answer.

"I'd be delighted."

"Good. Perhaps you can teach me what little game you and Calderon are playing."

"Game?"

"I see. The lesson is already over."

"I'm sorry, I don't quite follow what you are saying."

"I suspect my nose wasn't rubbed in Raul's home life for no reason. In fact I should say there has been a somewhat concerted effort to teach all about Philippine political realities from my first dinner with Wicksburg to your little 'cook's tour'. So what do you want from me? An article on Filipino poverty? A column on Imelda's corruptions?"

"You're a quick study, Mr. Snell. Is that how they say it, quick study? I've always like the term. It may be dated now. I once wrote a play called *The Death of the Quick Study*. Did you ever see it, or read it?"

"No. But I understand what you are saying. You wish to add threat to insult. Ought to be a rousing lunch."

"Your interpretations are too grandiose. The play was about a fellow who learns that simple, immediate mastery of complicated issues is not enough. He wants to feel things deeply too, and discovers that mastering them quickly prevents that. So he resolves to be dumber."

"I don't suppose it packed 'em in."

"There was a degree of puzzlement over it by the critics, and you're right, it didn't last very long. But obscurity has its compensations. I've never suffered the pangs of being a public figure."

"Shall we move to the shade?"

"Very funny! Splendid! Things get too hot out here too quickly," Garcia answers.

We order Heineken beers with lunch. I opt for an omelet and Garcia chooses his favorite shrimp salad. The beer is absolutely ice cold, instantly sweating up the glass, beading it up. It is like swallowing delicious dry ice.

"You are right. We have been trying, in our clumsy way, to educate you," Garcia says after a while. "But please don't let our awkwardness interfere with the message. Things are horrible and will have to change here. Ultimately even the rankest cesspool becomes unlivable by all classes. We didn't want you to think Manila was this hotel and that bay and the Little Theater in the Cultural Complex. But that says it stupidly. Of course we knew you wouldn't think that, but most Americans really have no idea what the Philippines are. They have some image of lumber or pineapples, or maybe rubber when they think of our region of the world. Maybe they've heard of Jeepneys, and they know it's dangerous here. And they believe Martial Law is a way of bringing order to this hot madness. We wanted to extend your view a bit. The connection this hotel and Raul's charming home, I leave for other 'theoreticians' to explore. I merely wanted you to know the two halves. Not halves. Far from it. The one one hundredth here and the other ninety-ninths there. Am I making myself clear?"

"Perfectly, except on the fundamental point. What do you want from me? I'm willing to say immediately that my consciousness has been raised. But I still have the lingering feeling you don't fundamentally give a damn about my consciousness. So what is it that you want?"

"You keep putting me in an awkward, tentative position," Garcia says, smiling, drinking more of his beer. "They never make this sauce hot enough." He stirs a side dish of a white and green shrimp sauce.

"Is it a political-sexual connection? Is that it? Raise political consciousness and I'll end up going to bed with you, is that it?"

"Fascinating idea," Garcia replies. "Tell me how it would work. Despair over poverty would make you more receptive to the ministrations of this old queen? I like that a lot, but I doubt it would really work. In any event, alas, it was not what we had in mind."

"We?"

"Myself, Mr. Mendoza, Mr. Calderon, and," Garcia pauses, watching me eagerly, "and Dr. Mohrstein. Oh, there are others, too, but you don't know them. Count yourself lucky."

"Mohrstein, the grandmaster?"

"I'm afraid you'll be hearing a lot of Dr. Mohrstein. Lots is being said, even now. Of course it doesn't make our media, because it is, after all, news, and news is forbidden. But the western press is reporting him as missing or defected, for example. The Soviets think he has been kidnapped. The reality is somewhere in between, I think."

"I don't quite follow."

"Neither do I, but, in any event, Dr. Mohrstein isn't the main actor. David M. Spendip is."

"And he's being kidnapped right now?" I suddenly feel immensely paternal about Mikey.

"Hardly. Far from it. That so far as I know has not even been contemplated. You can rest assured on that point."

"Something else is being planned?" I ask, watching Garcia carefully.

"Well, lots is being discussed. And that's where you could be helpful to us."

"I'm sure."

"No, in truth you seem to have the flexibilities, the perspective about this silly game that could be very helpful to us."

"What silly game?"

"Chess, of course."

CHAPTER 30

"This is about chess?"

"Yes, in one sense. I mean it begins with chess and hopefully leads to rather more critical issues."

"You're being remarkably cryptic."

"Deliberately, alas. Bear with me. Let me ask you a few questions about Mr. Spendip, if you don't mind. For example, does he have any political consciousness?"

"None whatsoever."

"I knew it! I knew it. The others have such a pipedream. On the other hand, you could say he is very anti-Soviet, couldn't you?"

"He thinks the Russians cheat at chess. Yes, he's anti-Soviet to that extent. But if you think he cares about Soviet treatment of Latvia, Soviet policy toward China, Soviet support for anti-Americanism, you're wasting your time. He couldn't care less. He couldn't know less. He couldn't be interested in less."

"Very effectively put. And precisely my position, I might add, in our discussions."

"Our discussions?"

"Discussions with Mr. Mendoza and others. Ah, the others, they are indeed the problem. They tend to see things with such clarity. Oh, that I had their clarity."

"And these others?"

"Oh, not to worry about them, I suppose. Although, ultimately I should think they probably are the only ones worth worrying about. They use me. Oh, how they use me!"

"How can a Genius in a G-string be used?"

"You are unnecessarily cruel. It will be your undoing, if I had to prophesize that. In that sense I think they will find you a worthy antagonist, if it comes to that."

"I'm tiring of these riddles in riddles, in riddles."

"It is nothing to my own enervation. But to return to the main point. Suppose one wanted Mr. Spendip to do something. On what grounds should it be asked of him?"

"You mean, where he is vulnerable? Is that what you mean?"

"I don't think so. I mean what is persuasive to him? Could he be recruited on the grounds that the Soviets cheat and therefore something has to be done about it?"

"What are you talking about? Mikey plays chess. That's all he does, all he thinks about."

"Precisely! Precisely, and that is precisely where he can help us, but how do we ask?"

"Ask what?"

"Ask him to lose to Mr. Calderon," Garcia says slowly, distinctly, but not looking directly at me.

I burst out laughing. I cannot stop myself. "That's the most absurd request you could make, the one that's impossible. Utterly and absolutely impossible! Worse than impossible—literally unthinkable! Jesus, have you no sense at all? Mikey still cries over, still weeps over a knight fork costing him the exchange four years ago. He still cries over it. Ask him to lose? He'd sooner castrate himself at the pool bar." I point in the direction of the red-haired woman.

"Arresting analogy. I wonder why you chose it." Garcia says.

"Ha, ha, heh, heh. Jesus! Out of the question. Not even in the remote possibilities. A pure act of God wouldn't budge him." I go on laughing.

"Then you won't help us?"

"Help you? Why the fuck should I help you?"

Garcia stops eating, wipes his mouth slowly, puts his napkin in his lap. I get the sense he's very unhappy with these remarks. Very unhappy. "I'm sorry," he says, "I've bungled this very badly. We perhaps should talk about something else. I'm really sorry to bring all of this up. I've done it quite wrong. I see that. Would you like another beer?"

"Sure."

"Garcia waves to the waiter, then scratches the back of his head.

"Have you bet a lot of money on the Interzonals?" I ask.

Garcia looks at me incredulously. "Is that what you think?"

"It's a reasonable assumption. You want help arranging a Calderon victory. You want Mikey to throw a point."

"Reasonable I suppose, given the way you think. But an absurdity, Mr. Snell, an absurdity. Let's not talk about it. All right I've made a terrible mistake. Let's not compound it with some dismal, absurd discussion of betting. Betting, indeed!"

"Okay. Okay, where is Reyle going to take them? What sights is he going to show them?"

Garcia waits for the beer before replying. "He dreams of showing them the same sights I showed you. He dreams of converting them."

"Converting them to what?"

"To changing all of this," Garcia waves toward the bay.

"Is that what Calderon is, an ideologue? A revolutionary?"

"No. Not really, as the others have noticed. Not really, but sometimes. Sometimes all of us are receptive to change, don't you think?"

"You keep mentioning 'others'. Who the hell are these others?"

"The only people who truly care for this great miserable country, the boys in the mountains who dare to seek change: the NPA. They're the final cleansing element."

"I'm a little confused. What is the NPA?"

"Rightly so, given my botched explanations. The New Peoples Army, NPA. But let's stop lest I compound the misunderstanding. But answer me this, if we wanted Mikey to do something for us, how crucial would Mrs. Spendip be?"

"Absolutely crucial. But if you're thinking of working on Vera to get Mikey to lose, I want to be there when you try. I really want to be there. It would be the greatest slaughter in history. She'd eat you alive."

"Not lose. Not lose, then. Forget that aspect. Just do something for us. What would persuade her?"

"Bring money," I laugh. "Lots of money!"

"I see," Garcia says, looking peeved. Then his eyes brighten in the sparkling light of the terrace. "Speaking of which," he says, suddenly animated again, as if spying something that will retrieve the whole disastrous conversation. "Speaking of which, I think your yacht is in!" He points to the sleek white, port-holed beauty slipping between two moored tankers.

Chapter 31

Garcia adds, "And, if I'm not mistaken, some lovely creature, a mermaid, is on the bow."

The yacht makes its turn, comes abreast of our view, but it is still too far away for me to tell. "We should have binoculars. I don't suppose you have any?"

"No, but that's remedied," Garcia claps his hands and when a waiter comes, carries on a spirited conversation in Tagalog with him. The fellow comes back with Nikon binoculars. Garcia takes them out of their slippery black case and hands them to me.

"You have very sharp eyes," I say adjusting the lenses. It is indeed Pam, resplendent in a bronze bikini, sitting up at the very point of the bow. She's as brown as a Filipino, sleek, seal-smooth. Golden and luscious on this white mounting above the cookie tin of the grey-blue bay.

"You seem excited," Garcia says.

"You're right. My ship has come in at last."

"Then forget my awkward presentations earlier, will you?"

But I don't answer him, merely keep watching the glistening, oiled shoulders soundlessly gliding toward the hotel's docks.

Over dessert and yet one more Heineken Garcia returns to his theme. "I must apologize for handling things so badly. But you should not simply dismiss what I'm saying because I have said it so badly, phrased it so poorly. Or offered it to you in a way that seems to have made you angry. Perhaps I displayed what I wanted to do in the worst possible light."

"Hardly, I still don't have a clear idea what you want, or why you want it. Or what you're doing talking to me in the first place."

"We need an ally in talking to Mr. Spendip."

"About losing?"

"Yes."

"That's the one thing you can't talk to Mikey about. It's not in his vocabulary. He won't understand anything you say. And why should he? What kind of cheap flim-flam is it, anyway? If Calderon wants to win, why doesn't he study hard enough to win?"

"It really has very little to do with Mr. Calderon's position. In fact he's planning to trade an early victory for a later loss, so that Mr. Spendip's score will not suffer."

"You mean beyond the two victories he could probably get."

"A double victory against Calderon is very problematic."

"I don't see why. Mikey has beaten him before."

"That was before Mr. Calderon's play became, what shall we say—Mohrsteined?"

"So in addition to defecting or being kidnapped, Dr. Mohrstein has become Calderon's tutor in drawing? This is getting more bizarre by the moment."

"Bizarre or not, I can assure you the people connected take this with the utmost seriousness. It involves one of their members. A member presently held by this government under conditions that could be charitably called abominable. And important member, but one this government does not even know it has. Do you understand?"

"Absolutely not."

"A friend of Mr. Calderon's a friend he would very much like to set free from this, this incarceration."

"And beating Mikey will open the cell door?"

"Precisely, in a manner of speaking," Garcia pushes aside his plate and hunches over the table. "It all has to do with a proper second. Calderon has no official second now. An early victory in

CHAPTER 31

the opening rounds over a player perhaps favored to win, over the only player with clear championship potential, I might add, such a victory would enable him to name his own second. And if done discretely and quickly with a minimum of investigation, with a maximum of celebration of Filipino honor, Filipino possibility, then Mr. Calderon's second could be freed for the tournament, perhaps freed period. The government has no real case against him. He was merely collected in a routine sweep of some outlying areas. In fact apart from his chess ability, the fellow has no traits inimical to the government."

"It has a rather improbable cast to it. Wouldn't simply asking for him be sufficient?"

""There wouldn't be a timely and possible public pressure such as would be occasioned by a signal early victory."

"And why wouldn't the government be very suspicious of asking for a prisoner?"

"Routine roundups make mistakes all the time. Besides the government has no reason to suspect Mr. Calderon, who is, after all, apolitical in the extreme. He shares with Mr. Spendip that enviable condition."

"He's apolitical but hangs around with Mendoza and Garcia-Lopez who are, who are, what? Let's see—Mendoza is so apolitical he can't come back into the Philippines. And Garcia is so apolitical he tells me not be photographed with him. What kind of nonsense are you selling? If Calderon wants to get a cheap victory, I suggest you start with Vera and bring a whole lot of money, and maybe talk about how the Russians do it, and Reyle will throw the point back later in the tournament. At least you'll get listened to."

"Well, that is blunt but helpful advice. I feared that, to tell the truth. I suggested as much. At least with Mrs. Spendip we would be bargaining, haggling, and Filipinos understand that very well."

"Yeah, we'll see who gets the cheapest deals in the Central Market."

"You think a political exposition of the situation here, an appeal to save people in a great deal of pain, an appeal to end suffering and misery would not be well received?"

"The problem would getting Mikey or Vera to hear it. If you mention suffering, Vera will tell you about her deprivations and she'll drown out any recitation you had planned. If you showed her pictures of mutilated bodies, she'd tell you that's what her ex-husband and the Baltimore court system had in mind for her. She'd ask for copies to send to them as evidence she knew what they wanted to do. Do you understand?"

Garcia shakes his head.

"I suspect you don't. Ask Mendoza about her, about them."

"Would you help us in discussing money with her?"

"Hell no! I won't help, period."

"Suffering means nothing to you either then?"

"Please, please don't insult my intelligence. All I can see is that you guys want Mikey to throw a game to Calderon. Everything else is a lie, isn't it? On that basis I wouldn't help you. Even if I understand perfectly what you were doing, I don't think I would help you. What would be in it for me? Why would I want to touch it?"

"I don't wish to insult you. Not at all," Garcia says, "I have some limited information about Mr. Mohrstein. I'd be willing to share it with you. If you knew what I could give you, that information would put you in the position of 'scooping' the wire services, the special correspondents, everybody. You are welcome to it, if you want."

"I'm not much of a newspaper man. I wouldn't know what to do with it."

"I thought as much. Said as much. It seems we have almost nothing to trade with, is that it?"

"Seems so. Which is not to say I don't wish you luck with Mikey."

"Would you and Miss Snow and the Spendips come to my house for dinner tomorrow night?" Garcia says quickly.

"As part of the campaign to convince Mikey?"

"For dinner. Although, perhaps Mr. Calderon will begin the negotiation there. I can't predict what will happen now. But mostly just for dinner, and for a chance to meet her." Garcia points toward the yacht.

"You don't lie very well," I answer.

"Given that, a personal failing for which I am deeply sorry, will you still come?"

"The gardens are lovely and the architecture is personally done?"

"Yes. At the time I hadn't the funds to do everything I had hoped for, but you will see powerful touches—better than the sorry excrescences of Locks in for Imelda. And I shall have my cooks prepare an authentic repast, and perhaps with luck we should have some innocent pleasure afterwards.

"Your pleasure is innocent, then?"

"Oh, always," Garcia says, laughing. "Always. You will come?"

"Why not? Pam, I'm sure would be interested."

"She will like some my statuary, I'm certain of it." He shoves the binoculars toward me again, and indicates I should go down to the dock and await the arrival of the yacht. Ostentatiously he picks up the bill himself. "I will come for you myself tomorrow at six, if that is all right."

"I can hardly wait," I answer getting up and waving goodbye to him.

The cement dock is the longest one. There are three others, wood structures that already provide power, water, and anchorage to about ten similar yachts. I walk along the cement figuring that Pam is still perhaps forty minutes away. There is no shade on the end of the dock and it's not clear if I can stand the sun for so long. Two older gentlemen are fishing off the right side of the dock. They wear large umbrella-like hats and have, in any case, skin as dark and tough looking as could be imagined.

Apparently Pam has gone below. There is persistent sweat which leaks into my eyes, whenever I use the binoculars. I put the robe hood up, but even so, the top of my head seems to be steaming. It is impossible to judge how far away the yacht is, but there is nothing ambiguous about the sunshine. I decide that were I to wait longer, Pam would only find a sunstroke victim on the dock, one quite unable to celebrate her arrival.

I go back to the room and take up a watch of sorts by the window. In the air-conditioning the binoculars work much better. It will only have been about ten days since I've seen her, but I find myself entertaining rather strange notion that somehow she will be sounder, more healthy, vibrant in the Manila hot glow. Perhaps Ned will have found a better pharmacist, able to mix portions so as to bring something out in her personality that was not there before. A bad sign, such fantasizing.

There are other bad signs. The water in the pitcher tastes plastic and unchlorinated. My newest Barong shirt has been torn under the arm. The new rubber thong sandals raise a red blister on the top of my left foot. At the pool bar the red-haired woman has simply put her head down on the bar top. That does not seem to interest the other patrons.

In another half hour the yacht does draw parallel with the cement dock, then turns and makes for berthing area at the end of the wooden docks. I sprint to the elevator and get to the special oversize slip at about the same time the yacht arrives. Pam is topside again.

This time in an orange sun dress with straps that tie around the back of her neck. She is very tan indeed, apparently very steady, holding only the guideline running off the davits to a small lifeboat swinging suspended on the top deck. She seems solid enough, but the odd smile she gives me signals an automatic response I know too well.

"You look very good," I shout as the line fore and aft are secured to cleats on the dock.

"Yes," she answers, "a lot of sunshine."

"You don't get seasick?"

"Not this trip. I was on the evenest of keels. My inner ear was asleep the entire time."

CHAPTER 31

Ned comes up. He walks beside the dark skinned Captain who sees to be nodding at everything Snow is saying. Suddenly Ned spots me and shouts, "Welcome aboard! Not much of a welcoming party." He then points to a large shielded electrical socket on the outside of the front bridge cabin. Hotel attendants bring a power line to the socket.

"You like it?" Ned says, gesturing to the yacht.

I jump aboard. Pam comes down from the upper deck to the fantail where I am standing. "Missed you," I say.

"Really?" she answers, giving me a slow kiss that feels almost flabby in its relaxation. "Well, here I am and I have some things for you. Do you want them?"

"Sure."

She hands me two black leather wallets made from the same plastic stitching of her Tampa stay. "I made 'em both on the way over. Sometimes it takes a lot of work just to pass the time. It's so boring some times, but Hillary was a good Canasta player."

"Then they came along?"

"Oh yes. They're below. Waldo doesn't feel well. Come on, I'll take you down."

Waldo is slumped in the second twin bed of his cabin. He looks ashen.

"Hong Kong flu, I'm certain of it," he says, sitting up a bit.

"Not seasickness?" I ask.

"Your solicitude as always overwhelms me," Waldo says. "Not seasickness. I don't get seasick. We went shopping in Kowloon just before we left. I never wanted to go the Kowloon side. Place is disease ridden. You tell in a minute. But no! The best bargains are on the Kowloon side, so of course we have to go over. Some place called Mong Kok. I've never seen so damn many people and everyone infested with special Chinese vermin."

"You ate some street food?"

"I could have. Who knows where they get the stuff they feed you there."

"Well, if you didn't eat it directly, you probably didn't eat any. How long have you been laid up?"

"The duration. The duration."

"He started feeling better the minute the engines stopped," Pam says.

"That may seem to be the case, but in actuality I have some variant of flu. I'm certain of it," Waldo insists. "Is the tournament going off as scheduled?"

"Yes. Sure Why wouldn't it?"

"Why wouldn't it?" Waldo asks somewhat incredulous. "They do have news censorship here," Waldo says, delighted with that prospect. "So I wonder if it is news, if nobody knows it's news?"

"What is the news, Waldo?"

"Some Russian Grandmaster has defected or something or other. Calderon's opponent, the coach of the Russians at the tournament, the senior fellow. Nobody knows where he is. Moscow claims he's been kidnapped."

"By whom?"

"By Filipino radicals. Maybe by Americans. You name it. Maybe by the local chapter of the VFW. I don't suppose you've heard anything of this."

"No," I answer. "They don't print anything in the newspapers here, except weather reports."

"Just our speed," Waldo says dismally. "Maybe we'd have a future here, given the competition."

"You could have a very short, very fiery future by starting a real newspaper here."

"Better quick expiration than a lingering death from some Asian germ, some insidious Oriental gas."

"You going to move to the hotel?"

"Absolutely not. You know what the charter of this thing costs? I'm not adding a hotel bill to it."

"You must be really sick," I say, "to talk about the cost of things. Very unlike you, Waldo. Has Hillary left you?"

CHAPTER 31

Waldo sulks, and Pam squeezes my arm as precaution against pursuing an evidently sensitive topic. "No," Waldo says sarcastically. "Hillary hasn't left me, though she probably wanted to. Still wants to. Nothing so traumatic."

"Well, good. I wouldn't want to add financial destabilization to our other problems in Manila."

"What problems?"

"Oh, I'll talk to you about them sometime when you're feeling better. Nothing really serious. More comic than anything."

"Perhaps that's the way to approach Southeast Asia—as a comedy," Waldo says.

"Yes," Pam agrees, "you can see the humor everywhere in the faces of the people."

What people has she seen? "How big is the crew on this thing?"

"I don't know. Maybe 12, maybe 20. I don't know. The captain's a Samoan—"

"Yes," Pam says, "the very first Samoan I've ever met. George somebody or other. He used to be in the U.S. Coast Guard. He's been everywhere."

"I see why you didn't miss me."

"That's not true," Pam says. "I did miss you. But sometimes it helped just to talk with George."

"Ah, George. You and George. Terrific!"

"Believe me, this thing pitched around too much for any real exercise," Waldo tries to reassure me.

"I suppose they fed you well, Waldo. And Hillary waits on you night and day."

Waldo shrugs. "They feed me all right. It's keeping it down that takes work."

"I'm sure things will be very quiet here. Come on, Pam, I'll show you the hotel and you can take a hot bath, if you like."

"There's four heads with bathtubs here," Waldo counters.

"But we have marble in the hotel. You ought to check it out, Waldo."

"Maybe tomorrow."

On deck Pam insists on confiding in me. "Waldo and Hillary are having a horrible fight."

"About what?"

"About his being such a baby. Of course he's seasick, but he denies it. If he got off the boat he'd feel better immediately. He did really carry on so."

"And Hillary let him get away with that?"

"She couldn't stop it. He was uncontrollable. Throwing up everywhere and then insisting that he knew what was wrong with him. Really amazing. I've never seen him like this."

"That's why Hillary's not around?"

"She moved into another cabin and paid one of the crew to sit in with him."

"True love."

"Well, he really was unbelievable. He couldn't keep even a few crackers down."

"Maybe you should have given him some of your pills."

"That's the point. He could have taken any number of things. Daddy had all kinds of drugs from Hong Kong. You can buy anything there over the counter, and he had all kinds of things, but Waldo insisted he wasn't seasick. He still insists he has the flu. But he never ran a temperature. He stopped letting us take it after the first day. He really enjoys his ill health."

"I'm sorry," I say, feeling somehow guilty for Waldo's behavior.

"Oh, let's get off here. I want to try a nice hotel size bed," Pam says, looking suddenly radiant in the sunshine.

She slips twice on the dock, once more near the pool, once again getting out of the elevator.

"Maybe your inner ear woke up," I suggest.

"Maybe," she answers, "can we put it to sleep again? I really do feel as if I'm sloshing around a bit."

"Lie on the bed and I'll see what I can do. I'll always take care of you."

"Did I say how much I missed you? All of you!" She says holding her arms up as if to stop the ceiling from collapsing.

Chapter 32

Pam and I come back for the command Captain's Dinner about three hours after we had gone to my room. Captain George looks resplendent in his nautical double-breasted jacket and yachting cap, a sartorial excellence somewhat clouded by the grey, soiled work pants he wears, and his heavy, steel-tipped shoes. Still there is a wardroom of sorts, a rather small stateroom with some dirty green carpet and one central table covered in white cloth and with seven straight-backed chairs around it. There is even a small bar set up on the left, beneath four large maps thumbtacked to the wall. Ned makes gin and tonics. Captain George is drinking San Miguel beer from the bottle. His hair sticking out from the cap looks remarkably thick and greasy—buttered wires. Pam immediately sits down at the left corner of the table and takes her father's drink smiling.

"You kids getting reacquainted?" Ned says with mock joviality. His wife, Evelyn stands by the bar and holds a small glass of what looks to be Campari and something else, most likely soda. She wears a peacock eye dress in dark blue and appears more tan than anyone else, except Captain George. Hillary stands near the Captain. Waldo has not surfaced for this soiree.

"Waldo likes to imagine he is suffering so," Hillary says, "so that others can't enjoy themselves. In point of fact as soon as the engines stopped his color started coming back. I don't know why he doesn't face the fact that he can't stand the sea. Plenty of people can't. Their great merit is they don't pretend about it. They take planes and meet you and everyone, everyone is happier. So instead of pleasant company and, heaven forbid, a little help along the way we, we have a martyr aboard. It's discouraging. Perhaps, Paul, you'll talk to him, would you?"

"I'll be happy to try, but my conversations with him tend to be rather one-sided."

"Yours and everyone else's. I've seldom seen such a self-obsessive. It is really rather tacky," Hillary continues.

"So we have one extra plate," Ned says, indicating to the cook's helper, a Filipino who looks about twelve years old, to take one place setting away.

"Should I take Waldo something?" I ask Hillary

"Let him stew. I told him ten thousand times that if he got up on deck, if he took some fresh air, he'd cure all his problems. But a cure would interfere with his celebrated dependency."

Captain George rather loudly pats his end of the table, apparently signaling everyone to sit down. I sit beside Pam.

She turns to me and whispers, pretending to get something out of her pocketbook on the floor between us. "Isn't he so magnetic?"

"And so articulate."

She laughs. Ned and Evelyn sit opposite us, leaving Hillary the other end of the table away from Captain George. Suddenly the lights go out, and the Filipino brings in a lighted candelabra. In this light George, who has taken off his cap, looks immense, brooding like John L. Lewis—great hooded eyebrows beneath mounts of well-oiled hair? Evelyn takes her napkin up and puts it in her lap. George watches this with interest, and then copies the action.

The first course consists of some shrimp lying weakly on stale cabbage leaves. The sauce comes in a white china pitcher.

"Is there some wine with this?" Hillary asks firmly.

In a voice that is at once guttural, soft, yet threatening, Captain George says quickly, "Beer." He claps his hands.

"Filipino beer is wonderful," I volunteer, hoping to stem some sort of confrontation. It is an unnecessary gesture. Clearly Hillary is not about to clash with this fellow. Nor for that matter is anyone else. Captain George eats with his spoon, using the fork merely as a block or rake to get the food on the spoon.

Eventually the first course gets cleared away. Ned makes fresh drinks for everyone. The beer finally comes and then slowly, carefully the Filipino brings out the main dish, a chicken and rice conglomeration covered in a brilliantly yellow sauce. Each plate has a mound of raisins on the side. Captain George, however, receives no plate at all. After we are served, still nothing has been brought to the Captain, who motions for us to start. I notice no one demurs. Indeed, there seems to be a bit of a premium on finishing the meal quickly.

"Has anyone heard anything more about Mohrstein?" I ask.

"Who's Mohrstein?" Ned asks.

Captain George sits with his hands folded on the empty space in front of him. He attempts to smile, as we variously nod to him, acknowledging his deprivation.

"Waldo knows," Pam says, smiling. "He knows all about him."

"Oh, is he one those chess players?" Ned says.

"Precisely," Hillary answers, "one of Waldo's minions. Part of Waldo's empire or trailer court's following or whatever."

"A Russian," I say, "and apparently defecting, or maybe kidnapped."

"There is some difference," Ned allows.

"Yes, that's why I was hoping somebody had heard something more. News here is quite controlled. I didn't know anything about it."

"What's so threatening about a single Russian chess master?" Ned says.

"That's what I don't understand. But maybe the New Peoples Army got him to defect."

"Oh sure," Ned says, clearly hoping the conversation will go elsewhere.

Suddenly the Filipino is back, this time carrying a large white china plate which holds on it a single deep bakelite bowl. Captain George will be fed, after all. The steward puts the plate and bowl down in front of the Captain and then swiftly—too swiftly, I think—glides away. What is in the bakelite bowl? What little delicacy has the rude Captain ordered for himself, but not for his well-paying passengers? I arch up a bit, peer into the bakelite dish. It seems to be full of fish heads. And when Captain George begins to chew on the first one, that impression is confirmed.

"Oh God in heaven!" Evelyn who sits nearest the Captain cannot contain herself. George looks at her with peculiar toleration. Will the Captain speak? There is almost twenty seconds of silence. Perhaps the fellow is offended by Evelyn's response?

But soon enough George says, "What I eat!" He points at the bowl. "What I always eat." He takes another fish head up on the spoon and chomps directly through the eye and jaw line. The crunching sound momentarily fills the universe of the wardroom. I can see Evelyn stifle another exclamation.

"In Nepal, Pamy, you remember the half-baked rats people used to sell in the streets. You were really frightened by them. And I didn't like them much either, although I heard they were very tasty and not bad for you, either."

"It's a shame they didn't have rat heads," Hillary says.

"Mohrstein's famous for drawing games. He can draw in almost any so called 'lost position'. His genius is for finding draws, perpetual check, total *zugswang*, that kind of thing," I say.

"There used to be some older master who was famous for that, wasn't there?" Ned says. "Yes, a guy named Schlecter or Sheltinger, or something like that. I remember reading about him. Is Mohrstein that good?"

"I think so," I lie. "Maybe Waldo would know for sure."

"Perhaps someone ought to take a little of the Captain's dinner down to Waldo," Hillary says, chuckling.

"How will Mikey do?" Ned says to me.

CHAPTER 32

"He might win, or he might come in second. It will depend a little on luck."

"Luck? In chess?" Evelyn says.

"Sure," Pam answers, "after a certain level of play then everything becomes luck, you know. Whether you sit comfortably at the board, whether the room is cool or hot enough, whether you really remember all those opening variations."

"Seems like you could control those things, Pamy."

"I suppose," Pam says, trailing off.

"Mistakes at the Grandmaster level have to be luck—they can't be much else." I assert. "If your concentration fails, you're unlucky, I guess."

"Or unprepared," Evelyn insists.

The little contretemps might have escalated except that Captain George seemed to respond immediately to any tension nearby. He slapped the table top again, actually bouncing Evelyn's plate toward her a bit. "You want more?" he asks, apparently rhetorically. We decline.

"Well, when does all this silliness start?" Evelyn asks.

"In two days," I answer.

"And when do the pairings get made up?"

"Tomorrow morning. Everybody plays everybody else twice. A round robin. Once in the first half of the tournament and once in the second.

"Sunday morning mixed doubles," Hillary says, laughing.

"Precisely," Evelyn says.

Captain George noisily spits some larger fish bones into his bowl. The china plates are taken away.

"Did you notice that the dock help were all speaking English." Ned says. "Does everybody speak English here?"

"Yes," Pam answers, "at least that's what I've read."

"Why do they speak English?" Ned asks.

Hillary's response is delivered flatly. "We occupied the country for fifty years, you know."

"I know that, but why do they speak English? They must have their own language. Or Spanish. Spain occupied the place for centuries."

"Why don't we ask our Captain?" Hillary says.

"I'm Samoan," Captain George answers. "I been here three times before. Never left the ship."

"There, you see," Hillary says.

"They have a native language, at least for this island, Tagalog, or maybe a mixed 'native language' called Filipino," Pam says.

"Well, what is for dessert?" Evelyn interrupts.

"Fruit," Captain George says, getting up from the table. "I have to go back to work now." He speaks slowly, as if rendering judgment on the little party. "You can stay as long as you like." He crosses over to the bar and yanks up a bottle of expensive brandy. He places it loudly in the center of the table, makes a kind of half bow and leaves.

"Charming dinner companion," Evelyn says. "Such a cosmopolitan fellow. Makes you want to travel to the Seychelles or anywhere with him."

"I thought he was great," Pam says.

"Very capable," Ned agrees. "You see how he docked this thing?"

"He converses like he docks," Evelyn continues.

"Oh, I don't know. Maybe you have to rope him in."

"Yes, yes, that's it exactly. You have to rope him in. Help him out to bring him close to you."

"Pamy!" Ned says too loudly.

I get up and find at the bar six small shot glasses that can serve for the brandy. Rather awkwardly I pour each glass by walking around the outside of the table.

Ned holds up his would-be brandy snifter, ""To young Spendip's smashing victory. To American honor and victory!' Ned shouts and then smacks back the full shot. "Say, that's not half bad stuff. Not half bad. Paul, gimme some more of it."

CHAPTER 32

When the dinner party breaks up Pam and I go visit Waldo who sits up in bed and reads a fat paperback on the Kennedy assassination.

"You know there definitely was some hankpanky with this," Waldo pats the cover of the book. "You all have a splendid meal?"

"Exciting," I answer. "How about you?"

"So, so. I'm feeling stronger, but I'm still running a fever. I can always tell—a certain lethargy, a kind of feeling that it might be better to stay in bed. You know, that kind of thing."

"Captain George was wonderful," Pam says, "He eats fish heads, just like that. He puts them in his mouth and squnches them up as if they were delicious."

"I've hear fish cheeks are the best part. Head, I'm. . . whole heads, maybe not."

We fall into peculiar silence standing by Waldo's bed. Finally Pan says quietly, as if to break the spell. "Mikey's ready, I think."

"You've talked with him?" Waldo asks.

"No, but Paul says he's ready, don't you, Paul?"

"Sure."

"Well, good. Column will write itself, won't it, while we're here. We can put it on the cable or phone it in, or mail it in and run a week or two behind. I don't think it makes much difference."

"You're not interested in scooping the opposition?"

"Snelly, who is our opposition? I've given that a lot of thought lately. And I don't have a clear answer. In the absence of clear answers, I'll guess I'll go back to my reading. It's like a thriller." He says, waving us toward the door.

"You want anything?" I ask as we are leaving.

"My wife's supposed to take care of me," Waldo says not looking up from the paperback.

Pam does not come back to the hotel with me. Apparently at Evelyn's insistence. Can it be home rules will apply on the other side of the world? In the very center of hustledom?

Vera seems uninterested in the question.

"Lotta poor people around here, you know that?" she says coming into my room through the fire door.

So Calderon's little educational campaign has made something of an impression. "He took you to some dirt-floored shacks, did he?"

"Yeah, yeah," Vera says, "course I seen a lotta places without plumbing. Not so many kids around, though. Lotta kids here. Everybody's a kid here. Not my idea of a tour of this city."

"What did Mikey think?"

"He liked it. He was pretty busy working out a twist in the Philador. I don't think he noticed. I began thinkin' it wasn't such a hot idea getting him upset before the matches. You don't think Calderon did it deliberately, do you?"

"Possibly. I don't know."

"Well, if dinner tomorra is going to be a re-run, I'm not going. Neither is Mikey."

"Dinner I think will be quite the opposite. A glimpse of Philippine luxury and high life," I say, wondering myself if Garcia really qualifies for that category. "I don't think you should worry about that."

"I'm not so sure Mikey needs that either. Maybe betta we stay here. Eat quietly in the hotel."

"I think we can come back early, if that's an issue."

"The only issue not getting Mikey's concentration fouled up. Ya understand?"

"Sure."

"Really? Do ya really? I don't think nobody understand except me and Mikey. We been to a lotta matches for a long time. And the few days before a tournament, they gotta be quiet, and, and, . . ." Vera stops for a while, apparently weighing things carefully. "And non-political. Something political going on here. Something political."

"I agree."

"You do, eh? Then you know something?"

"Not really. Except maybe there is some political connection between Calderon and Garcia and maybe Mendoza and maybe Mohrstein."

"Mohrstein? He's back in the Soviet Union."

"Maybe, or maybe he's here. Waldo says nobody knows where he is. The Russians say he was kidnapped."

"And by Garcia?"

"I doubt that," I answer, laughing.

"Maybe I'm gettin' Mikey into something he shouldn't be gettin' into."

"How are you doing that?"

"By agreeing to go to this dinner tomorra."

"So cancel out. Garcia will understand."

"Yeah, maybe we better do that. But you think we can be back here early?"

"Sure."

"Mohrstein's missing?"

"Maybe."

"We don't have ta stay long, right?"

"Vera, we don't have to go."

"You think we oughta go?"

"Well," I reflect a bit, "I'm sure it will be interesting."

"Interesting," Vera seems to turn the word over in her mind. "Yeah, interesting." She sighs, as if in the next few seconds she will impart some burdensome secret to me. But before she speaks, Mikey is at the doorway.

"I got the answer to closing the bishop file in the Dutch. You wanta see it?"

And they gather each other up and are gone.

Chapter 33

Garcia's house is a kind of multi-level, rattan antique shop with an extraordinary view of Manila and the bay. The sunken living room is strewn with rattan couches and chairs mounded over with thick blood-red bolsters and cushions. Wicker birdcages twirl slowly from their ropes attached to thick beams some thirty feet overhead. There are low stone tables and passing directly through the center of the room is small stream, a little river that moves silently but clearly across and around specially arranged rocks.

Two thirds of the way across the living room there is a jutting second level holding a large oval dining table and twelve chairs. Extending up from that level is a circular wrought iron staircase that leads to a wide balcony following the contours of the outer wall of the house. It is clear that further up the hillside there are other rooms that attach to this central living-dining space through a corridor at the south end of the upper interior balcony. The wall facing Manila is glass from floor to ceiling.

Garcia, shirtless, wearing a sarong tied with a rope, stands on the upper balcony and motions for us to come up. His skin is very tan and almost, it seems, injected with something to stretch it taut. I imagine for a while that he takes massive doses of cortisone.

"I do concede," Garcia says much too loudly, as if he is already drunk or hyper stimulated, "that the benefit of this country or, rather, the future of this country—far from my own benefit or future—rests with these young stalwarts in the mountains." Garcia points to four sullen young men in jeans and T shirts at the other end of the balcony. "They're the only ones who really seem to care. What is Marcos but a pale imitation of me, with lots more power and fewer appetites? Ah, his poor kidneys. And Imelda smells, did you know it? At that time of the month her odor is all over Luzon. I can come here at night and catch a whiff of her. And outside it's positively overwhelming. She stinks to high heaven. The trouble with most women."

I wonder how Vera is enjoying this. Pam seems transfixed elsewhere. Is she watching the troops on the balcony? Clearly she seems to be staring at them, but there is a goofy-jawed attention to her stare, as if the vision rested somewhere about halfway up in the air, halfway to the fellows holding their arms and listening to Garcia and watching us with such skepticism.

"Do come up here, and we can all go outside. The air is very clean tonight," he laughs. "Maybe Imelda is in America—where she belongs. Really! Doesn't she? In a condominium in Houston, or in a houseboat, in a mansion in New Jersey—isn't that so?"

Suddenly Garcia points beyond us and shouts, "Reyle! You lead them up. Bring them to the heights—where they couldn't go without your guidance."

Calderon has been sitting in the back of us, near a polished copper chimney that opens over a circular fireplace. He gets up rather grudgingly and steps across the river to take us up. "Good evening," Reyle says quietly, "I'm afraid Silberio is overly stimulated by proximity to real fighters, rather than those sluggish Metro Manila guards."

"Whadya mean?" Vera says.

"I mean Silberio has probably taken too much of whatever he takes when the New Peoples Army comes here."

"These are guerrillas?" Vera asks.

"He thinks they are. I suppose I think they are. They think they are. So, let's say they are."

"Are they gonna kill us?" Vera asks.

Reyle laughs. "That's a good question. Maybe after dinner they'll tell us."

"I'm serious, 'cause we just came to dinner. We didn't come to get involved in some guerrilla war. Ya understand?"

"Mrs. Spendip," Garcia bellows out, "this is my home. My home. Welcome to my home. Here my rules prevail, and anyone who comes to my home is peaceful, is upright, is dependable, is happy, and is unarmed. Isn't that correct?" He turns to the troops at the other end of the balcony, but they seem to ignore his speech. "In any event, I promise you that tonight the quarrels of my sad country are suspended, suspended between hope at one end." He points to the troops, "and real delivery at the other." He gestures toward Mikey, who is earnestly studying the guerrillas on the balcony. He seems quite interested in them. "But do come up before we lose the sunset. The last light over my bay is the grandest light in all this planet. There are drinks on the dining table. Pick one up and do hurry. Do hurry."

The invitation to drink brings the fellows from the mountains across the balcony and quickly down the circular stairway, so that they get to the dining table just as we do from the level below. There is an awkward moment or two, when it is not clear if we should introduce ourselves. Garcia solves the threatened impropriety.

"You are looking at Mr. A, Mr. B, Mr. C and Commander 6. Fine looking fellows, aren't they? My country is assured in their strong grip, don't you agree? And, and—wonderful to say—since most of them have been fighting in the mountains since they were ten or so, almost none of them speaks anything approach Metro Manila's English. So you can call them anything you like and none will be the wiser. Will they, eh Commander 6?" Garcia leans over his railing. "But get your drinks and come up."

The drinks are tall Planters Punches and very, very strong. Mr. A offers one to Mikey who immediately accepts. A wears an impressive knife holder on his belt. I can see traces of a thick wooden handle and what looks to be a curved, fold-out blade. Something like a linoleum knife.

CHAPTER 33

"Don't drink that," Vera says.

"I know. I know," Mikey says, sipping to see what it tastes like. "Tastes great!"

"Yeah, well, just don't drink it." Vera refuses hers. "Come on." She starts up the circular staircase.

Mr. B offers to shake Mikey's hand. Almost involuntarily Mikey looks around for Vera, but she is midway up the stairway. They shake hands. B half bows, then throws one arm around Mikey's shoulder, as if to welcome him into their brotherhood of insurrection. Mikey takes a long drink and smiles.

Pam picks up her drink. "Oh, it smells like Florida," she says, suddenly turning back waves of nostalgia, I can tell.

"Well, it ain't Florida," I answer.

"Yes. Yes, I understand that."

"Unless there is a Tampa Liberation Front. Maybe there is. Probably there is, but Garcia is one of a kind."

"I don't think so," Pam answers, "but we're each one of a kind, I guess. Isn't that the case?"

"Let's go upstairs."

"Mikey!" Vera shouts from the balcony. "Come on up here, and I told ya to stop drinkin' that."

Mikey looks up at his mother, then at his new companions. They clearly seem puzzled by these directives from above. "Yeah, yeah," Mikey finally says, and still holding his drink he motions to the troops to climb the stairs. Each of them picks up another drink and then begins sprinting up the steps, holding the drinks out to avoid spilling them. A game, apparently: run with two drinks to the top of the monument and there, through the narrow, four-person space, out through the small slat window, find—what? True liberation?

"We shall go outside. And then I will show you my splendid garden, my splendid statues," Garcia says. He leans over and embraces Pam. I wonder if body lotion, tanning cream or dye, will rub off on her lavender blouse from the Central Market. "So good to see you, Miss Snow. And how is your father? I don't believe I ever talked directly with him, but my relatives did. Certainly did. I see the boys are up to their usual tricks." Garcia waves at the troops who have moved beyond him, glass in each hand.

The outside balcony is far wider than the inside one, really a wooden deck extending as a roof to the lower level of the house, and then a narrower bridge to the upper levels further up the hill. The main room inside had been cooler, but even the steamy outside air is not unpleasant. Or perhaps the Planters Punch has allowed me to make adjustments. Mikey has gone up ahead with the troops, who now unpack what look to be automatic rifles from a collection of them on the second tier.

I catch up with Garcia. "Are those real?" I ask pointing at the rifles.

"Ah, yes," Garcia answers.

"I thought your guests were unarmed."

"Inside they are, usually—unless I forget. Is Spendip a gun buff?"

I am almost afraid to answer, so intent does Mikey seem on the display presented to him. B kneels down and proceeds to demonstrate how to field strip the weapon.

"What kind of rifle is it?" I ask Garcia who calls out the question in Tagalog to C standing by the stack of weapons.

"He says, an AK-47, a fresh batch."

"Are you the contractor?"

"Mr. Snell," Garcia takes hold of my shoulder, pushes rather hard against it, as if he really needs support, or is testing me in some way. "I am used in all sorts of ways by these people. All sorts of ways. How they use me!"

"I thought you might be hedging your bets against their takeover."

"Sometimes I tried to convince myself of that. It's by far the best way to look at it. But in point of fact, my motivations, one or the other, make no difference to them now. Or to me. What's done is done. And cannot be undone, ever—or at least not peacefully or even satisfactorily. So I am resolved, good Buddhist that I am,"

Garcia laughs, "to yield to what I cannot change or alter anyway. To flow away with these fellows and see what comes of it."

"Mikey!" Vera shouts again, "be careful with those things. And stop drinking."

Mikey doesn't answer, merely waves his hand at her, as if she were an annoying child he needed to calm by petting.

"Miss Snow," Garcia says, "if you look beyond that ridge you can see the furthest tip of Corregidor. Do you know about Corregidor?"

Pam smiles and nods.

"A lot of butchery there," Garcia says. "My aim, apart from their aim," he motions to the troops, "my aim is quite modest, Mr. Snell—to preserve a bit of flexibility a bit of venue (such a good word, *venue*) in a world of increasing stricture. Another good work: *stricture*. And preserving a little venue sometimes requires me to link arms, not to say legs, torsos, or what have you with those who have somewhat antithetical views of the world."

"Especially if they are younger," I add.

"Because they are younger. Our obligations to youth—that is what this dinner is all about."

"I thought it was about Philippine hospitality."

"Of course. Of course," Garcia says. "That is the beginning of everything. Everything. But everything has its price, doesn't it, Mrs. Spendip?"

Vera looks at Garcia and smiles too broadly, then continues to watch Mikey.

"Where's Cavite?" Pam says.

"You're interested in Cavite?" Garcia answers, "How remarkable. What is the attraction?"

"The Spanish fleet was there when Dewey came in. They Spanish boats moved there to save Manila from shelling. I remember reading that, studying that. They would have been safer under their own artillery in Manila, but they didn't think the city should be shelled."

"Exactly—the very reason they lost!" Garcia says. He points along the bay line to a little knob sticking out of the water. "On the other side of that, about three more miles, hidden in the fog. Are you an aficionado of naval battles?"

"My daddy used to read to me about Admiral Dewey and the Spanish fleet. Sometimes at the ranch we would read for hours and hours, if it was raining, during the rainy season."

"On hot nights like these," Garcia says. "Such hot nights. Let's take off our clothes." He immediately unties his rope belt and drops the sarong, revealing only a purple G-string-modified jock strap. "You see on a night like this," Garcia says. But Pam is still watching the fog bank and Vera has moved up the walk way to get closer to Mikey who is bent over now, assembling the weapon under the enthusiastic directions of B.

"It is my fate to be unappreciated by people whose opinions I value greatly," Garcia says suavely, gathering up his sarong and retying it.

"I didn't know you valued Vera's opinions so highly," I answer, "or my own."

"Well, she is a headstrong, but rather clear-minded woman, and those are hard to find, aren't they, Mr. Snell?"

"Dewey didn't lose a single man," Pam says. "Four hours of shelling not even a hit on his forces."

"Something of an exaggeration, but in the main acceptable. The Spanish, bless them, were less than competent in their tasks. Rather like those fellows." He points to the group around Mikey. "They had guns on Corregidor and when they opened up on Dewey, they were about a mile short, so they 'corrected' their sights on the next shots. This time they were miles long. Dewey was probably encouraged at that point, unlike me." Garcia concludes hoping to recoup in history what he had lost in flesh display.

"They aren't going to shoot those things, are they?" Vera asks.

"Rest assured, they will not. Gunfire would attract attention, and whatever else those fellows want right now, attention does not figure in their game. On the other hand, they do seem to be

CHAPTER 33

drinking a bit. But then they always do here. Who was it said alcohol and gunpowder make a very combustible mixture? Or was it alcohol and gasoline?"

"Mikey!" Vera shouts, "stop drinking that!"

Mikey and his new buddies merely laugh at this last imploring.

"I don't believe what is happening here," Vera says.

"There's really nothing to worry about," Garcia insists. "We're all as innocent as farm animals here. But you haven't really seen my statuary and the light is failing. Let's be quick about it."

"Mikey, come on!" Vera shouts, but Mikey merely waves her down again.

"Let him play with his companions. He appears to be a true armament fan."

Garcia leads down an outside redwood stairway. The garden slopes away from the house, and the grass on the hillside is treacherous. We have to inch down sideways. Once we are off the slope we have trouble seeing.

"These three," Garcia points to three white alabaster monkeys, "were commissioned by friends of mine when I started the main portion of the house. They represent the variant Filipino style on the standard see no evil, and so forth. Actually, they've become one of less favorite displays."

Vera stumbles, and gets up after Pam and I pull on her right arm. She decides to go back into the house and Garcia shows her a special path back to the lower level.

"It is treacherous, isn't it?" Garcia says after she leaves.

"Yes," Pam answers, "very treacherous. Daddy says life here is very treacherous too."

"A wise man," Garcia answers. "And now for one of my favorites."

He leads us beyond three small pine trees to a fairly level area. There is a small white cement pool and beside a statue of a four-foot tall angel of rather epicene features, except for the foot-long erect phallus coming from the middle of the sculpture.

"Now, Miss Snow, you must tell me. Other young ladies I've had out here insist they get wet looking at this statue. Is that the case really?"

Pam looks at the statue all right, but I recognize the drifted-off gaze that comes into her eyes.

"You seem impressed," Garcia says.

But Pam is un-conversational.

"Are you stunned? Is that it? Overwhelmed?" Garcia laughs.

For a moment I can feel a rising fear, surge of anxiety that she might be once again listening to those private voices that snap off the outside world. I move closer to her, worried that she might fall asleep once again.

But at the worst moment of worry, Pam says clearly, "Dewey never had any intention of helping Aguinaldo, did he? I mean he said he was going to and he brought him from Hong Kong, but when it became critical, Dewey cooperated with the Spanish against the Filipinos who wanted independence, didn't he?"

"I didn't realize you were such a history buff," Garcia says, "didn't know young Spendip was such a weapons buff. What are we going to do with both of you? I wonder. Give Mikey ancient weapons and let him reenact the war for you, firing over the American's heads while they advance from Cavite, pretending to be firing at the Spanish, but actually shelling a deserted fort, as per worked-out instructions."

"Yes," Pam says, "I've heard that, a kind of mock battle to confuse the Filipinos into thinking the U.S. was really going to liberate Luzon from Spanish rule."

"I ought to get you a job at one of our sorry universities. But you haven't answered my question about the statue."

"Oh, I don't get wet, not very much anyway. Not lately anyway. Not ever actually," Pam says easily.

"I see," Garcia says, "perhaps it is dinner time. Let's go back up."

Chapter 34

On the path Pam continues her recitation. "And when they finally caught Aguinaldo, it was through a ruse or something, wasn't it? A phony ceasefire."

"Yes, a typically American trick," Garcia says. "The white flag of decimation. You seem to know a great deal about our miserable history."

"Daddy used to read to me about the Spanish-American war. But before I came I was reading a good history of the Philippines."

"How industrious," Garcia says. "I suggest you wash up down here," Garcia says, when we get to the living room. Then come up. I'll be getting the others to the table. Sometimes it's an iffy proposition, I can tell you."

It must have been with the lure of an extra drink that Garcia got the outside decks cleared, for we sit with fresh Planters Punches at each place. Mikey sits in the middle of his new armament buddies. Vera sits directly opposite and conspicuously puts her drink to one side. She motions to Mikey he ought to do likewise, but he ignores the directive. B brings a 45 caliber pistol on to the table and quickly disassembles it, showing Mikey how each part, each spring, fits together. Pam has her hands palms down on the table as if to make it rise in a séance. Her forearms extend too far on the table cloth and she looks momentarily like flesh sphinx watching the NPA fighters. Garcia, clearly unhappy with the pistol on his table, never the less deals with the problem by swilling feverishly at his Planters Punch. When he's through, he signals to Vera to hand him her drink. She does so and then reaches for Mikey's but C snatches it up before can put hands on it. He holds it away and shakes his finger at her. Then he hands it to Mikey who takes a long quaff.

"Well, I see we've brought our entertainment to the table. Really! You really go much too far in these matters, Commander 6. Have you lost control of your group?" Garcia's mix of desperation and obsequiousness impresses no one.

"Yes, we need to deal with the reason for this dinner," Calderon says too loudly. He sits next to Pam, who has yet to move from her frozen Sphinx position.

"What reason?" Vera asks.

"Ah, such charming naiveté," Garcia says to Vera, nodding at her in a way that suggests they both know perfectly well what is to follow.

Two Filipino women bring in platters of mounds of yellow rice and seafood, mostly shell fish.

"Mikey," Calderon says, "this is Commander 6."

"We met. We met. I know him," Mikey says, still fiddling with the strewn parts of the 45.

"Would you like sometime to meet Commander 2?"

"Sure. Why not? I like these guys. They know a lot of stuff about these." He fits a long spring into a dark carbon tube that apparently fits into the gun's disassembled barrel.

"I would like you to have that opportunity. So would he. He is essential to our purposes. Do you understand?"

Mikey continues the assembly of the weapon until both B and C simply take hold of Mikey's wrists and compel him to set the partial pistol down. They indicate he should listen to Calderon.

"What's with the physical stuff?" Vera says hotly, looking at Garcia.

"It's okay. It's okay. These guys are okay," Mikey smiles and laughs with B and C.

CHAPTER 34

"You can help us. You can help Commander 2. Would you be willing to do that?"

Mikey stirs his rice, takes another drink of punch.

"Stop that!" Vera shouts.

Suddenly Pam says, releasing the table, "Didn't they use water torture during the war?"

"Which war?" I ask, heartened that Pam has apparently rejoined us.

"Miss Snow's war, what else? Yes, my dear, you are once again entirely accurate. General Funston, I believe, the grand interrogator. You force water down a fellow's throat. You fill him up till it's just about to explode its way into his lungs, you flood it down his throat so that it comes out his nose and pretty soon he's ready to tell you anything."

"You seem to show a great deal of enthusiasm for the topic, a great deal of knowledge," I add.

"Oh probably no more than Miss Snow, certainly not more accurate. "Garcia nods to Pam. "But if to create a bit of flexibility, a bit of venue during these times, if we have to link arms with General Ver, so be it. Filipinos are not so judgmental and hidebound as you Americans."

"General Ver?"

"Marcos's Chief of Police, his chief inquisitor, interrogator, and torturer." Calderon says.

"And you're linking arms with him?" I ask.

"A figure of speech for playing his games, using his tactics on occasion, as the occasion arises," Garcia says slowly, then takes another long slug from Vera's drink.

"The political lines seem to be blurring."

"Not blurring. How could these fellows," Garcia motions to the NPA troops, "be indefinite? Not likely is it?"

"There's nothing indefinite about the NPA," Calderon says.

"In a struggle like this one, when it gets most intense, it may be difficult, perhaps impossible, to tell one side from the other. The struggle itself makes the rules. But you needn't worry about that Mr. Snell, should you? Only those Olympian few who claim to sit outside of history need to do that. Only those privileged few." Garcia smiles toward Calderon. "For the rest of us, it's business as usual. Up with the sun. Murder all day long, till an evening repast, a little interim of rest."

"And Commander 2?" Calderon says.

I'm not sure whether Mikey has followed any of this. Pam has cocked her head, as if absorbing every detail.

"Ah yes, the venerable Commander 2. Incidentally not the sort of fellow to enjoy even such a tame dinner as this. Purist. Puritanical and so forth. Some of these fellows in the mountains become, ah, what shall we say: inflexible? I have no doubt, however, where the future belongs. But inflexible—not the sort of people you would have much to do with for any reason. More evidence of their natural governing talents, I suppose. But about Commander 2, Mikey. The situation is as follows. Three weeks ago in a routine roundup north of here, a rather routine arrest of a mass of villagers, routine incarceration, Marcos landed Commander 2. Although he hardly knows it, at least not yet. Sometimes the processing of these roundups takes a week, sometimes a month, once, a half year. Nothing so far as we know is being done to resolve the issue with the two hundred presently under arrest. Now as soon as he was arrested, Commander 2 presented himself to the authorities as a student and as a second for Mr . Calderon—his premier second, which, indeed, he may be. Isn't that right, Reyle?"

The NPA group seems bored with Garcia's recitation. It may be that Mikey will go back to his pistol.

"At the same time, and according to plans worked out for such a contingency, Mr. Calderon reported to the authorities here that his second was missing, and that would make his attempts in the Interzonals somewhat deficient, or less than highest quality, given the nature of international competition nowadays. Am I getting it right, Reyle? But just as naturally the officials here, being good Filipinos, were not much interested in a case in the northern area, and indeed are not much interested in anything, unless one of two

CHAPTER 34

things happens. And Mikey you ought to pay attention to this, since this where you come in. If one of two things happens: one, either a lot of money changes hands at all levels here in Metro Manila and in the north, so that officials in both places are motivated to expedite matters and release Mr. Calderon's second. And we are naturally enough pursuing that route, although lately we've had a bit less money that we had planned on to spread around." Garcia smiles at Vera, and Mikey watches that smile very carefully. "Or two, if official pressure is brought to bear on the issue. If, for example, a single telephone call came out of Malacanang Palace, the matter could be settled in an hour. But to stimulate officials of that rank we would need something of real magnitude, something of what passes in this sad country for a public opinion matter. Now, if Mr. Calderon in the early rounds of the tournament achieves a spectacular victory, then he might be able to suggest, discretely of course, that his second's presence was essential for his continuance in the tournament. Or he might suggest, not so discretely, in public that the good President's arbitrary arrest policy has gathered up his second and prevented the Filipino people from seeing one of their own become a challenger for Atashian's title. He could threat to discuss this in public. A phone call might follow immediately. Especially since our very macho President lately seems intent on proving Filipino worth in the world. Are things becoming clear, Mikey?"

"Yeah, I'd have ta say they're crystal clear," Mikey says.

"Well, what do you think?" Garcia says.

"I would return the point when we meet for the second time in the tournament," Calderon says quickly. "So at least you'd be even on points with me."

"Probably one down," Mikey says, not smiling.

"It might be true that you could beat me twice in one tournament, but statistically that doesn't have a high probability, does it?"

"Mikey don't care for statistics," Vera says.

Garcia looks annoyed.

"Didn't some senator compare the Filipinos to wild horses that had to be broken before they could be ridden?" Pam says.

"Beveridge," Garcia says. "Your knowledge continues to dazzle me, Miss Snow."

"You got mine already," Vera says.

"Not that kind of beverage," Garcia laughs. "The distinguished senator from, where was it? The Midwest someplace. During the hearings about General Funston, he said something outrageous about the Filipino people needing American discipline before they took up democracy. Yes, we need to be broken like a horse. And how these have done it!" Garcia says pointing to the NPA group. "How they have broken me."

"It could be argued the Russians throw points all the time," Calderon says. "We might be simply countering what they do every day in every tournament."

"Maybe," Mikey says, "but there's no percentage in our arrangement."

"Only that I get my second and they get their Commander 2."

"And our sad country gets another chance to eliminate its dictator, its excesses," Garcia adds. "Surely, Spendip, those are important percentages. Surely they mean something to you. Surely the welfare of your new friends means something to you."

Mikey shrugs but doesn't say anything; then he looks at me. "What do you think?"

After a moment I say, "I think it might be a scam. A cheap way, a novel way, to get a point. How do you know Reyle won't play for a win later on, and the point you gave away will be the difference between winning and losing the challenge?"

"Such a cynic, Mr. Snell. Disgraceful!" Garcia says. "Whatever else is going on here, I can assure you that simply trying to build up Reyle's score is not in anyone's mind. In no one's mind."

"Not even Reyle's?" I ask.

"I resent that, Mr. Snell," Calderon says somewhat wearily.

"You resent it, but I notice you don't repudiate it."

CHAPTER 34

"It don't make any difference," Mikey says. "The first four players could throw him their games and he'd still end up last. He hasn't got a chance, with or without my point."

"Tactful as always," Garcia says, "and more than a little arrogant."

"And probably accurate," Vera says.

"So where are we?" Garcia asks.

"Eating our rice," Pam answers. And we do that. There are bits of ginger and chicken tucked away in the mounds.

After a few minutes B turns to Mikey and says in awkward English, "You please help us, please." Mikey waves him down with a hand gesture.

The two women servers come back with salad plates, bits of cantaloupe and pineapple and avocado spread out on sheets of lettuce. Garcia orders beer for everyone and ten bottles of San Miguel quickly appear.

Mikey says, "I knew there was something wrong with the Mohrstein game. You worked something out with him, didn't ya?"

"That's true," Calderon says, "you're the first person to notice it—probably the only person."

"I knew it. I knew it. Mohrstein just doesn't move like that. The rhythm, the emphasis, the whole style was wrong. It leaps out at ya. I knew it. I knew it."

"Something more carefully could be worked out," Garcia says.

"It would have to be a whole lot better than the Mohrstein game, a whole lot better."

"Then you're willing?" Calderon says anxiously.

"I don't know," Mikey answers.

B repeats his injunction for help, but again Mikey waves him down. "Let's finish putting the 45 together," Mikey says and B obligingly leans over and indicates which pieces go where.

When the gun is back together, Mikey points it at me. "You think it's a scam, a trick?"

"Will you point that someplace else?" I ask. "Either way it seems to me they've gotten you upset enough to maybe get a point out of it, haven't they?"

"Mr. Snell, you really amaze and appall me. Do you want me to go back through it all again, would that help? You persist in seeing this as a very limited operation to enhance Reyle's chances—which even Mr. Spendip concedes are rather limited, with or without such elaborate machinations. Why not accept the situation as we have described it? What can be your objection? Why are you so skeptical?"

"Well, let's see. You've asked us to believe in Commander 2 up north in jail some place. Why not call up the Palace and demand action? Reyle's the best chess player in the Philippines, in all of Southeast Asia—that ought to give him clout enough at the Palace. How can one more game make a bit of difference?"

"You know nothing about the Philippines, nothing about the Palace, nothing about our situation."

"That's true. I sure as hell know nothing about what is really going on here. Nothing at all."

"You don't understand the necessary personal psychology of getting things done here. And the accident of public pressure or threatened public pressure, or the momentary elation of victory. The little intoxication that might flow through our leadership, if they actually thought the Philippines was going to achieve a challenger to the Championship. All avenues have to be pursued. And all at once. Of course pressure is being brought to bear now, but not enough and not fast enough. We have deadlines of sorts."

"Like what?" I ask.

"When Mikey and Reyle will meet for the first time, for example, and when the thorough processing of the arrestees will begin, or when the entire government topples, to be replaced by a stringent gang led by Imelda and Kokoy or any of his wonderful friends." Calderon says.

CHAPTER 34

"Reyle's prospects, his score, is the least of the worries here—the absolute minimum least. Even Mikey concedes that. Don't you?" Garcia says.

But Mikey doesn't answer.

"It was Douglas MacArthur's daddy that eventually subdued the Philippines, wasn't it?" Pam says.

"Score another point for Miss Snow's historical knowledge. Indeed it was and a far more dashing figure than the son, and far more ruthless, I suspect. In the MacArthur tradition then, is that it, Mikey?"

"I'd like to try field-stripping the rifle again, up there." Mikey points toward the roof.

"Well, I'm sure you can. Absolutely sure that can be arranged, but I really think we need to discuss what you are planning to do with regard—"

"All right! All right!" Vera suddenly shouts. "You had your little chance to make a pitch and you made it and it's time for Mikey to make up his own mind. And he don't have to do that, do ya Mikey, now or any time that you say, does he?"

"In view of the time constraints," Garcia says.

"If we are going to work something out," Calderon continues, "we really need to know whether we can get started on working it out. I must insist on that."

Mikey gets up from the table as do A, B, and C. Holding the 45, Mikey quickly walks toward the staircase, then sprints up a few steps. On the first turn he swivels back and through the bars, softly says to Calderon, "You work something out. I'll look at it. I'll try to help these guys." Then he runs up the remaining steps, sprints down the balcony and the doorway to the roof.

"There's your answer," Garcia says to Calderon. "There's your answer."

"It's absurd," I cannot stop myself from observing.

"Absurd, ya think it's absurd?" Vera says in a way that signals interest in my terminology, if not my sentiments.

'Mr. Snell, Mr. Snell!" The voice is quite strange, improbably, but there is Commander 6 standing and speaking my name in English—rather clear, unaccented English. "You had better shut up. You had better. You really had better."

"Didn't one of the American Governors of the Philippines become President?" Pam says, hands still on the table like the Sphinx of Metro Manila.

"Taft," Garcia answers. "Taft. Taft," Garcia repeats, "or maybe Leonard Wood. Did he become President?"

Chapter 35

"How much are they paying?" I ask Vera through the fire door at noon the next day.

"What the hell are ya sayin'?"

"What the hell are you doing? I really thought you were all the way behind Mikey's career."

"I am. I don't know what ya talkin' about."

"You have no idea?"

"Nah. None."

"You didn't say a word about the little proposition yesterday. Last night's festivities didn't bother you a bit."

"Mikey thinks it's a game. I knew he wasn't goin' for it. I told 'em they could make their pitch."

"Even if it screws up his concentration?"

"Why don't ya let me worry about that? You got enough problems without taking on Mikey. Why don't ya just write your columns and leave us alone?"

"What are my problems?"

Vera points toward the bay, in the general direction of the yachts.

"Okay, okay. But for somebody who worries about whether Mikey gets enough sleep, for somebody who gives me sermons on concentration and remaining non-political, you seem pretty casual about the psychological warfare going on here."

"Ya just lemme worry about that. We can handle that. We have handled it. Now if you don't mind, I'll just close this door. I got some things to do." Vera eases the fire door shut, and I hear the levers come down, sealing it.

I decide that Vera has been recruited. And if Vera has been recruited, can Mikey be far behind? Evidently not, for at two o'clock he comes down to the pool and tries to recruit me.

"I need ya take me to Calderon's place," he says, still ashen in the burnishing Manila sun, still wearing jeans and polo shirt. He carries his climate everywhere he goes, I decide. I once knew a fellow in the Coast Guard who made judgments of people by their complexions. Mikey would have qualified for revered status in the fellow's listing of acceptable professions, acceptable character—"Poolhall. Very poolhall. Never try to hustle this type."

"You need me?"

"Yeah, I don't know where it is."

"And so you need a guide."

"Well, they want you to be there, too. They think you're opposed."

"You're not opposed?"

"I want ta look at what they got for a game. It's an interesting problem. I know I can set up a better game than Mohrstein did. That's for sure. And I get the point back. The Russkies do it all the time. And maybe I get one of the AK-47s."

"What do you want with an AK-47?"

"Scare the shit out of people in D.C.," he says jovially.

"They aren't legal. You'd never get it out of the airport."

"I know that. I know that. Come on, show me where Calderon's place is."

"Can we take Pam?"

"Nah, she'd be bored. We're just going over a game, makin' sure everything goes smoothly."

"Are you just going to do it? You talk as if making things run smoothly was the only consideration at this point."

"I want to see what they come up with. Now hurry up."

CHAPTER 35

I think about calling Pam from my room but decide she would indeed be bored. I expect to be bored myself. But at the outset, at least, nothing is boring. First off there is a usual, gagging, jostling, terrifying Jeepney ride to Calderon's hotel. And then once we are there, more than a little surprise: Mendoza sits on the second bed in the semi-maroon darkness.

"Hello," he says, getting up to shake hands with Mikey.

"I didn't think you could get into the Philippines," I say.

"I'm not in the Philippines. I'm in Malaysia, in K.L. at my brother's place. Do you see?" he laughs.

"And you came in by parachute?"

"Something like that."

Calderon sits with his back to us at the rattan desk in the far corner. Beside him a tall, spindly-looking fellow looks over his shoulder. They appear to be working on a document of some kind.

"The game will be finished in a minute," Mendoza says.

"What did they work up?" Mikey asks.

"I'm not sure. They're putting the final touches on it now. But it's reasonable. Not inspired, but reasonable. And that's all it has to be."

"Dr. Mohrstein," Mikey says, walking up to the tall fellow. "I always wanted ta shake your hand after a victory, but I'm still not gonna get the chance," Mikey says with a strange exuberance.

Mohrstein turns around. He looks as if he's come straight from the Death March. His suit drapes around him, as if trying to find enough bones to hook on. I remember that Mohrstein is a fruitarian.

"Isn't your government looking for you?" I say to no one in particular.

"His government knows exactly where he is," Mendoza assures me.

"So who is looking for him then?"

"Your government and Marcos's," Wicksburg replies, "but neither will find him, I think."

"Probably neither wants to," I continue.

"That's a possible interpretation," Mohrstein says, thoughtfully. "Makes a good bit of sense. So it's just the media that thinks things are terribly critical."

"Let's look at the game. I haven't a lot of time," Mendoza says.

Mohrstein pulls the paper off the desk and brings it over to the first bed, where there is a chess board set up. A kind of Dracula-esque figure in a long blue serge suit, Mohrstein puts the sheet down, takes off his flesh-colored glasses, rubs his nose, then the region below his right ear. "We're planning a Queens pawn opening—"

"How do you know who gets white?" I ask.

"You haven't seen the pairing? They were published this morning," Wicksburg says. "Calderon gets white. They play the first day. It couldn't be better. A good omen!"

"A Queen's pawn with a variant of Queen's Indian Defense," Mohrstein says.

"I almost never play it," Mikey says.

"That's the point. It's going to be one of your patented surprises. But you'll make a small misstep in mid-game, then a terrific defense in the endgame. But finally material will carry the day."

"What kind of misstep?" Mikey says. He starts playing out the moves. "Just like Smyslov-Tal in Riga," Mikey says, quickly going through the first fifteen moves of the opening.

"Exactly," Mohrstein says, impressed evidently by the automatic command Mickey has of MCO. "But now comes the innovation, one that seems actually a pretty good change. I planned on using it myself at some point, but it requires a different style of play. Your style." Mohrstein pushes an unlikely pawn forward, offering it as a gambit. "Now after due consideration, Reyle will accept the pawn and then you get to play some fancy fireworks. A couple of sacrifices here and here," Mohrstein brings down first a knight, then a bishop. "And then Reyle finds this ingenious defense, a massive shift to the back rank of just about everything—very in keeping with his essentially defensive play, don't you think?"

"How about I try this?" Mikey says, moving a rook over.

CHAPTER 35

"Loses even sooner," Mohrstein says. He reels off verbally a series of moves and Mikey nods his head, takes the rook back to its original square.

"We have you doing the following, which seems overwhelming but actually leads, after some very clever, defensive moves, to a wholesale liquidation, putting you right into endgame. But despite the pawn loss, your endgame looks promising, given the mobility you have and solid pawn chain on the King side. However, at long last, Reyle simply demonstrates that he can hold, and the pawn advantage wins. You like it?" Morhstein asks.

"It's a whole lot better than your own 'loss'—who thought that one up?"

"Neither one of us," Mohrstein says ominously. "But that's not important. You are the only one so far to question it."

"This one will be done better," Wicksburg says.

"Ya right about that," Mikey answers, again with a kind of buoyance that seems strange in the cool maroon semi-darkness. Mikey picks up the game sheet, quickly rearranges the pieces and plays through again. When he gets to the mid-game, he stops. "You have me playing this and this, and this," he says, "but I'd play it more naturally in the reverse order. Fill the file first and then bring the Queen in. Leads to the identical position, but it should be done this way. If I bring the Queen over first, we could get into a struggle for the file, if Reyle weren't so passive." Mikey smiles, "So let's reverse the order, okay?"

Mohrstein and Calderon hunch over the board, play through the sequence three times and agree to change the game sheet.

"Then on move thirty-four, Reyle has a check, but you don't let him use it. Why? Seems like the logical thing to do. People will want to know why?"

"What? Using what piece?" Mohrstein asks.

"The rook can come in, 'cause if the bishop takes it, there's a standard sacrifice leading to smothermate in five moves."

"The rook can come in?" Mohrstein says, worried. He plays through to move 34. "You're right. We never saw it. Now what?"

Wicksburg says, "The question is would Reyle have seen it over the board? Isn't that the question? We aren't trying to create a masterpiece. We're trying to duplicate a plausible victory, given the styles of the two players. Reyle isn't looking at this point for counter-attacks, or greater complication. He's looking for simplifications and survival. Why would he want to initiate the morass a peculiar *en prise* check would create? He wouldn't be thinking along those lines."

"Yeah," Mikey says, "and bringing back the knight seems to hold everything and of course there's Reyle with a rook he's gotta move. Okay. Okay. I just wanted us to look at it."

I am impressed and worried that Mikey seems to have taken charge of the game's creation.

"We need to indicate where the pauses are for "study,"" he laughs at the term, "so the forty moves work out all right. And then you figure about twenty more moves in the second session?"

"Twenty-two," Mohrstein says.

"Let's try to cut that back, so we both can get some rest for the next round. Besides we can review it after the first session."

"No," Wicksburg insists, "we've got to know now what's happening and in how many moves. We can't meet again after the tournament has started. We simply can't risk it."

Risk what, I think.

"Okay, okay," Mikey agrees. "Let's take a look at the second session moves."

I sit on the other bed, think about slumping back. Mikey, Wicksburg and Calderon go through the endgame moves. I am aware that Mikey is making changes, adjustments in move order, but mostly their conversation blurs out of comprehension. I don't notice an AK-47 anywhere. Perhaps a disappointment for Mikey?

Why is he so readily agreeing? Surely he knows the value of a full point in the tournament. But there he is cheerfully complying, suggesting changes, enjoying the ritual more than its originators and benefactors.

CHAPTER 35

"I got one other idea," Mikey says as they start to put the board away. "Instead of playing the Queen's pawn first, I want Reyle to play the Queen's bishop pawn—an invitation to English, then I'll answer with pawn to King three, an invitation to the French. Then Reyle can answer with pawn to Queen four and we'll be back on sequence."

"You never play the French defense," Reyle says.

"Right! I want them to start worrying about why I'm offering to go into the French. I want them to spend the next few days worrying themselves sick that I've got some new prepared wrinkles for the French. It'll keep their seconds busy chasing phantoms all week."

Mohrstein laughs, "It has a certain appeal, I suppose. Why not?"

"Okay, then I think we ought to play through it once with the clocks to make sure we got everything down pat," Mikey says.

"Good idea," Wicksburg says, "very thorough."

"Characteristically thorough," Reyle agrees. "Tonight here?"

"Better not be here," Wicksburg says. "We'll find a place and notify you. Leave this evening open."

"Yeah," Mikey says, "now, how about my weapon?"

"Commander 2 left this for you," Mohrstein says, smiling. "But just to play with here. You can put it together a few times, if that is what you want."

"That's what I want," Mikey says, eagerly taking up the suitcase and flipping it on the bed.

It occurs to me from my prone position that I would be a perfect target—easily cut in two by a short burst from such an automatic weapon.

I catch up with Pam in the late afternoon in the would-be wardroom of the yacht. She sits rather glazed-eyed, with a large green fruit drink in front of her.

"Waldo any better?" I ask.

She nods, cocks her head. "Waldo is wonderful. Just wonderful! He took me to lunch today in the Central Market. But then he said he felt tired. But we had a wonderful, wonderful time. He's so attentive. He never leaves me alone for lunch."

"Were we supposed to have lunch?" I ask.

"I don't know, were we?"

"I see. Well, I had to go some place with Mikey. He's going to do it."

"Do what?"

"Toss Calderon the opening point. I can't believe it. And Vera seems happy with that decision."

"What decision?"

"To give the point up. Are you all right?"

"I feel, I feel really quite wonderful. Captain George was telling me about his experiences in the Coast Guard. He's retired from the Coast Guard, did you know that?"

"I didn't know Captain George spoke much at all."

"Well, it's a funny English, a Samoan English, but he was everywhere in the Coast Guard. Everywhere. He was even on icebreakers. I'd love to go on an icebreaker. Way up north on an icebreaker, where it's so cold you can't even urinate outside because it freezes before it hits the ground."

"George tell you that?"

"No. I read that somewhere, or maybe Waldo told me. Waldo is always telling me wonderful things."

"You want to have dinner at the hotel?"

"Let's have dinner in your room."

"Room service, eh?"

"Right. Room service. Service in your room," Pam repeats. "Sometimes the best grapefruit are available only from Room service, did you know that. I think that's true, although I can't be sure."

"Why don't we go to my room and discuss it."

"Yes let's do that. Let's do that."

I put the green drink in the galley refrigerator. Two stewards are asleep in tilted chairs outside the meat locker. We agree to look in on Waldo before we go to the hotel. But he is fast asleep, the paperback on the Kennedy assassination open on his steadily rising and falling stomach.

"Do you think," Pam says when we get to my room, "that there is some part of you hidden down deep that you're afraid to let come out? Some part of you that is terribly shy?"

"Shall we look and see?"

"I'm serious. Some little part of you that thinks if it came out people would begin to laugh. Or maybe if it came out, you'd feel very frightened, or at least upset. Maybe just very tired. It's tiring keeping it from coming out sometimes."

"If you've got something way down deep that I haven't handled, I'd like to get started on finding it," I say reaching for the straps of her sundress.

"No. No, not till after dinner," she says easily.

"Before and after dinner, okay?"

"Sometimes I think it's the anticipation that spoils everything. When I am looking forward to something, then that's when things start to go wrong. I was so looking forward to our trip to New York. You see, and then that little part of me way down deep knew that it couldn't really connect with what was happening there, never really could. It was always staring at what was happening. Amazed maybe, but mostly very, very shy."

"Okay, okay. First a little dinner. What will it be? Roast beef? Salmon steak?" But I recognize it is a losing battle against this increasing distraction. Not even large shrimps cooked in garlic with a massive side order of noodles seems to help. Not even four bottles of San Miguel beer.

After dinner when we are in bed Pam says softly, "I think it might be happening again. I'm afraid of that."

"You can tell when it's coming?"

"Sometimes, not often, but sometimes. And when I can tell, it's much worse. That's what's so frightening about it. It's like, it's like whatever that little part is, it's broken free, floating around and getting stronger and stronger, more and more shy so that sooner or later I know what I really am. Do you know what you really are?"

"I'm here with you."

"Yes, that's true, too. You are here, but where am I?"

"Here in this mammoth bed with me, aren't you?"

"No. No, no. I'm way up north where it's so much cooler, isn't it? Way up north where it's cold enough to sleep the clock around."

"Maybe sleep is the enemy. Maybe we ought to stay awake."

"Yes, stay awake with me. Stay awake with me till tomorrow, will you?"

"Okay. We'll stay awake and then no more buzzes for Pamy, all right?"

"You sound like my father."

"I am your father."

"Oh father, father," Pam says. "What will it be like in the morning? And where will I be?"

"In Connecticut, child."

"Yes, yes—that's where I belong," Pam acknowledges, falling asleep.

Chapter 36

At eleven-thirty I am awakened by insistent knocking on the front door. So Mikey has played through the moves and wants to share his memorization with me, I think, getting into the hotel robe. But it is not Mikey. Rather, little Raul hands me a piece of paper.

"Isn't it a little late for you?" I ask him, but the question only further heightens the interest of the guard on the floor. He gets up from his folding chair. Hurriedly I open the paper.

The note is full of Garcia touches: "I hope I did not disturb your sleep. Inveterate night owl that I am, I cannot conceive of anyone turning in before midnight. Be that as it may, a matter of some urgency has come up regarding the first match. Could you please meet me at the Pensione Filipina, a combination nightclub and hostel not ten minutes from your hotel. Young Raul has been commissioned to show you the way. You owe him nothing more than the considerable I have already given him. I will be at the bar, hopefully by the time you arrive. Thanks so much for enduring this inconvenience."

"Where did you get this note?"

"From my master."

"I know that, but where was he when he gave it to you."

"In Mabini."

"Well, wait for me by the elevator. I'll get dressed."

Pam does not wake up. In fact, I lean over to check her breathing, so inert does she seem. I think about scribbling a note, decide against it, start to exit and realize I must leave her some information. I scrawl the name of the place and tell her I am meeting Garcia. *Home soon* is the way I end the note.

Raul seems intent on getting me directly to the place as quickly as possible. He trots along three blocks of Roxas Boulevard and then turns left into side streets. We pass a huge sort of folk village with open markets still selling goods. Why have I never been here before? Then we come out into a three block area which seems almost dropped out of the suburbs of Jacksonville. Open lawns, heavy trees, and across a vacant lot the quite neon blinking of the Pensione Filipina's sign. Raul points at a wooden latticed door at the corner of the building. "My master is inside, waiting for you." Then he waits and I give him a couple pesos. He turns and sprints off.

There seem to be no cars. No Jeepneys passing by. Not much noise. The vacant lot is covered with heavy gravel and there is no way to walk across it silently. A warning then of imminent intrusion? Is that the reason for the poured gravel? I hear music, guitar and bass, and a straining baritone voice—soft rock tones.

Garcia in dark brown trousers and a green Barong short sleeve shirt stands at the bar. The bar top is implanted with silver dollars over which a half-inch of Lucite has been poured.

"If the truth were known," Garcia says, "I was hoping you weren't coming."

"That's a helluva greeting, after your note. What is happening?"

"Nothing pleasant, that's for sure. I did not arrange this meeting. Commander 6 thought it was imperative. I am merely carrying out my directives, faithful and well-used retainer to the end. If I had it to do all over again, Mr. Snell, I would have declined the original liaisons, beguiling as they were, as thrilling as they were. I continue to be used disgracefully. But I separate myself from what is going on here tonight. You must understand that. I am not involved, but of course I am. And here you are, involved now, too."

"What is happening?"

"Savor that statement, Mr. Snell. Savor it. Believe me it's the noblest thing you will have uttered in life. You want to know what is happening. So be it. Let's get on with it."

"With what?"

"Follow me, Mr. Snell. And say goodbye to your childhood."

"Sometimes you more than a ham," I answer following Garcia out the bar.

We go up a highly polished wooden staircase to a second floor. There is very little light. The walls are polished, dark-stained mahogany and only a teardrop illumination of twenty-watt lightbulbs mark a few of the doorways off the hall.

"Rooms for hire, but nobody uses them now. Lent to me for four hours." Garcia says, "But it's too hot and no air-conditioning. Ours is the second to last on the right."

"Is Commander 6 waiting for us there?"

"Yes. And others."

I stop midway down and speak in a whisper. "Okay, why don't you tell me what's going to happen. What's this about?"

"I'm not sure, but then I'm all too sure, if you follow me. A little demonstration for you, to show you how 'sincere' how 'committed' these people are."

"Demonstration? Of what?"

"Ah, not to be afraid, Mr. Snell. Sooner or later all the games end like this. Come along. I can promise you a cheap thrill. Manila is full of them, but this one may be the best money can't buy." Garcia takes my arms and steers me down to the door. He knocks twice. Mendoza pulls the door open. He, too, takes my arms and pulls me in.

The room is dark. Even my adjusting eyes have difficulty picking out other people near the bed. I am aware that there are others in the far corners, along the heavy drapes that shut out the neon of the Pensione's sign. Through those curtains the sign appears only as a large vague rose colored smudge. There is a rather high, sagging double bed in the center of the room. And on it someone is resting, a rather weathered, very tan fellow, maybe a dockworker, maybe forty years old, somebody used to a lot of sun. He is lying on what appears to be a kind of painter's drop cloth, only vinyl and clear. You can see the ribbing of the tired bedspread through the plastic. And there are towels under his shoulders, and under his head and knees. His face looks a bit bruised and swollen. There is a sinister three-inch wide strip of adhesive over his mouth. Commander 6 fits yet another piece of tape over that one and winds it around the back of the fellow's head, bringing back the end so that it laps over the lips yet a third time. When he lifts the fellow's head to perform this seal, he cradles it in almost maternal fashion. Then the commander lights a cigar.

The aroma is instantly thick and acrid. "Your Cuban embargo has done wonders for our market," he says, drawing several puffs on the cigar until its glowing end is the most visible point in the room. In the instant of using his lighter I notice that, indeed, there were six others standing along the walls and all holding weapons of some kind. Perhaps Mikey could identify them.

"We got the impression," the commander says, "You didn't believe us. You thought we were proposing some sort of scam. Scam, such a word! But we are serious. We really are very serious. We will get our Commander back. We will! Especially here that is difficult to understand. It's hot here and the coconuts hang in the trees, and the water is easy and swimmable. But that's not our interest. This man failed us."

He blows smoke in the fellow's face. I can see the man's eyes watching the cigar with a terrified fixation. The commander obliges him. He puts the cigar out on the fellow's left cheekbone. The tobacco smell yields instantly to the scent of flesh barbequing. The stink is overwhelming. There is a neat, charred hole in the fellow's cheek, and he rises off the bed, bouncing. Only then is it clear his legs are strapped to the heavy footboard, his hands handcuffed to the springs. There is an interminable squeaking, creaking, as the fellow rises off the bed, sinks back, arches and swivels, pulls at his restraints. I hear his mangled moaning through the thick tapes, but it is like the sound of an argument three apartments away.

Then Commander 6 takes out a large pair of pliers from his fatigue jacket on the chair beside the bed. The room is stifling hot—the slowly-turning overhead fan meaningless. He opens the pliers and shows them to the fellow whose eyes are full of tears. The eyes follow the pliers again with hysteric interest.

"Scam?" the commander says.

"Jesus!" I say, and almost on that utterance two rifle barrels come across my chest.

"We are serious," the commander says, "you ought to know that."

"Mikey ought to know that, too." Mendoza adds.

"Is this your idea?" I ask Wicksburg, but he jerks his head away from what is happening. Answer itself.

The commander has taken a large pinch of the fellow's flesh below the tape on his chin and he is twisting the pliers so that part of the lip, then the sheet of flesh along the jaw simply tears away with a slow, sputtering, adhesive sound. Gouts of blood rush down the fellow's neck, on to his shirt. Blood spreads out on the towels. Of course, the plastic—such sanitary soldiers.

"My God!" I begin to feel weak, have difficulty standing. But the commander is implacable. He motions to two others who come over to the bed. They bring up short, maybe fifteen inch, galvanized pipes and instantly bring them down on the tops of the fellow's kneecaps. The sound is unmuffled. I can hear the chipping, splintering noises of shattered bone. The body springs off the bed. There is again that awful squeaking, creaking, would-be thrashing movement, and the muted arguing, arguing, arguing through the tapes. The pipe wielders move up the torso and at the next command smash the edges of the fellow's hip.

"Do you think this a scam, Mr. Snell?" The commander shouts at me. He takes the pliers and yanks off the fellow's left ear. He shoves it in front of my face. Hands take hold of my arms.

"Why are you doing this?" I shout.

"Shut up! Why do you think this is a game, Mr. Snell, a scam? Everyday people are dying like this. Our people. This is the norm in our fighting. Commander 2 will die just like this. Do you understand? Except Marcos's scum are better equipped, more painful, more interesting. Isn't that the word, Garcia? Interesting. Or can't you talk through your orgasm?"

"Mikey thinks it's all a game," Mendoza says.

"But it's no game, is it, Mr. Snell? Is it?" The commander turns back to his work. The fellow's eyes are glazed but spinning, watching the pliers as the commander moves around. "You want piece of flesh, Mr. Snell. Which one is your piece of flesh, Mr. Snell? Which one has scam written on it? You want to pick it?"

I cannot hold the nausea back. Semi-chewed shrimp and noodles reassemble themselves on my shirt, across the top of my pants, and then onto the floor.

"God!" Wicksburg says, moving away from me.

"You still haven't chosen a part, Mr. Snell. Pick something please."

The spinning eyes watch the pliers, then me, then the pliers again. And blood gushes from the hips, the jaw. Even the burned hole on the cheekbone is pumping away madly now.

"What Mikey's doing for us is no game," Mendoza says. "You leave him alone. Just let him work with us. We are serious people. Very serious. He needs to know that. He needs to understand that."

"You're murdering bastards, that's what I see."

"You see retribution for betrayal. That's what you see, Mr. Snell. Very simple justice. He was helpful to us with Mohrstein, an intermediary like you. But then he was very helpful to General Ver about us. So pick a part of him for separation."

"For God's sake, why don't you finish him off," I say softly.

"You were helpful to us with Spendip. Don't be helpful to Ver and don't let Mikey play games with us," the commander says.

He slowly pushes the end of the pliers into the fellow's right eye. There is a terrible popping sound. "You're right. There's a mark between a lesson, an instruction, and sadism." The commander drops the pliers on the fellow's chest, and holds out his hand like a surgeon. Into it someone slaps a wooden-handled, folded linoleum knife. The commander opens it and quickly cuts the fellow's throat. More blood soars out the neck, and for the first time clearly distinguishable groans, hissing, hacking coughing sounds come of that bouncing, creaking body.

Others undo the handcuffs, unstrap the ankles. Then it becomes clear the plastic is in fact an enormous bag, such as might have encased a sofa. They bring the bottom edge up and the gushing broken carcass, the bloody towels, are all gathered up in a neat satchel. Cords bind the top and two sentries carry the body like a rug out of the room. The bedspread looks barely ruffled.

The commander tosses me a towel from the rack beside the bed. "When we're gone, clean up your puke," he says disdainfully.

And then they are gone, as I swab off my shoes and a small residue ellipse on the floor. I dry heave my way to a waiting Jeepney.

The light in Waldo's port hole is still on. I can lie along the dock and knock on the thick glass. Finally Waldo opens it.

"I've got to talk to you."

"You know what time it is?"

"I don't care what time it is. I gotta talk to you. Can you come out here?"

"Why not come aboard?"

"I've been sick. I'd stink up the boat."

"My God, Snelly, are you all right?"

"No. No, I'm not. Come out here, please."

"Right away. Right away," Waldo tosses the paperback and puts on a robe. The light goes out. In a few minutes he is standing on the dock.

I am sitting on the edge, dangling my legs next to the yacht. Waldo squats down beside me.

"You smell terrible," he says. "Some Filipino garbage?" He asks.

"No, I just watched somebody tortured to death," I say slowly. "Let me tell you what is going on."

There are moments of slow silence, moments when Waldo looks at me skeptically, incredulously, then shakes his head and asks another question. There are moments when I can't stop talking all around the point, beyond the point, and then quietness again. I am aware that Waldo is distancing himself from what I say, distancing himself from the whole, untidy story he hears, but I am also aware that gradually he comes to accept more and more of it.

"Mendoza was there? He watched too?"

"And Garcia."

"I don't know him."

And I go back through it all, the visits, the luncheons, the propositions, and Mikey's preparations. And again I feel Waldo easing off, drifting away, as if to recollect a private reserve. So I pause again. The scent of vomit lingers between us and seems a kind of validation for even the most implausible assertions. And after a while like absolution itself, Waldo sighs, "How could you be carrying on this madness without ever mentioning it to me. Without ever consulting with me?"

"You were sick."

"You see how sick," says. "And here you are."

"What am I supposed to do?"

"We need to develop a plan of action," Waldo says, getting up. He tightens the belt of his robe. "We need a definite plan."

"Should I tell Mikey?"

"Not yet. Maybe not. Probably not. I don't know. I don't know. First things first. Throw that shirt in the bay. Chuck it right down there. I'll be back in a minute." Waldo goes back aboard.

Cross Creek to cross creek, I think, dropping the pullover into the water next to the yacht. Waldo comes back with a small wet towel and a short sleeved blue dress shirt. It's acres big on me.

"Swab off your trousers and go back to the hotel. They're probably through with you for tonight." He says with rather too much assurance, I think. "I'll contact you in the morning."

"The tournament starts at 10:30 a.m."

CHAPTER 36

"I know. We have to have a definite plan. A definite plan, actually." Waldo deliberates a bit. "You go back to the hotel. If I need you, I'll call. Get some sleep, if you can. Make sure Pam is all right. Actually, I guess what I'm leaning toward is waking Hilly up. Things are, are serious, I guess. And we need a plan. I'd better wake Hilly up. You go on back. We'll be in touch first thing in the morning."

I nod, start back toward the hotel. The dock seems wobbly. When I am about forty feet from the yacht, I hear Waldo's loudly whispered voice, "Paul, Paul."

"What is it?" I turn around feeling disconnected, rubbery legged, still nauseated. Residue of vomit swirls up everywhere. "What is it?"

"Paul, that's one of my favorite shirts—Hilly's too. Be careful with it, will you?"

Chapter 37

Hillary arrives early and is clearly dressed for traveling. She stands in the doorway and clarifies the situation. "We're going to assume that things are pretty much as you reported them to Waldo, give or take an embellishment. Was someone butchered in front of you, actually murdered?"

"Tortured and then murdered."

"There's not a chance, I suppose, a prank was being played, a little shocking game for the foreigners?"

"Not a chance. The blood was real. The gagging sound I'll never forget."

"Skip the graphics. Let's say things are as you have described them. It's time to leave. We are linked with you and you have been threatened. Was the Spendip boy threatened too?"

"I guess so. I wasn't following everything clearly."

"He wasn't there, was he?"

"No."

"My guess—just a guess—would be they will leave him alone. If they had really wanted to intimidate him, he would have been there. So you are the more likely victim. We are linked to you, not that I particularly regret it. Although in this case I suppose I do regret it. We just got here. When threats are tossed around, especially in places like this, I always, always, get out. So we shall get out. And I advise you to do the same, Get Pamela up. I want her to leave immediately."

"Getting her up may take a bit of doing. She hasn't been too well the last day or so."

"Oh, no. Not really?"

"I am afraid so."

"It never rains, but the whole damn heavens open up. Poor Pamela! She had no business coming here, but try to tell Ned that." Hillary walks by me and goes over to the bed. She bends over Pam, whispers something to her, then leans in closer, whispers again. There is no response that I can discern.

"Do you think you could get her to the boat, if you had to?"

"Sure, but I don't think getting out is all that necessary."

"You don't? Why?"

"I've been thinking a lot about it. I think last night was a kind of insurance policy. They seemed to be worried that I was going to talk Mikey out of throwing the point. But Mikey's not planning to do that. As soon as Calderon has his point, they should be happy. And there'll be no reason to continue threats. Nor reason to punish anybody."

"You don't think so?"

"No. Once Mikey has lost the game, then all of our bargain will have been fulfilled. I can't see how there will be anything but elations all the way around. They wanted to make sure Mikey would do something for them. But it was all so unnecessary. Mikey had already decided to do something for them. My God, he spent most of the last two days, including last night, memorizing the game that he and Reyle are supposed to play this morning. He's already shown he's going through with it."

"And his mother?"

"She's been bought off. It must have taken a pile of money."

"So it's your position that all we have to do is wait for the end of the first game between Mikey and, and who is it?"

"Calderon, the Filipino champion. And that game has already been worked out. I was in on most of the sessions. Mikey worked on it like a chess problem. I really don't think there is any difficulty. At least I can't see any."

"Ah yes, no difficulty—except the one my father used to talk about."

"Your father?"

"Yes, he always used to say, always used to tell me, 'Hill, people who don't have what you have sooner or later want to see you dead. Never forget that.'"

"They want to see us dead?"

"Sooner or later they mean to kill us all. It's rather simple and logical. In their place I might want the same thing. But I am not in their place, and I have no interest in lingering anywhere near it. We get underway in less than an hour. We have to get Pamela to the boat. And I strongly suggest you get out of here, too."

"You mean with you?"

"Preferably not. You are, after all, the marked man, but if you do come, we'd find room for you. But we are absolutely leaving within the hour."

"It would be better for you, I stayed?"

"A case could be made for that," Hillary says, opening the closet and pulling out Pam's dress. "I don't suppose she brought an overnight bag."

"No. A case could be made?"

"Well, if you disappear, doesn't that raise the suspicions of whoever you've been dealing with? I really thought you had some judgment. And who have you been dealing with? You might be right—if little Spendip follows the scenario, then perhaps there really isn't any problem at all. I would never deliver myself into that fellow's whims, however. So if I were you, I'd leave immediately, even before we do." She begins calling to Pam, jostling her. "Mikey seems a little young, a little strange, to be holding your life, don't you think?"

"Do you think I should tell him what happened last night?"

"Do they expect you to?"

"I guess so. I can't be sure. I'm not certain what they want."

"Another fine reason to get out. You can tell him, if you want. If you think he's going to renege, I certainly would tell him. But if the game has been worked out, and everybody's happy with the scheme, then, then, I suppose there's no reason to tell him."

Hillary puts two hands behind Pam's head and slowly pulls her upward. The motion is so reminiscent of Commander 6's little embrace that I feel nausea stirring again. "What Spendip knows is not so important as what he does. You're the agent in this ridiculous affair. If the goods arrive, then there's no problem. If they don't arrive, nobody blows up the goods. They fire the agent. In fact, of course, they could hardly blow up Spendip. Think of the publicity on that. What would they get out of it? It would be like publicly shooting a baby. But nobody will care if you turn up in the bay with your throat gone. Lend a hand, here, will you?"

We draw Pam upright. She smiles at us and opens her eyes a bit, seems only tired, not toppled.

"I certainly would tell him, and in the most lurid terms possible, if you think he's not going through with the deal."

"I'm sure he's going through with it."

"Fine, then there's no problem. But if I were you, I'd be in a cab to Manila International Airport right now. But I'm not you, thank God. Pamy! Wake up! We're going back to the boat. We're going home. Do you hear? Home. We're leaving Manila. This morning. In an hour we're going home."

"I'm not the agent in this. I'm not. I've stayed out of that role. I'm an observer." I try to convince Hillary.

"I wish we were recording this, so I could play that sentence back to you when this is all over—if you're around. Listen, if Mikey does what you say he's going to, then you all can enjoy the Manila sunshine for as long as you like. Pamy! Paul and I are going to get you dressed. Can you help us?"

"Of course I can help you," Pam says softly, falling back toward the pillow.

"Splendid, Pamela, splendid! One more burst of energy. Bring yourself forward. That's right. Actually, I think we'll skip the dressing. Use the robe. We'll walk her down in the robe."

I get the robe from a chair and slip Pam's left arm into the sleeve.

"Put the other arm in, Pamela," Hillary says, greatly encouraged that Pam is now talking. We bring her to her feet.

"I can stand," she says rather dopily. "I'm only a little tired. That's all."

"How is it?" I ask.

"How is it," she answers.

"Stop engaging her. Move her toward the door," Hillary says.

"Come on, love," and I ease her a step at a time. Hillary puts an arm around her waist. I have hold of her around the back and under right arm.

"Please, please," she says.

""No pleases, Pamela. Pleases are for after we get aboard. After we are out of here."

Vera is waiting for us in the hall. "She sick again?" she says.

"I suppose," I answer.

"Well, look. You coming with us to the theater or not?"

Hillary stops and nods toward me, a directive to answer that question. "Yes, yes, of course," I say. Hillary smiles. I have apparently hit on the correct response.

"Mikey's playing through some variations off the English now, but he's ready."

What does ready mean for Vera? "Good," I answer. "I'll be right back as soon as we get Pam back to the boat."

"How come her folks aren't here?"

"We traded invalids," Hillary says stonily.

"Hehn?" Vera asks.

"My husband is sick too," Hillary continues. "Could you get the elevator?"

CHAPTER 37

"Yeah," Vera says. "You coming back?" she asks again after we have arranged Pam in the corner of the elevator, under the brightly polished spherical mirror.

"Of course," I answer. "All my things are here."

"Yeah," Vera says, nodding at us when the door closes.

We make an awkward trio, wobbling our way across the terrace, pausing at poolside for a little rest. Perhaps Vera watches from the tenth floor.

Pam says, "Is Waldo this much of an invalid?"

"Worse," Hillary answers, "a conniver—the worst sort of conniver. He may have found the perfect place for his skills. But he's too locked in to see it."

"You mean Manila?"

"I mean Manila—a conniver's Elysium, wouldn't you say?" Hillary laughs a bit. "Come along, Pamela. You're doing splendidly. But we still have a ways to go."

The tankers have departed and the bay stretches out like fresh tin foil from an infinite roll over the horizon. Where are the jagged saw teeth to tear off an appropriate boundary? What are the boundaries of the bay, I wonder. It stretches to the ends of the earth. If you spent every day looking at it, would you know where the sky was? Wouldn't the universe be turned upside down?

Captain George stands by the bow spring-line on the dock. He isn't wearing his cap or his double-breasted jacket. All business now, hustling to shove off, is that it? We limp down toward him, and Ned Snow comes running to meet us.

"You're a brick, Hilly. A brick. Come on, Pamy. Come on, Honey. We're almost there," he says.

"We ready to cast off?" Hillary asks.

"As soon as you get aboard."

"Everything else set?" Hillary says.

"Everything," Ned replies.

"You coming, Paul?" Ned continues.

"I don't think so."

Ned looks relieved. "I can't believe what's been going on around here. Just can't believe it."

"You could have believed it last night."

"I suppose so. I'm glad you were the one with the front row seat on that one. Those kind of displays bother me."

Bother you, Ned?

"It was like dismembering a pineapple," I say for no reason I can understand.

Ned looks at me strangely. "Pamy's not doing too well?" he asks Hillary.

"She's all right. She's cooperative least, and no martyr. No cloying martyr."

Captain George waves us aboard, and as soon as Pam, Ned and Hillary are steady on deck, Captain George lifts his foot. The forward spring-line snaps off the cleat and the yacht swerves almost perpendicular to the dock. Captain George in an agile leap follows the spring-line aboard. In two more grasping vaults, he is in the bridge.

Ned holds Pamela up. Hillary steps behind them and waves to me over their heads. Ned waves Pam's arm in a broad swirl. Ned is still waving Pam's floppy arm when the yacht turns to the west, gradually removing them from sight. Does Waldo wave from his porthole? Des he issue any communiqués from his stateroom, any last minute advice? Probably not, I decide. Doubtless the exact details of Kennedy's autopsy are more interesting to him. Snell is only just one more corpse daily washed up on the seven thousand islands of the Philippines.

Chapter 38

"You share a cab with us?" Vera asks as soon as I come back out of the elevator.

"Okay. Sure. Mikey ready?"

"Mikey's always ready," Vera says, steadying herself down.

"Pam's slipping away again, I am afraid."

"That one's got problems," Vera says. "We're gonna get some coffee downstairs. Meet us in the lobby in about, what? Thirty minutes?"

I take a shower and debate packing up. It might expedient, if things do go awry, but how could I carry my things with Vera and Mikey? Instead, I decide to take my passport.

Mikey and Vera are waiting by the front doors of the lobby. Mikey hands me the score sheet. "I don't want to get caught carrying this," he says, laughing. "You can follow the moves, if you want."

Vera has gone ahead to get a cab. She insists on waving one herself despite the doorman. There is a line of cabs all the way out to Roxas Boulevard, but Vera manages to get a cab to pull out of the line and double park in front of the main entrance. She waves us out, then scrambles into the front seat herself. Only as I open the back do I notice that it is a Green Archer taxi. By then it is too late.

"Come on, Mikey. Ya don't want to be late. They'll start your clock."

The doorman seems to join the other cabbies swearing at us, as we head back out to the boulevard.

"I hear Tarlac has intestinal flu," Vera says.

"Yeah? Where'd you hear that?" Mikey says.

"Mr. Garcia called this morning to wish you luck."

I bet he did, I think.

"No kidding?" Mikey says.

"I told him you made your own luck. And ya do, Mikey. Ya always do."

"Yeah," no sweat." Mikey says.

We pass the American Embassy. So far the cabbie has followed Roxas Boulevard to the Cultural Center about a half mile down the road. I keep waiting for him to turn off, plunge us into the rancid alleys of Mabini, park the cab and butcher us all. Maybe Garcia was wrong about these Green Archer fellows. In the last stretch of open space before the Center, I can see the yacht out on the cookie sheet of water and moving slowly, fixedly, toward the deeper cuts. Nobody on deck. No more manipulated waving. Has Pam settled into deep sleep? Pennants fly from the guide line and I have an unsettling feeling of abandonment watching those weak flags attempt and fail to flutter in the limp and steamy air above the bay.

We are five minutes late getting to the Little Theater, but the welcoming speaker, the grand Imelda herself is over a half-hour behind schedule. Everyone waits for her entrance. Mikey takes his seat on stage and Vera and I find places in the fifteenth row, the appointed row for seconds. The rest of the theater is packed. Amazing. About two thousand people are on hand for the opening ceremony. Part of Imelda's fan club or her paid retinue? Perhaps real chess enthusiasts. It is impossible to say. There are several small lap boards in evidence, however. And for twenty pesos you can rent an earphone that will give a commentary in English or Tagalog.

There are six large demonstration boards mounted on the back wall of the stage. Six tables are down front. The brass punch buttons of the clocks on the tables catch for a moment the soaring

CHAPTER 38

sunlight coming in off the bay. Then somebody pulls the curtains, blocking the enormous windows on the east side of the theater.

Suddenly the crowd explodes in applause. And coming down the back aisle straight through the center of the theater is a retinue of white suited fellows. In the middle there is the grand Imelda herself, wearing a gleaming white silk dress. The loudspeakers explode in what I take to be an introduction to her in Tagalog. More cheering from the audience—almost ecstatic levels of yelling. About half the audience is on its feet. Arms shoot up in the cool, air-conditioned air. A myriad of Bolshevik salutes. When I turn around to watch, I notice Garcia about ten rows back and toward the east side. He smiles and gives me the thumbs up signal. It is not clear whether that is for Imelda's arrival or for something else. Then furtively Garcia holds his nose. Imelda's passage shuts the view off.

Three of the white suited attendants hustle forward, get up on the stage and stretch out a long white silk ribbon. Imelda takes her seat at the center of the first row in the orchestra. There follows an opening prayer by a resplendent Archbishop. I am reminded of a myriad of high school assemblies. What do the Russians make of this? Then there is another long Tagalog introduction to Imelda, drawing extended cheers at four different moments. The twelve chess players patient in their chairs watch this with expressions, it seems to me of disdain. At length Imelda comes on stage. The audience gets to its feet and falls silent. All of this seems carefully orchestrated. She says only a few words in Tagalog and then takes an enormous chrome scissors, walks to the center of the stage and dramatically snips the ribbon. The attendants immediately roll up the two halves. There is more applause and Imelda bows, comes back to the side microphone and reads a message from the President himself.

Through that message Mikey stares toward the back of the stage, contemplates, apparently, the demonstration board for his table. Then each competitor is announced. About half of them stand to acknowledge brief applause. Mikey merely waves to the audience. He and Calderon are the only ones without ties.

Then the stage is cleared. Demonstration board handlers move into position and the command to start echoes in the theater.

Calderon wears what appears to be a new cream-colored Barong shirt. He leans across and shakes Mikey's hand. I unfold the score sheet Mikey has given me. Vera looks at it.

"What's that?"

"The score of the game they're going to play."

"Sure," she says, "sure, sure."

I begin to get a very uneasy feeling. Calderon will start with pawn to Queen bishop four, apparently English opening. Mikey will respond with pawn to King three, an invitation to the French defense, and then Calderon will reply, pawn to Queen four, setting the course for a Queen's pawn opening. Mikey will respond, pawn to Queen four and by indirection a very conventional Queen's Gambit Declined will have been achieved.

Right on script Calderon plays pawn to Queen bishop four. Commentators undoubtedly noted there was no surprise here, since Reyle often used the English, although he would probably be happier in a traditional Queen's Gambit opening. Mikey does not immediately respond. Very good, I think. Quick response would indicate lack of option consideration. One can decline the English in a number of ways.

"Ya can put that away now," Vera says to me, before Mikey moves.

"What?" I ask.

"Ya can tear that up now, if you like—"

"What do you mean?"

"Watch!" She gives me an endearing nudge in the ribs. But it feels as if my side and both lungs are caving in. I have difficulty breathing. The blood rushes around. I can feel my pulse soaring. Gouts of blood I'm certain are about to pop right through my cheekbone. My knee caps shatter.

"Watch what Mikey does to that schmuck." She says again.

Mikey takes up the King's pawn and starts to advance it, but instead of pushing it ahead one square to King's three, instead of

CHAPTER 38

offering the passive, highly defensive position of the French Defense, Mikey pushes the pawn to King four. Vera chuckles under her breath. Pushing the pawn up to King four invites Calderon to explode the center and forces the game into wide open, highly risky, combination-ridden lines—precisely the kind of complicated, dangerous slugfest Mikey loves. He offers to liquidate the center, offers to engage Calderon in a hysterical quick development and immediate attacks against mutually exposed Kings. He rams Calderon into the type of game Calderon instinctively avoids, instinctively fears. And he does it by springing a triple surprise. First he jettisons the schedule of moves rehearsed (certain to confuse and perplex Calderon), second he slams the game into a wild, relatively uncharted but highly complex and risky opening line, and third, having accomplished those first two points in itself signals that he undoubtedly holds a prepared variation no matter what course Reyle takes. Surely Mikey would not whimsically sail off the prearrangements without knowing ahead of time where the depths and reefs were. It is as if at the start of a regulation boxing match, Mikey has touched gloves with Calderon, dropped back and then triple kicked him in the gonads.

"Sweet, sweet," Vera says, nudging me again.

Reyle begins a peculiar rocking motion, rolling toward the board and then away from it in his chair. He watches Mikey, who only smiles at him. After the posting of the pawn to King four, there is substantial murmuring in the audience. Would that I had spent twenty pesos to hear what the commentators are saying. Doubtless something like "fireworks on Board Five. Fireworks on the first move. Another patented Spendip surprise."

It is inconceivable that Reyle will take up the challenge and play pawn to Queen four, offering to explode the center. But not to do that leads to a loss of initiative, in which White gets a kind of reverse Sicilian Defense and all the attacking chances rest with black. Mikey's move may be unsound, but clearly he is banking on the shock element and a prepared variation on top of the shock. Calderon continues to rock back and forth. People around us have switched from duplicating the Levy-Tarlac match on Board 1 to Mikey's game. I hear more murmuring and rearrangement of pieces. Mikey has indicated he intends to win the game directly or lose directly. Whatever the King's pawn move does, it seems to reject altogether the possibility of a draw.

Reyle puts his hands to his jaw, rests his elbows against the edge of the table. I wonder if he even sees the board yet. Has he stopped drowning yet? He must reassemble all his traditional skills, see the position for what it is, disregard any superimposed idealized rehearsed game and do all that with the notion doubtless zinging around in his head that he has been played for a sucker. Maybe more than he can accomplish in the time limits.

On the other hand, in only three minutes, three minutes to redirect his energies, rediscover his possibilities, Reyle plays pawn to Queen three, accepting the loss of initiative, accepting the passive position Mikey has tossed him into. Mikey immediately, instantly, plays pawn to King bishop four. The quickness signals prepared variation and the move itself announces that Mikey cares not a whit for caution. He means to attack and attack, mount pressure after pressure. The move signals that somewhere in the next twenty moves or so Mikey has a super combination waiting for the right configuration to turn up. Mikey is familiar, the move says, with all the lines of this hyper-attack, familiar and exultant.

"Sweet. Sweet," Vera says again.

I am aware in the general murmurings in the theater, in the excitement of rearranging boards, that my name is being called. "Mr. Snell. Mr. Snell!" somebody seems to be saying. "Mrs. Spendip. Mrs. Spendip!" Yes, it is Mr. Garcia at the end of our row. I turn to watch him.

"Mr. Snell," he says loudly, "what is going on? What is happening?"

Before I can respond, Vera turns and gives Garcia his answer. She swivels in her seat, half rises to face him. People around us have already stood to get a clear view of the demonstration board. Vera raises her right arm, fist clenched and turned toward her. She thrusts the arm up and slaps her left hand sharply on her upper arm just below the bicep. She repeats the gesture to dispel any confusion Garcia may have had.

"What does that fag expect for a lousy five grand?" Vera says sitting down.

I am afraid to look at Garcia. I feel for my passport in the jacket on my lap.

"You and Mikey kill me," I say to Vera with more than a little ambivalence.

"Nah, it's him," she points to Reyle, "we're gonna kill. Gonna put him right out of this tournament! Put him right out!"

I slump down in my seat and try to watch the demonstration board. After the initial shock of Mikey's King's bishop pawn move—there is actually a smattering of applause when it is posted—people seem content to sit back down.

The next half hour goes by with painful slowness. It is clear Reyle has lost the thread of the game. He scuffles around in his own back rank, seems merely to make half-hearted preparations for the onslaught Mikey builds up. More pawns on the King side come down the board and Mikey doubles his rooks on the King's file as preparation for blasting that lane open. Reyle rearranges more of his pieces on the back rank, as if the King were gathering his children just before the conflagration consumes them. Such passivity invites devastation I decide.

"Look, Vera, I gotta use the toilet. Be right back," I say.

I get up, climb across her, away from Garcia's side of the theater, and start up the aisle. Is he watching me? Is Commander 6 in the balcony? My walk becomes a trot. I think I catch a glimpse of Garcia's powder blue suit in the other aisle moving toward the back with me. But I am not about to wait around to see. I hit the maroon swinging doors at the end of the aisle running. I hold my jacket like the baton relay runners pass, one to the next. The main lobby is slippery marble and open golden sunlight. My feet go tapping on the surface and I keep up the run to the vast, automatically opening doors. I don't look back, but I hear a voice shouting from somewhere, "General Funston! General Funston!"

The doors are exasperatingly slow, but soon enough I am on the pavement. No taxis, not even the dubious shelter of a Green Archer someplace. And Roxas Boulevard looks to be three football fields away. I ball up my jacket and start running down the sloping lawn. The grass is spongy, the few Royal Palms are no cover in the lush, green-sheared tundra. Is Garcia on the roof with a high-powered rifle? Is 6 on the grassy knoll to my left, waiting to coordinate his rifle shots with Garcia on the roof?

My throat feels on fire, but I manage to run fast and faster. And at the Boulevard I get a red Nissan cab to pull over, though the driver is skeptical of the sweat soaking through my shirt and my heavy panting.

"Hey, Joe," the cabbie says, "Don't worry. Don't worry so. I know the fastest way to the airport."

I manage to get a Garuda flight coming in from Jakarta bound for Hong Kong, where a Pan American connection will be waiting. "Just for you, Mr. Snell," says the clerk, "just for you." She smiles and brushes away drops of sweat on the Visa charge sheets.

I have to change a traveler's check to pay the exit tax. There is a difficult and unnerving delay as immigration and customs process one hundred and seventeen departing Japanese businessmen who seem to be bearing away most of the Central Market. The officials appear relieved and uninterested that I am carrying nothing.

At a newsstand in the transit lounge I purchase five Philippine handkerchiefs and use them like towels in the gleaming men's room. My shirt is sopping wet, but there is nothing I can do about that. But then it hits me, I can buy a new shirt. The duty free shops are nearby and littered with Barong shirts. Of course!

I tuck in the sopping shirt and make my way to the friendly, avaricious duty-free boutiques. I sort through acres of banana-fibered Barongs, each more expensive than the last. Financially I am forced to settle for a Hanes T shirt with "Florida" and "Have a Tampa!" stenciled on the front. I wad up the sopping shirt and

CHAPTER 38

throw it in the trash in the men's room. The second shirt abandoned in Manila.

Across from the restroom is a door labeled "Members only," and I hear what appear to be familiar voices. I ease the door back a bit. Yes, at the bar I can see a white-flannelled leg.

"Snelly! Snelly!" Waldo booms out. He is standing next to Ned Snow. "Snelly, come on in. You made it. You made it! Have a G & T."

I step in. No official seems to be around to hurry me back out of the place.

"Don't worry. Don't worry," Waldo shouts, "you make your own here."

"What happened to the yacht?"

"Part of Hillary's master plan. The Coast Guard met us with a forty boat off the Embassy and we transferred to JAL."

"How'd you do that?"

"Two things going for us. First class fares, and, a medical emergency." Waldo points to Pam who is in a wheelchair at the end of the bar. She is apparently sleeping.

"Jesus!"

Hillary comes across the rooms and says, "Mikey played for a win, I take it."

"Yes."

"Competition," she says, "I love it," and makes herself another Bourbon and soda.

"You taking JAL too?" Ned asks.

"No. Indonesian to Hong Kong and then Pan Am."

"Well, guess we'll beat you to the states. We stop at Tokyo and then hop to New York."

"Go ahead, make yourself a drink," Waldo says. "I guess you can tell I'm glad to be off the boat."

"We're all glad you're off the boat, darling," Hillary says.

"Kind of miss old Captain George," Ned adds. "But maybe we'll be back. Next time, without chess."

"Yes, indeed," Waldo says loudly, "who would have thought it's such a dangerous sport."

Amid their chuckling, I go down the bar to Pam. A nurse stands about eight feet in back of the chair. I squat down to look at Pam's face. She appears to be out cold. Head hanging down so that her jaw almost touches her chest. She has an endearing, goofy smile on her face, a smile that refuses to comment on anything beyond the little, insulated private bliss that gave it birth.

Chapter 39

It is four-thirty Friday and Waldo and I are at the Hane Country Club bar. Waldo has his left armpit wedged in against the padded lip of the bar top.

"You know, Snelly, you know," he says, "I told you they were a whacko lot. Every one of them. I mean if they're any good. And let's face it, Mikey might be the best of all of 'em. But whacko. And it was bound to come out sooner or later. That news conference was a disgrace."

Mikey had pulverized Calderon in the opening match, a shellacking from which the Filipino did not really recover. As Vera had promised they did put him out of the tournament, although he lingered through the remaining rounds, a large vulnerable target for the five other opponents. Mikey coasted off that opening victory and threatened to storm through the remainder. He pulled opening surprises in the next two games and won them resoundingly, but against Dr. Levy, in a drab variant of the Ruy Lopez Mikey seemed to lose his bearing. The game drew and that started a run of draws. Meanwhile Tarlac began picking up wins from his fellow Russians. A victory, rather short, rather too short, against Ivanov put Tarlac over the top. Mikey called a news conference and harangued the Russians for throwing matches to Tarlac. But, of course, he had no proof. He did insist it could be done with a minimum of preparation and memorized moves.

"I mean he sounded like a whining punk. You know what I mean? That cry baby stuff will never go over well here," Waldo says. "If he doesn't get out from under that woman, he's never going to grow up. It's a shame. Talent like that needs to be matched with some maturity. 'Course it never happens, not with American champions anyway. Why do you suppose that is?"

It is clear Waldo requires no answer to the question.

"Shall we try the early bird dinner?" Waldo says.

Lately Hillary has not been coming. She spends a lot of time visiting relatives in St. Louis or shopping with her sister in San Francisco. "It's just a phase," Waldo explained a couple of weeks ago. "Women go through them all the time," he said.

Pam entered what it think of as a five-key-holder phase. That's longer than a three-wallet phase, maybe even longer than a four-wallet phase. We spent about ten days in New Canaan, Golden Hills-ing it, since it was so convenient to Kennedy airport. But then there was a quarrel between Coffee and Belasco about treatment and fees. So she was moved to Tampa. Coffee thought it would be better if she were closer to home. I resigned from writing the column while we were in New Canaan. I expected that Arnie and Phil would immediately cancel it, but I underestimated their vindictiveness. They surprised Waldo and me by hiring a retired accountant at the Brandon-Mercer Trailer Park and had him expand the column to five times a week. Once in while Arnie brings in some fan mail. People apparently write in and say things like "It's a relief the Tribune finally got a chess columnist who knows something about chess."

Mikey and Vera probably came back to D.C. I've lost touch, although I remember reading in a barber shop a gossip magazine that showed Mikey at a commune in South Carolina. A religious commune, I think, one that specialized in making pottery bowls.

I don't miss the column and Arnie and Phil seem to enjoy giving me boring, dead-end assignments. Probably they'd fire me, if they could.

CHAPTER 39

Pam was home for a month and about twice a week we went for drives in my Fairlane. The silences between us became long and strangely less threatening, less uneasy. I began to think we could have a life like that. Drives in the evening and silences, little plans for outings in various parts of the state. And it wouldn't have been so bad either, but abruptly she fell over another ledge. Currently she is back in Tampa and it looks to be at least a five-key-holder phase, although I haven't gotten a single one from her yet.

"You going up to see her again, Sunday?" Waldo says over his melon.

"Yes, sure."

"It's none of my business, but if you want my advice, I'll tell you you'd better let her go."

"Why is that?"

"Cycles," Waldo says, excitement rising. Lately Waldo has been very interested in cycles. Life cycles of products and newspapers and now apparently romances. He scratches a long, arching curve on the table cloth with his fingernail. "You see the rise here?"

"Yes."

"That's where things were. I wanted you to try there and you did. And I appreciate that. So does Hilly, though she'd never say it. It made sense there. Pam was on the upswing. But, but," Waldo pauses, moving his finger along the top of his indented cloth curve. "But the tide's running out. It's the downslope. Nothing you can do will change that. Bluntly put, I don't think she's going to get any better. I think it will only get worse. I think they ran out of treatments six months ago. Does she know you when you come?"

"Yes, of course."

"I think she gave up. I don't blame her. I'm not judging her on that."

I say, "We all give up, don't we. Didn't you?"

"Eat your melon and have a little respect," Waldo laughs. "Remember who's paying for it."

Who is paying for it?

"Snelly, what I'm trying to say is that for your own good, you need to get on with life. Visiting Pam is a way of standing around. That's what you're doing, standing around. Visiting her is very nice, very thoughtful, but it's a little gesture. Just that, a little gesture. Little gestures make no difference. They don't change anything. They don't help her. And they don't help you. So let it go, will you?"

"I'll think about that."

"Don't think about it. Do it." Waldo says. He eases a pit from the melon out of his mouth on to the spoon.

I wait for him to pursue the theme, confidant that he cannot stay away from it, but, as always, he is too crafty for me. He takes the spoon and inverts it over his water glass. The pit eases off, clicks on the water surface and then drops down in a slow whirl to settle below the ice cubes at the bottom of the glass.

"What do you think of that?" Waldo says, beaming. "Isn't that something!"

www.ingramcontent.com/pod-product-compliance
Lightning Source LLC
Chambersburg PA
CBHW071339150426
43191CB00007B/786